Learning at the Back Door

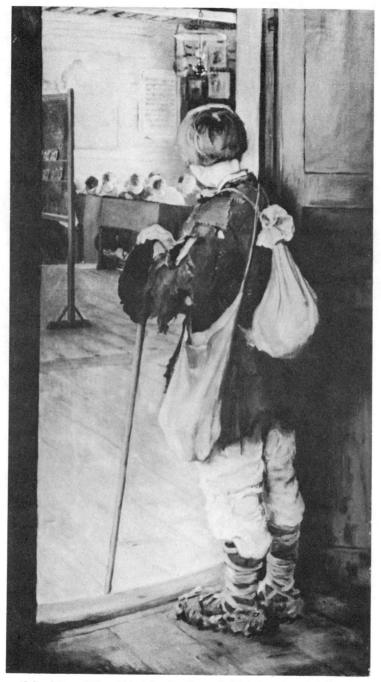

"School Door," Klyushkin (after Bogdanov-Belski), Russian, 20th century
Elvehjem Museum of Art, University of Wisconsin-Madison
Gift of Joseph E. Davies

"Learning's Open Door," Michael Smith
University of Wisconsin Photo Media Center, 1980

Learning at the Back Door

Reflections on
Non-Traditional Learning
in the Lifespan

Charles A. Wedemeyer

THE UNIVERSITY OF WISCONSIN PRESS

Published 1981

The University of Wisconsin Press
114 North Murray Street
Madison, Wisconsin 53715

The University of Wisconsin Press, Ltd.
1 Gower Street
London WC1E 6HA, England

First printing

Printed in the United States of America

ISBN 0-299-08560-0

Sir John C. Eccles, *The Understanding of the Brain.* Copyright © 1973 by Sir John C. Eccles.
(excerpts)
Roger Reynolds, "The Man Who Fell to Earth," *Reader's Digest,* January 1980. Copyright ©
1980 by The Reader's Digest Assn., Inc. (excerpts)
Carl Sandburg, *The People, Yes.* Copyright 1936 by Harcourt Brace Jovanovich, Inc.; copy-
right © 1964 by Carl Sandburg. (excerpts)
Sir Peter Venables, *Report of the Committee on Continuing Education.* Copyright © 1976
by The Open University Press. (excerpts)
Nicholas A. Wheeler, "Toward Safe Routes to the Strange Future," *The Chronicle of Higher
Education.* Copyright © 1978 by Editorial Projects for Education, Inc. (excerpts)

Library of Congress Cataloging in Publication Data
Wedemeyer, Charles A.
Learning at the back door.
Bibliography: pp. 243–250
Includes index.
1. Nonformal education. 2. Continuing education.
I. Title.
LC45.3.W43   374   80-52301
ISBN 0-299-08560-0   AACR2

*To Mildred Brown Wedemeyer,
whose loving support, caring solicitude,
and willing assumption of many responsibilities
made this and other projects possible,
this book is lovingly and gratefully dedicated.*

Contents

Figures and Illustrations   xi
Acknowledgments   xiii
A Personal Note   xv
Preface   xix
An Introductory Note About Terminology   xxv

Part One
The Rise of Non-Traditional Learning

I   A New Urgency Regarding Learning   3

II   Learning at the Back Door   18

III   Teaching, Learning, Schooling, and Knowledge   32

Part Two
Non-Traditional Learning and Its Implications

IV   Distance and Independent Learning   47

V   Open Learning   60

VI   The Implications of Non-Traditional Learning   74

Part Three
Technology and Special Processes
in Non-Traditional Learning Systems

VII Technology and Non-Traditional Learning   95

VIII Instructional Design in Non-Traditional Teaching
      and Learning Systems   116

IX Building and Evaluating Non-Traditional Institutions
    or Programs   132

Part Four
Learning from a Lifespan Perspective:
Its Ends in a Learning Society

X Lifespan Learning   161

XI Education for What?   180

XII Back Door Learning in the Learning Society   199

Notes   223
Selected Bibliography   243
Index   251

Figures and Illustrations

Frontispiece 1   "School Door," Kluyshkin, after Bogdonov-Belski   ii

Frontispiece 2   "Learning's Open Door," Mike Smith   iii

Figure 1   Essential Elements in a Teaching-Learning Situation   38

Figure 2   A Real Time-Space Teaching-Learning Situation:
The Classroom   38

Figure 3   A Teaching-Learning Model to Accommodate
Physical Distance   40

Figure 4   Phase I: Faculty Development   124

Figure 5   Phase II: Software Development   127

Figure 6   Phase III: Hardware Procurement   129

Figure 7   Three Phases of Instructional Design   130

Figure 8   Conceptual Matrix for Non-Traditional
Institutions/Program   142

Figure 9   Model of Teaching-Learning Relationship Between
Non-Traditional Learner and Distance Institution   149

Figure 10   The Learner Is Central   150

Figure 11   A Planning Matrix for Modeling a Non-Traditional
             Teaching and Learning Institution   157

Figure 12   Sources of Deliberate Education and Learning
             in the United States   169

Figure 13   An Estimate of the Relative Intensity of Three Kinds
             of Lifespan Learning at Different Times in Life   178

Acknowledgments

There are many mentors who enriched my understanding of nontraditional learning. Their publications are cited throughout this work and in the Bibliography. I am especially grateful to Fred Harvey Harrington and Donald R. McNeil for continuing support and encouragement.

Among my Wisconsin colleagues, Jack Ferver, Robert Clasen, Wilson B. Thiede, and James Duncan were always tolerant of my concerns and always helpful.

Fellow workers in the vineyard throughout the world are an exceptional group whose knowledge, friendship, and sustained interest contributed much to my understanding of the field. Only a few can be mentioned here. In the United States, Ripley Sims, Mary Lou McPartlin, Ted Estabrooke, Gayle Childs, and John Davies; in England, Frank Jessup, Walter Perry, and Walter James; in Sweden, Börje Holmberg; in the Federal Republic of Germany, Otto Peters, Günther Dohmen, and Karlheinz Rebel; in Canada, Coolie Verner, Roby Kidd, and Allen Tough; in Australia, Ian Mitchell, Kevin Smith, John Birman and Rupert Goodman; in Venezuela, Hiram Padron, Alberto Gibbs, and Pedro Vasquez; in Argentina, Andrew Joseph; in India, Bakhshish Singh.

My students were a special group whose intelligence and enthusiasm brought much new knowledge to the field. I am especially indebted to Michael Moore, Habeeb Ghatala, Tom Brady, Frank Nabwiso, Joseph Ansere, and Martin Kaunda.

To two former secretaries, Jan Noyola and Judy Johnson, I am grateful for unfailing support in the preparation of the typescript for this book.

The following publishers and organizations have kindly granted permission to quote from copyrighted sources: Adult Education Association of the United States of America, from *Adult Education*; Editorial Projects for Education; *Educational Technology*; Elvehjem Museum of Art; Harcourt Brace Jovanovich; Institute of Electrical and Electronic Engineers; *International Encyclopedia of Higher Education*; International Congress of University Adult Education; Institute for Research and Training in Education; Jossey-Bass Publishers; *Journal*, American Dietetic Association; Macmillan Publishing Co.; McGraw-Hill Book Co.; National Research Council; National University Extension Association, from *Continuum*; Open University Press; *Public Telecommunications Review*; Reader's Digest Association; State University of New York Press; UNESCO Institute for Education, Hamburg; William Morrow & Co.

A Personal Note

Every man must scratch his mark. Public monuments and facilities bear the graffiti of those who have had to reveal their names, loves or fantasies to posterity. For we extend ourselves, in part, through our marks.

—Roger Fransecki

I had the great good fortune to grow up in a home where reading and learning were continuing activities. Although our home was modest, it was rich in books, magazines, and an atmosphere of excitement with respect to finding out things, solving problems, and knowing about people and events past and present. Learning, despite my early deficiencies in arithmetic, German, and chemistry, was pleasure. My parents never stopped learning and were, I realize now, models of middle-class mobility by reason of self-initiated learning.

We did not have anything so grand as a "library" in our home, but we did make extensive and continuous use of the public library. As a boy, I filled my coaster wagon with all the books the librarians would let me take, and pulled the load home, anticipating at every step the thrills and enjoyment that would be mine in the days ahead.

Our books at home were mainly the classics of English and American literature, and books on science and scientific discovery. How proud we were, when, infrequently, there was a little extra money that could be used to buy a new book or magazine, to have our parents solemnly discuss with us what we might want. We quickly discovered a basic difference between books of lasting worth and those of temporary interest. The classics (we didn't use that term then, of course) we read over and over, once we were ready for them. If we weren't ready, we merely put them aside to try again later, confident that, when we were ready, the book would open itself to us, feed insatiable curiosity, and fill us with awe, pleasure, fear or excitement.

Naively, as a boy I thought that was the way all children grew up with their families.

But as a teacher of English and science, and as a school administrator — with most of my experience in schools that served what today would be called "disadvantaged" youth — I learned how crippling the effects of early language deprivation can be in youthful learners. I taught English by university radio in the thirties, in addition to regular duties, hoping to extend and enrich reading and learning to people whose lives without these activities would be progressively more barren and unrewarding.

In the Navy in World War II, I worked with others in developing new and efficient ways of teaching Naval personnel to fight and survive. Ships and personnel were dispersed throughout the world. Learning had to be carried on under the most adverse wartime conditions. Hence there was a high premium on innovative methods that would assure rapid, effective learning — in a way a proving ground for the non-traditional learning systems that would spread through the world in the next thirty years.

It was perhaps inevitable that my career in the university would align me most comfortably with University Extension (that's where the action was, and generally still is, in extending opportunity to learners most in need) and with the Department of Continuing and Vocational Education in the School of Education, where my colleagues and graduate students could help to create a body of knowledge about non-traditional and independent learning through the lifespan.

Innovation was still necessary, and I was not afraid of technology because my early learning had enabled me to perceive technology as a means for achieving fundamentally humane purposes. Records, tapes, radio, television, the telephone, moving and still pictures, the computer, teaching machines, and the satellite — all became tools in studies, experiments, and continuing programs that would strengthen and reinforce print, writing, reading, and learning, for learners near and far. The spread of interest in this work took me to many countries, where I discovered anew the social, economic, and personal consequences of arrested development and wasted human resources. The unsolved problems I observed there generated among the inhabitants a growing despair, which became callous indifference, anger, or anarchic hate because of lack of opportunity to learn, to grow, to mature — to become what each one wanted to be.

I had hoped that this book would, in some small way at least, present a "field theory" of non-traditional learning through the lifespan, noting and analyzing the dynamics of all the forces — educational, social, cultural, psychological, technological — that are involved in the various kinds of learning employed during the lifespan. That the book falls short of this goal does not dismay me too much, for I know that others will eagerly take up the beginning suggested here, reviewing, modifying, improving, and someday bringing closer to reality a fully developed field theory.

No doubt some readers of this book will disagree with what they find here. It is extremely difficult to think about common things — teaching, learning, motivation, communication, rewards, content — in a context other than that provided by one's own experience and the givens of one's culture. In a lively dialogue on a proposed change of instruction, a respected academic colleague turned to me in frustration and said, "But it's self-evident that the teacher must be in charge and make all the decisions."

Perhaps a useful feature of this book is that almost nothing in it has seemed self-evident. The viewpoints expressed here are just that — viewpoints. In an emerging field of knowledge there are no absolutes. The theories suggested may best be considered in the light of the Principle of Tolerance which long ago was expressed at the University of Göttingen: all knowledge in any area contains error and uncertainty. Tolerance is needed to accommodate uncertainty, for nothing can be so precise as to eliminate all error completely. An informed tolerance enables us to appreciate that all knowledge is both limited and subject to eventual correction.

Madison, Wisconsin   July, 1980

Preface

"We have poured billions of dollars into our present highly structured instructional bureaucracies. But only recently have we begun to experiment with supporting learning resources, open to all, which truly place themselves at the disposal of learners."

— Ronald Gross, *The Lifelong Learner*
(New York: Simon and Schuster, 1977, p. 167)

As learning becomes more important to individual and social survival, the kind and quality of education a person obtains for himself becomes more urgent. If traditional ways of learning do not satisfy urgent needs rapidly or equitably enough, other ways are found. These other ways of learning are usually called *non-traditional*. Used by more and more learners across a wide range of ages and levels, non-traditional learning replaces, extends, supplements, or builds upon learnings acquired in traditional ways.

The many different kinds of non-traditional learning, in format, content, purposes, length, level, and difficulty, comprise (even at this early stage of development) a wide diversity of choices and options for learners. This diversity requires an active role for learners in the voluntary selection of learning transactions, and a willing assumption of primary (though sometimes shared) responsibility for progress in learning. The mechanisms of non-traditional learning are open to all, and, in the market economy in which they operate, are more accessible to learners than traditional ways of learning. Non-traditional learning has the potential to bring about profound changes in all of American education.

The need to learn, implying satisfactory access to suitable instruction, was once identified with childhood and youth. It is now acknowledged to be lifelong. Yet most of traditional education is still geared to that earlier child–youth priority as though the need of people to learn lifelong had never been discovered. Although the past century has brought explosive and revolutionary change to nearly every aspect of human life, educational change is still evolutionary, and its tempo is glacial. Nevertheless, the changes that have occurred, when extrapolated into the near future, seem to signal continuing and significant departures from the traditional.

The many kinds of non-traditional learning bear different names: distance learning, independent learning, open learning, external studies, correspondence study, home study, radio education, television education, satellite education, self-directed learning, and so on — the operational denotata of various ways of "learning at the back door." A broad and inclusive view of the entire non-traditional field is difficult to structure because the terminology used is generally overlapping, unspecific, and inaccurate. To call the category that includes all these diverse ways of learning "non-traditional" is not very accurate either. But, however inaccurate, the term is widely used and must be employed in any discussion of the field. The traditional–non-traditional dichotomy, applied to learning, preserves certain myths and fallacies.

For example, that which is traditional is assumed to be older than that which is non-traditional. It is assumed to be closer to the primitive, the original or natural way of doing things. It is assumed to be better, widely understood, and accepted. Caleb Colton, an Englishman commenting on innovation (i.e., attempting something that deviates from the traditional) stated, "We ought not to be over anxious to encourage innovation, for an old system must ever have two advantages over a new one; it is established and it is understood." This "bird in the hand" mentality perpetuates the traditional, provides some stability against too-rapid change, but also does mischief in preserving myth and fallacy.

Our traditional ways of learning are actually relatively recent. Traditional learning is "remembered" from the recorded and experienced past, preserved as an artifact in our culture and institutions, and perpetuated by custom and law. On the other hand, non-traditional ways of learning have, in some respects, roots that go back beyond the traditional, and are closer to older, more natural ways of learning. While traditional learning is certainly established, whether it is well understood is moot. The surge of interest in other ways of learning by increasing numbers of learners suggests that traditional learning is not entirely accepted.

As to traditional learning being inherently better, the evidence is by no means convincing. Comparative studies over the past fifty years have consistently indicated that non-traditional learner achievement is at least equal, and in some respects may be superior, to the achievement of learners in traditional schools. Critics of such studies are quick to point out that comparisons of achievement sometimes fail to control hidden variables that affect achievement. Learner motivation, for example, is often cited as a probable explanation for the equal or superior achievement of learners in non-traditional programs. Or the fact that non-traditional learning is "harder," requiring more study, self-direction, and responsibility, is cited as a variable that affects compared achievement. The self-selective feature of non-traditional learning is also cited as a probable factor in the equal or superior achievement of non-traditional learners. "Non-traditional learning works for some, but not for all," is the common defense of traditionalists.

If these comments are turned around, the critics of comparative studies seem to be saying that because traditional learning is weak in learner motivation, self-direction, and learner responsibility, it cannot be compared with non-traditional learning. Nor does there seem to be evidence that traditional learning works well for all learners. The steady decline in learner achievement in traditional schools, as measured by national tests, discredits the assumption that quality learning is inherently and exclusively the product of traditional ways.

While non-traditional learning is not new, there are novel aspects to non-traditional learning. The use of modern communications media, for example, often provides an aura of surface newness or modernity that obscures more fundamental change — change reaching back to fundamental principles of communication in learning that are older, conceptually, than traditional education. A change of the communication medium in learning may not, by itself, be a really significant departure from the traditional, except of course among the tradition-bound. The new media are also used in traditional institutions; so media per se are not reliable indices of the important differences between the traditional and non-traditional.

The true differences are to be found in the capacity of non-traditional learning to tolerate and exploit physical distance between teacher and learner; in the invention or rediscovery of learning models that transcend the traditional; in a new understanding of the learning environment, so that a learner does not have to be in a specific place at a specific time to enjoy opportunity and access for learning; in a new perception of time with respect to the stages of learning; in the consistent effort to place the learner in the center of the teaching-learning process, with more active and responsible roles; in roles for teachers that link teaching with more truly professional activities; in concepts of instructional design and institutional development that are based more on fulfilling learning requirements and activities than on teaching requirements and activities.

But perhaps the most important difference between traditional and non-traditional learning is the almost unhampered opportunity and access to learning that may be enjoyed by learners who follow the non-traditional route. In a nation which has so long cherished opportunity for all, this feature cannot be dismissed as unimportant.

Non-traditional learning cannot any longer be dismissed as some behavioral aberration peripheral to "real" learning. It is not merely a crutch or surrogate for the convenience of a few learners who couldn't succeed in traditional schools. For most participants, non-traditional learning is not even an alternate way of learning; it is the only way open to them that is reasonably compatible with their needs and life situations.

"Learning at the back door" is, of course, a metaphor that heightens our perception of the discriminations inherent in a front door–back door world of education. People of quality use the front door; lesser folk carry out their tasks at the back door. There are different accommodations provided for, and different values attached to, the learning activities carried out at each door. Yet there is nothing in our history that remotely justifies the derogation of any kind of learning as second class, when undertaken with purpose, initiative, energy, and resourcefulness. Indeed, the self-made (usually meaning the self-educated) person has been one of our most enduring folk models. Abe Lincoln, learning basics alone, by firelight, was regarded as inferior by the professionals who confronted him, but we take comfort that it is Lincoln's wisdom and compassion that triumphed and survived.

Learning at the Back Door is not focused on any particular age group or institutional level because non-traditional learning occurs throughout life. However, because non-traditional learning is more visible, and perhaps more vulnerable, at the post-secondary, higher, and adult education levels, institutions and practices at these levels are referred to more often than others. The importance of making the learner the center of the universe of learning is stressed throughout, and a tentative theory of non-traditional learning in the lifespan is evolved, touching a wide range of subjects grouped into four parts.

For example, in Part One ("The Rise of Non-Traditional Learning") the new urgency of learning, and the changed societal contexts that make lifespan learning an imperative, are examined. The motivation for learning that characterizes human beings, the discontinuity of learning theory from a lifespan perspective, and the relationship of non-traditional to traditional teaching, learning, schooling, and concepts of knowledge are reviewed. An alternative to the classroom teaching-learning model is proposed. A different concept of learning environment is suggested.

In Part Two ("Non-Traditional Learning and Its Implications") *distance, independent, open,* and other kinds of non-traditional learning are analysed. Their characteristics, their overlapping and imprecise terminology, and their implications are probed for their probable effect on traditional as well as non-traditional systems of learning.

In Part Three ("Technology and Special Processes in Non-Traditional Learning Systems") the role of technology in diffusing opportunity to learn and providing access to instruction is discussed, and the importance of media in the communications aspect of learning is approached from the point of view of humanizing learning. Principles and procedures for instructional design, and institutional development and evaluation in non-traditional learning systems, are presented with a discussion of learner role behaviors as the desirable basis of institutional development.

In Part Four ("Learning from a Lifespan Perspective: Its Ends in a Learning Society") a "lifespan" view of all learning (traditional and nontraditional) is suggested. Regardless of system or method, whatever is learned is uniquely internalized, evaluated, and acted upon according to both short- and long-range needs and purposes. It is proposed that the learner meets different situations throughout life by employing three different kinds of learning behavior, defined here as *survival, surrogate,* and *independent.* Recognition of these behaviors constitutes another way of perceiving lifespan learning. Finally, it is the ends of all learning which mock the foolishness of the ancient academic dispute over a liberal arts versus a technical education. The possibility exists that non-traditional learning may be the flux that will bring these contents together in a useful blend. A conclusion summarizes the themes and viewpoints found in the book.

Learning at the Back Door is not a how-to-do-it book. Rather, it is a what-to-do and why-to-do-it book. There are many good books, reports, and articles on how to do the things that are called non-traditional, distance, open, and independent learning. There is growing competence and expertise in this field throughout the world, and a rich and diversified literature with such writers as Erdos, Holmberg, Mackenzie-Postgate-Scupham, Flinck, Dohmen, Rebel, Gooler, Perry, Sims, Knowles, Tough, Gould, Cross, Bååth, Moore, Peters, and others contributing to the advance of knowledge.

Furthermore, descriptions and inventories of non-traditional education continue to appear. For example, a new world Inventory of Non-Traditional Education is being published by the United Nations Educational, Scientific and Cultural Organization (UNESCO), "an attempt to gather the various experiences of the last two decades (which) resulted in the creation of new types of institutions and forms of higher education. . . . The Inventory contains information on about 500 innovative systems, institutions and programmes. . . . " (UNESCO Adult Education Information Notes, no. 2, 1979, p. 5.) Another report, "Tomorrow's Universities, New Ends and Means," by W. Werner Prange, David Jowett, and Barbara Fogel, is in preparation to summarize and interpret the important 1977 Wingspread World Conference on Innovation in Higher Education.

But there has been comparatively little treatment of what and why, the basis of theory. Hence, except in isolated instances, this book is not concerned with specific programs, institutions, or innovations, but rather with the hypotheses, analyses, and generalizations that contribute to theory.

Non-traditional learning — cut off as it has been from the educational mainstream — has been forced to go it alone for too long, to struggle for survival in an indifferent-to-hostile educational environment. In such an enterprise, operations come first, and theory has to wait. Society and the traditional schools have been among the losers, for many of the theoretical and applied features of non-traditional learning have profound significance in the reform and improvement of the regular schools, colleges, and universities.

An Introductory
Note About Terminology

Most educational terms had their origin in the evolution of traditional schools. In the context of non-traditional learning, however, school-based terms take on different shades of meaning. The bulk of the terms used in the chapters which follow are in fairly wide, but not necessarily consistent, use. Hence it may be useful to indicate the kinds of terms used in a consideration of non-traditional learning, and to define some of the basic terms at the beginning. Later, definitions of these basic terms will be refined, and additional terms introduced according to the purpose and context of subsequent discussions.

Sometimes referred to more as an attitude toward learning than as specific programs, *non-traditional learning* is an umbrella term that covers learning that is usually carried on part-time, and is initiated by, and largely under the control of, the learners themselves. It is usually self-paced and self-evaluated. Learning programs generally subsumed under the non-traditional rubric include:

> *Independent Learning:* This term identifies learning carried on wholly or largely independently of outside direction or control, characterized by learner autonomy and distance from educational authority. Independent learners may be consistently engaged in learning, but not usually on a full-time basis. Specific programs for independent learners are called *independent study, home study,* or *correspondence study.* Instruction reaches learners via such media as correspondence, radio, television, satellite, telephone, or com-

puter. Such programs employ two-way communication between teacher and learner, and usually individualize instruction.

Distance Learning: This term describes learning activities in which learner and teacher are at a physical distance from each other. Learning is generally part-time, and otherwise similar to that called independent. In some countries, the terms *distance learning* and *distance education* are now used in place of such designations as *correspondence study, home study* or *independent study,* or the identification of programs by the communication medium employed, such as radio or television.

Open Learning: This term came into use in 1969 when the British Open University was founded. It, too, means providing part-time learning opportunities for learners at a distance, who operate with a degree of autonomy and self-direction, but with open mediated access to learning without conventional prerequisites for acceptance or accreditation.

External Study: Most often used in British and Commonwealth countries, this term means extramural or off-campus learning. External study programs may diffuse instruction for the distant, part-time learner via various media, and also use the classroom for certain purposes. In the United States, external degree programs have found some favor.

Learners from infancy to old age engage in learning on their own initiative, part-time, motivated by self-perceived needs, concerns, and aspirations. Such learners set their own goals, exercise a high degree of autonomy, and evaluate their progress at a distance from teachers and institutions. There is less of this non-traditional learning during the years when learners are required to attend traditional elementary and secondary schools, or when they are enrolled full-time in post-secondary, college, or university education. But after traditional schooling has ceased, the adult learner is confronted by needs for continued learning. Autonomy, independence, self-motivation, self-direction, and self-evaluation are important traits in continuing education. Institutions that cater to adult learning needs are not usually threatened by such learner characteristics, and establish programs for adults which tend towards the non-traditional. Thus the opportunities for learning are probably richer in many respects after the age for leaving school than at any other period. Programs are consciously developed for learners who do not fit traditional patterns, and who do not attend school solely because of some requirement. A cluster of terms is used to describe adult learning programs:

Adult Education: Programs for adults are generally intended for persons who have left the formal, traditional schools. Adult education, however, can be traditional or non-traditional in character, depending on the degree to which the institutional providers recognize the importance of such things as learner autonomy and self-direction, self-pacing, and self-motivation, and attempt to reach learners at a distance.

Continuing Education and *Lifelong Learning*: Often used as synonyms for *adult education*, these terms introduce a further concept, the continuity of all learning throughout life.

Educación Permanente (permanent education) and *Lifespan Learning*: The European concept of *permanent education* is similar to that of *lifespan learning* (preferred in this exposition of non-traditional learning). These terms are presently used primarily by providers and specialists in adult learning, but are increasingly important concepts in educational reform, providing a perspective on all the learning, traditional and non-traditional, that occurs in a jumbled sequence throughout the learner's life.

Learners, in order to meet their need for access to learning opportunity, for information resources, instruction, counseling, and guidance, have traditionally been required to present themselves in person at those schools where instructional resources and services are maintained for youth. Frequently a person cannot gain access to resources and services without satisfying entrance requirements and devoting full time to learning. For adults particularly, such conditions are formidable barriers. An exception, of course, is the system of *public libraries*, which long have had, and now stress, their special role in assisting the continuing education of children, youth and adults. The learning encouraged by libraries is essentially non-traditional. Libraries are not providers of learning programs in the same sense as, for example, *University Extension*, which originated many of the innovative programs for reaching learners who lacked access to traditional institutions. Some private, proprietary, and specialized schools have also been in the vanguard of providing non-traditional learning opportunity and access.

The great advances in rapid and effective communication have made it possible for people (learners and teachers, for example) to communicate across distances so that learners no longer must physically "go back to school" in order to continue learning. Different ways of designing instruction enable part-time learners to learn at a distance, and progress at a rate consistent with their needs and situations. The removal of space-time-age barriers to learning has imposed special design requirements for non-traditional learning, and generated additional terminology.

Educational Technology: Programs designed for learners in communication via correspondence, radio, television, telephone, computer, cable, and satellite retransmission require specialists in media, communications, learning theory, instructional design, evaluation, and other areas. The teams of specialists who develop and produce non-traditional courses, materials, and processes employ technology for educational purposes.

Technology of Use: Part of *educational technology*, this aspect of use identifies the special processes that are used in designing, building, operating, and evaluating non-traditional institutions and programs. In addition, teachers and learners have to learn how to use, for instruction and learning, the products, materials, and processes that are employed in non-traditional programs.

Systems Design and Development: The complexity of designing, developing, producing, operating, and evaluating non-traditional programs poses physical, technical, human, and operational problems. To cope with this complexity, the *systems design and development* concept has frequently been employed. This, too, is an important aspect of *educational technology*.

The terminology of non-traditional learning covers a wide range of subjects. Much of the terminology is imprecise and overlapping. In the chapters which follow, specific terms will be refined and contrasted with the meanings of similar terms in traditional and non-traditional education.

Part One

THE RISE OF NON-TRADITIONAL LEARNING

I

A New Urgency
Regarding Learning

There is a new sense of urgency regarding learning throughout society. Even as the effects of the lowered birthrate in the United States cause enrollments in elementary, secondary, and higher education to level off or decline, there is growing conviction that everyone has a need, and a right, to learn throughout life.[1] The idea of schooling, which has been culturally linked to the discrete time-place education of children and youth, is being replaced by the concept of lifelong — or lifespan — learning unhampered by place-time barriers, motivated by the changing and maturing needs of more responsible and self-directed learners.

A report from the National Research Council states:

"We seem to be on the threshold of a 'learning society' in which learning is regarded as essential not only for the survival of man, but also as a route to social and individual maturation, the key to personal development and adaptation to the social changes wrought by new knowledge and technology."[2]

Renewable Resource — The Capacity to Learn

In our complex, interdependent, and increasingly overcrowded world, it is becoming evident that the human being's continually renewable capacity to learn has been the least appreciated and least exploited human resource. Such massive problems as the rapid depletion of natural resources; the unequal distribution of food, health care, and energy; pollution; peaceful coexistence; and immature civilizing processes are basically

3

problems of human attitude and behavior. These seem capable of solution only through Continuing Education, which gives to learning of all kinds at all levels a survival priority that contrasts sharply with the generally low public priority and profile of continued learning.

The National Research Council report referred to earlier includes a brief scenario of the kinds of educational services that are needed and feasible in U.S. metropolitan areas in the 1980s.

Technology, which itself requires more independent and self-directed learning, can at the same time improve access to learning opportunities.

Educational services of the future should not only serve the full range of learners in society, but should also be concerned with the residual effects of less effective education. Not all children and youth received an adequate education in the past, and as they have grown into adulthood, they have carried with them the learning deficits of their school years. Since World War II, such deficits have become impediments to steady employment, job satisfaction, successful parenting, and effective participation in the affairs of a rapidly changing society.

Persons with learning deficits may have suffered some degree of learning trauma during school attendance, and therefore find it difficult to turn to standard schooling, which they expect to be ineffective in helping them.

Supplementary education services that are mere extensions of regular schooling at fixed places and times do little to improve access and opportunity for those who most need to overcome learning deficits, and tend to perpetuate barriers to their continuing education. Delivery of educational services to the home by telecommunications could overcome some of these problems as well as expand educational opportunities for a whole range of citizens. . . .

Instruction could be diffused through an interactive communications system. Access to services could be provided in the home, workplace, office, community center, library, museum, or other institutions as available and appropriate.[3]

The report of the National Research Council (NRC) presents a tantalizing picture of education in the 1980s, in which non-traditional learning will play an important part. Even if the human need for, and the technical feasibility of, the NRC education scenario is accepted, some basic questions must be faced before there will be progress from where education is today to where it should be in the future.

What changes are needed in the present structure of education to accomplish lifespan accessibility to learning opportunities?

Is the need for lifespan learning, implying non-traditional programs, understood in society's largely specialized and traditional institutions?

How will the new programs fit into the present child- and youth-oriented structures of education?

What new institutional and fiscal policies will be required to encourage the changes needed?

Can traditional institutions be expected to initiate non-traditional programs without continuing, as a matter of self-interest because of traditional missions, the downgrading of that which is not traditional?

What institutions have responsibilities to undertake the research, experimentation, and innovation necessary to develop the new programs?

Is there a theoretical base in lifespan and non-traditional learning from which ideas for research, experimentation, and innovation can be derived to guide institutional change and development?

These are questions which will not be greeted with enthusiasm by most members of the education professions. New education priorities threaten old priorities. The pie of subsidy may have to yield smaller portions to everyone. But there have also been leadership, innovation, and institutional responsibility.

Universities Have Special Responsibilities

Dr. Howard R. Neville, president of the University of Maine (Orono), noted the responsibility of universities to provide, on and off campus, courses for citizens that would help solve the problems of inflation, unemployment, pollution, drug abuse, energy conservation, health care, housing, crime, urban inefficiencies, and economic development. At the heart of many of these problems, Neville said, "is the under-development, under-utilization, and waste of our society's human resources."[4]

Many universities have undertaken innovations to change traditional ways in higher education, and particularly to reach out to new categories of learners. Ericksen reviewed 241 innovations of the Committee on Cooperation (COC) of Chicago plus the Big Ten universities. In a report on Ericksen's review, Schillace noted:

Innovations occurred at all levels of instruction from undergraduate to graduate programs and in all areas of curriculum. A great percentage of the innovations involved the application of technological aids to instruction or some instructional rearrangements tending toward individualizing instruction. In some, the innovations reported tended to be either aids for providing information to a greater number of students or an attempt to rearrange the learning situation so that the amount of learning required of the student at any one time could be better controlled to meet students' needs.[5]

Except for the extraordinary inter-university cooperation accomplished by the universities in the COC, the innovations are perhaps not greatly different from other university efforts at change, reform, and improvement. Schillace comments that "one thing sorely lacking in attempts to produce change and innovation in higher education is a conceptual framework or theory from which reasonable hypotheses about change can be spawned. If necessity is the mother of invention, then theory is the mid-wife." Schillace continues:

Most of the innovations seemed to be trial-and-error responses; they were not procedures developed on the basis of a consistent theory of how people learn and how they are to be instructed. If we think of these innovations as products of some creative process responding to systems of instruction in higher education, it would seem that the results are merely temporary solutions to short-range problems.

Most products of innovation in college teaching seem to be the result of an incomplete process of creativity, relying heavily on a primitive trial-and-error approach. Implicit, unarticulated and incomplete models of how man learns and is to be instructed are drawn upon.[6]

Schillace recommends a four-stage process for creative problem solving:

1. intensive information gathering
2. application of relevant and available technological and performance skills in the problem-field
3. bringing together relevant materials and tools
4. a period of cognitive "incubation" during which the problem solver encourages spontaneous processes that might bear on the problem

Operating without a theoretical approach, innovations in universities frequently apply a technological Band-Aid to regular instruction methods, on the assumption that traditional college teaching is the ideal standard, and all that is necessary is to put that on television, in print, on tape, or into the computer. What sometimes results is the misuse of the communications medium employed and a "ho-hum," more-of-the-same learning experience.

The Open University of Britain, however, has won acclaim from students, academics, and the general public for the quality and compelling interest of its innovations in mediated instruction. Nearly alone among the new non-traditional universities, the Open University spent much of its scarce lead time in the structuring of teams to prepare its courses, develop a rationale if not a theory for its innovations, consult with specialists, and train its academics and technologists to work together effectively and cooperatively towards agreed-upon objectives for content, teaching, and learning.

The driving force behind this creative endeavor was Walter Perry, M.D., Vice-Chancellor, now Lord Perry. Like the heads of other universities, little in Perry's medical and teaching background had prepared him for the leadership and management of a large, innovative university. But Perry allowed himself to acknowledge needs that lay beyond his own capacities. He had the confidence and humility to make a prudent assessment of himself as well as the task when the Vice-Chancellorship became open. Perry commented,

I had, of course, heard about the University of the Air. Like most members of the established university world, I regarded it as a political gimmick unlikely ever to be put into practise, and likely, if it were, to produce only a few graduates of relatively poor quality. The idea that I might myself become involved in it never crossed my mind. I had never been interested in adult education. I knew nothing of educational technology or of the use of broadcasting for educational purposes. I was wholly ignorant of the new developments in educational theory and philosophy that were challenging established patterns and practises. I had never been active in national politics and was not driven by any urge to extend educational opportunity to those deprived of it, although I would have been sympathetic to such an aim had it been put to me. . . .

The main attraction of the challenge was the extreme diffculty of effective teaching at a distance. I had long been concerned at the pitiably inadequate standard of most of the teaching that went on in the established universities. I had tried, in Edinburgh, tentative experiments in designing courses by teamwork. . . . It struck me that a similar approach would inevitably be needed in the context of teaching at a distance. If it could be made to work in that context, it should ultimately spread back into the established universities and raise the standards of teaching everywhere. This was the motive that, on reflection, decided me to apply for the job. . . .[7]

For most people, the values attached to learning are derived from beliefs acquired over the years. Values and beliefs are related to learning theory.

Values, Beliefs, and Theories

Our ideas about humanity and the need or importance of learning are culture-bound. Is man a free agent in the world? A helpless victim of inherited genes? The product of social and economic conditions that force him into behavior over which he has little control? Is the individual important, or is the group, composed of conforming individuals, more important? Is the individual born to serve the state, or is the state created to serve each individual? May the individual seek upward social and economic mobility through his own efforts, or are his class and status to be determined by the collective needs of the state? Who is to get an education, for how long, with what curricula and rewards, at what cost to self and state, for what purposes and at what quality levels, through what methodologies, opportunity and access systems, and under what controls?

These are basic questions that each society deals with in its own way from pondering its basic beliefs and values concerning human life on this earth. Furthermore, each citizen, each learner, acts out in his lifetime his own and society's concepts and theories of the purpose, importance, and priority for education.

The new urgency regarding lifespan learning does not make itself known to an educational world without implying the existence of theory. In fact, there are conflicting theories. Basic to any approach to human learning there must be a view, a philosophy if you will, of humankind. Developing theory involves looking at something, considering it, contemplating; deriving a belief, policy, process, or principles of action; making judgments, conceptions, propositions, or formulae that may be pragmatic, abstract, or hypothetical; or forming unproved assumptions.[8] Any learning theory would have little significance without a view of human beings, the learners. In fact, learning theories express such views, directly or indirectly. Learning theories are not only the product of thinkers, they find their way into public policy respecting education and deeply affect the way schools, teachers, and learners behave. The pendulum swings of public school policy over a period of twenty to thirty years result from shifts in theory. Schools may go from progressive education to basics, to something else. The changes in teaching, content, and learning standards reflect changes in theory.

The new urgency regarding learning throughout life represents another shift in our beliefs and theories about learning. Kulich, an adult education comparativist, noted:

One can say, generally, that up to the fairly recent wide-spread and readily available schooling for everybody, self-education was the prime way for man to cope with the world around him. The universal man of the renaissance, the highly skilled guild craftsman of the baroque period, are excellent examples of the self-learning adult. With the introduction of free compulsory education for children, following the industrial revolution, many educators have forgotten the need of the adult to continue on learning, although the working man struggling for his place in the industrial society and the North American self-made man provide us with ample examples of the self-educated adult. In our own time we seem to have gone the full circle, as in spite of the extended schooling period for our children and youth we have to rely increasingly on the adult's ability to engage in a life-long self-learning process.[9]

The full-circle shift described by Kulich reflects changing times, circumstances, values and theories respecting education. Kulich adds, "The concept of *education permanente* is slowly gaining ground. Life-long integrated learning can succeed only if we mobilize the human ability to learn throughout life in a systematic way. Independent study, and the self-learning adult, will have to form a considerable part of this integrated life-long system of education."[10]

If the non-traditional kinds of learning mentioned by Kulich are an integral part of the new imperative for lifelong learning, there is an unspoken assumption (value, theory) that man can make choices in his life, affect outcomes by taking responsibility, and carry on learning on his own initiative as well as in an other-directed mode. The history of formal institutionalized education, the rise of the learned professions, and the success and prestige of schooling in providing upward mobility through the industrial revolutions, for a time eroded the belief that the learner himself can successfully continue learning. When schooling ended, it was thought that learning (at least as recognized by the schools) ended. Adults, it was believed, were not capable of learning much after the period of schooling.

All this is now changing, but change is always accompanied by doubt, skepticism, and even antagonistic disbelief. Indeed, it could be argued that the indecisiveness of educational leaders in responding to the new urgency for lifespan learning reflects a division among professionals and academics, respecting man's need and capacity for continuing learning on the basis of self-initiated effort. As movements and convictions undergo change the remnants of different conceptual systems for learning exist side by side. This diversity compounds the confusion of teachers, parents, legislators, students, and the public at large respecting the importance and the purposes of learning and education.

In consequence, a laissez faire attitude may prevail in which the hard intellectual questions of reform or improvement are never really tackled, and educational talent and expertise are dedicated merely to tinkering with existing systems, without adequate theory, as Schillace noted.

A View of Humanity Underlies Learning Theory

To act decisively about learning opportunities, access, curricula, and rewards to meet the new urgency for learning requires conviction expressed in new and higher priorities for learning. How does each of us find conviction in the face of difficult questions at the base of learning theory? How do we "decide," for example, whether individuals are gene-shackled, environment-determined, or agents capable of free will in development? If we are gene-shackled, many would conclude more and better learning throughout life may be of little use. If we are environment-determined, many would conclude that the chief means of improving the lot of people must be to change the environment rather than to improve human beings through continuing learning. If we can exercise free will, be makers of our own world and selves, then many would see the importance of learning through life as an imperative, a conviction.

The view of humanity that people cling to affects convictions about education. Conviction is crucial if lifespan and non-traditional learning are to become a permanent and important part of American education. Where do we find conviction?

Do we turn to science and the scientific method for answers that will form the basis of our convictions? Or do we expect too much of science and the scientific method? Perhaps uncertainty, inaction, laissez faire in the face of the big questions is a safer retreat from the risk-taking (as Dubos put it) of man making himself.[11] Do we delude ourselves that science alone will tell us what we are, what we can become? Can we insist upon fact alone as a basis for our beliefs and convictions?

Thomas Henry Huxley pointed out that "Those who refuse to go beyond fact rarely *get* beyond fact . . . almost every step (towards progress) has been made by the invention of a hypothesis which, though verifiable, often had little foundation to start with. . . ."[12] Donald Campbell, in a paper that provoked wide discussion among American researchers, stated:

> We must not suppose that scientific knowing replaces common-sense knowing. Rather, science depends upon common sense even though at best it goes beyond it. Science in the end contradicts some items of common sense, but it only does so by trusting the great bulk of common-sense knowledge. Such revision of common sense by science is akin to the revision of common sense *by* common sense, which, paradoxically, can only be done by trusting more common sense.[13]

Campbell, following Kurt Lewin, is an advocate of a wise integration of qualitative and quantitative methods in research leading to social action. He proposed a process of "qualitative knowing" as an alternative to the usual quantitative-experimental approach, with renewed emphasis on the methods of the humanities because of growing doubt regarding the appropriateness of the natural science model to social science problems. He is not alone in delineating the continuity between common-sense and scientific knowing.

Man, so "Learning" an Animal

If, in despair over uncertainty, we opt for total skepticism or unfounded credulity, or retreat into a laissez faire mentality, we most assuredly give up "knowing," consistency, and initiative in the expansion and perfection of knowledge, and conviction in the maturation of theory.

The rejection of total skepticism, credulity, and laissez faire mentality clears the way for us to be responsive to the qualitative as well as the quantitative, with respect to man, so learning an animal. Can we select a middle ground and carry qualitative knowings into the scientific dispute over the nature of man, focusing on the larger areas of overlap between the extremes? There is evidence that we can do so, on both scientific and humanistic grounds. Sir John Eccles, researcher in physiology and biophysics, may provide the bridge:

There is much misunderstanding and downright error in popular beliefs today that environment is dominant. . . . We are still gravely underestimating the tremendous range in the brain performances apart altogether from environmental influences. The environment is important simply for discovering and using what we have inherited. This is the essence of the age-old nature-nurture problem.[14]

The relationship of genes and environment to behavior is still a critical issue. Sociobiologists believe that "the nature-nurture debate . . . did a disservice by setting up apparently competing hypotheses when the true picture is one of complementarity." Robert Trivers, for example, believes it is now well established that "Behaviorally, man is neither in thrall to his genes, nor totally emancipated from them." William Hamilton's kinship theory established a base for arguing "that there is an underlying mechanism that will, in changing environments, facilitate the selection of gene-based adaptive traits that affect physiology, and to some extent, behavior."[15]

The controversy on this issue continues. At the University of Minnesota, the reunited twins study initiated by Thomas Bouchard and involving an interdisciplinary team of seventeen scientists, is turning up new evidence of the importance of genes in determining behavior.[16] And Richard Dawkins in England has proposed that "memes" (units of cultural imitation from communication and learning) work with genes to affect behavior. Dawkins suggests that memes are chemical codings that are replicated by communication, and that culture may result from the bonding of genes with memes.[17]

But Eccles also believes civilization and culture are made by man, and reciprocally make man, and that "education is the means whereby each human being is brought into relation with [civilization and culture] . . . immersed in it . . . participating in the heritage of mankind and so becoming fully human."[18] He continues: "Each human being is a person with this mysterious conscious self associated with his brain. He develops his brain potentialities from his lifetime of learning . . . and so becomes a cultured and civilized human being . . . [different from] other animals that we can regard as 'things'. Without that interaction [between genetic

code and the environment] you could be a thing. . . ."[19] Here is a bridge —
a blend of scientific objectivity and qualitative knowing. We understand
the capacity and the importance of learning to the so-human animal.

The dilemmas of reasoning and faith we must resolve if we are to find
conviction respecting the reform and extension of education, call to mind
the metaphor Quine borrowed from von Neurath: "We are like sailors
who must repair a rotting ship at sea. We trust the great bulk of the timbers while we replace a particularly weak plank. Each of the timbers we
now trust we may in turn replace. The proportion of the planks we are re-
placing to those we trust must always be small."[20]

The metaphor provides an explanation for the slowness of change in
general, but it also illuminates Schillace's four-stage process for creative
problem solving cited earlier. Theory in part, then, is a process of establishing or determining trust in the design for change which is derived from
theory. "Design," Dubos notes, "involves also values, because free will
can operate only where there is first some form of conviction."[21]

The Survival Value of Bimodal Evolution

Wheeler, a physicist writing about our future survival, states a conviction about education that is reminiscent of Eccles and Dubos.

What does it mean to be educated? What has become — must become — of the
meaning of education?

The issue before us springs ultimately, as does so much else that matters, from
our perception of the relation of Man to Nature. More fundamentally, because independently of our perceptions, the issue springs from the nature of Man.

. . . .we are informed not only by the molecular structure of our genes, but by
the diverse instrumentalities (both formal and informal) of education. . . . Our
evolution has become, as it were, bimodal. . . . It is evolution not in the biologi-
cal mode but in the conceptual — the expression not of genes but of ideas — that has
made us what we have become. . . . What is clear is that if we are to survive, if we
are to become viable in our new habitat (from which there is now no retreat), it
will be by force of new ideas and values. . . . We stand, therefore, in collective
need of education.[22]

Formal or informal, traditional or non-traditional, our learnings through
the lifespan have a greater significance for our survival than ever before.

The Adult Sector of Lifespan Learning

Has the new urgency regarding learning — apart from experimental
programs and the continuation of older non-traditional programs — made
any real difference in the educational world? Fred Harvey Harrington,

historian and former university president, has presented a remarkably candid picture of the current higher education situation, especially in the education of adults. "There are indications," says Harrington, "that adult education is becoming respectable."[23] Furthermore,

Adult learners are at the center of today's most interesting innovations in higher education — credit for learning through life experience, credit by examination, drop-out and drop-in arrangements, special degrees for adults, weekend classes, all sorts of non-traditional experiments.

There is a new enthusiasm for off-campus or what is now called distance education. . . . A flood of books celebrates the external degree as the great hope for the future. . . .

Recognition that information and traditional methods become outdated overnight in our technological society has produced an amazing increase in noncredit continuing education for professionals. . . .

Although older students prefer practical fare because they have to make a living, there has also been an increase in liberal education for adults.[24]

Harrington notes that professors who work on issues necessitating problem solving (energy, poverty, environment, etc.) "have come to understand that research and campus teaching are not enough. . . . they must become adult educators" to make an impact. And, "while still pursuing excellence, higher education is showing renewed interest in creating opportunity and a second chance . . . for the disadvantaged," those who want a mid-career change in occupation, and a wide range of learners who were passed by in the regular schools.

But Harrington also points out that the battle for the acceptance of teaching adults has not been won:

Despite the gains, adult education is not yet recognized as a full partner in most colleges and universities. Attitudes include indifference, skepticism (especially as to quality), and even open opposition, most noticeable in the colleges of liberal arts. Past attempts to establish the education of adults as part of the fundamental responsibility of colleges and universities have more often than not failed. Continued failure is likely again unless those who favor a better deal for older students prove more effective than they have to date.[25]

There have been previous efforts to raise the level of adult education in the universities.

Each time, however, the predicted happy day failed to arrive; and each time the reasons were the same. There was a shortage of money, and there were admitted weaknesses in the programs designed for adults. But the key factor was the reluctance of educators to consider the teaching of adults as important as research and the teaching of the young; and there were no economic or social pressures strong enough to change this situation.[26]

Harrington reviews the low priority placed by academics on adult education from the 1960s to the present, and concludes, "Time has not changed that tune." Nor have the budget-cutting tendencies of universities changed, with Step One — cutting adult education — still standard in much post-secondary education.[27]

Although the sense of urgency respecting learning is broadly evident throughout society, it is not yet a matter of primary or even secondary concern among American academics whose careers, and hence whose inclinations, tend towards research and the traditions of teaching youth.

Three Questionable Assumptions

The future of educational change, as projected in the NRC scenario for new educational services to metropolitan areas in the 1980s, seems to look chancy. However, the appearance of chanciness is dependent upon three implicit assumptions. These assumptions, and a commentary on each, follow:

The First Assumption: traditional universities have to be the principal means for initiating and sustaining the changes needed.

The first assumption is not necessarily valid. In Britain, for example, a new institution — The Open University — was created to undertake needed changes when it was clear that the traditional universities would not or could not do so. In the United States, the consortium that is called The University of Mid America, now under the leadership of a new president, Dr. Donald McNeil, may become the regional non-traditional model that it was intended to be. Many other models that depart from the traditional university pattern exist (Minnesota Metro, Empire State College, the N.Y. Regents Degree Program, the University Without Walls, etc.).

But in some ways the most vigorous innovation in lifespan non-traditional learning may come from other sources. Almost unnoticed there has been a vast increase in the amount — and also the quality — of educational materials and programs available to learners of almost all ages. The providers of these materials and programs represent a rich and diversified educational resource frequently going beyond the traditional. For example:

Educational Institutions

University Extension. University Extension, also a legitimate part of the traditional university, is listed here because it has been in the forefront of encouraging lifespan and non-traditional learning since the first decade of this century. Its programs affect nearly all age groups. A university resource on the one hand (standing between the traditional academic departments and the learning publics), Extension is also a community-regional resource on the other.

Agricultural Extension and "Outreach" Programs.

Community and Technical Colleges.

Public School, Vocational, Agricultural, and Adult Programs.

Adult Education Agencies (national, state, local). Adult Basic Education, Literacy, English as a Second Language, etc.

Proprietary Schools.

Other Institutions

Education Distributing Networks. The Public Broadcasting Service, National Public Radio, local public radio and television stations, cable systems, and more recently the Appalachian Education Satellite Program, a satellite-cable system which diffuses the education programs of more than sixty colleges and universities, and which may expand its service from the Appalachian to other regions of the United States.

Professional Associations. Programs in healthcare, librarianship, education, management, economics, city management, accounting, etc.

News Gathering and Distributing Networks on radio and television, newspapers, big and little magazines, and publishing houses.

Unions, Cooperatives and Occupational Groups.

Business and Industry.

Churches and Religious Organizations.

Government (federal, state, local) Agencies with education programs in specific fields: health, agriculture-nutrition, the military, post office, commerce, business, employment, job training, safety, energy, conservation, the environment, minorities, women, crime prevention, etc.

Public and Private Libraries, Museums, Art/Music centers, and Historical Societies.

People Groups

PTA–PTO.

Consumer Groups.

Hobby Groups.

Other Special Interest Groups. Ethnic and cultural societies, political, environmental, energy, minorities, women, etc.

The list above does not exhaust the diversity of providers now supplying learners of all ages with materials and/or programs of almost every conceivable kind. The growth of this vast and more or less informal educational resource "beyond the traditional classroom" is evidence of the importance of lifespan learning. The situation may impel providers to use fresh and creative approaches, innovative models for teaching and learning, which would not be encouraged in traditional settings. Universities, the capstone of our formal education structure, have special prestige and responsibilities in the continuing education of learners, but they are not alone the arbiters of the needs, contents, and levels of learning that will serve the "learning society." Just as Chautauqua and the Ethical Culture Society served earlier Americans, the diverse array of providers of informal education today may encourage the universities themselves to take a larger part in the non-traditional learning that is going on.

The Second Assumption: University academics, and especially liberal arts faculty, have an inflexible and unyielding disinterest or hostility to needed change.

The second assumption is not necessarily valid. As the enrollment patterns of traditional colleges and universities continue to change in the direction of adult students, it is unlikely that traditional college and university attitudes towards adult learning will remain unchanged. In April 1978, the following U.S. Census Bureau information appeared in *The Chronicle of Higher Education*:

More than a third of today's college students are 25 or older, the Census Bureau reports.

In 1977 about 36 per cent of such students were at least 25 years old, compared with 28 per cent in the older group five years ago, the bureau estimates.

The Census Bureau's sampling of American households last fall found a particularly strong increase in the enrollment of older women.

The number of women aged 25 or older who were enrolled in college last fall was up more than 23 per cent over the previous year. In the past five years, the number of enrolled women over 25 has more than doubled.

For men, the trend was less dramatic: enrollment of those over 25 was up 2.9 per cent in one year and up about 34 per cent in five years.

Among students under age 25, enrollment of women declined more than 6 per cent in one year but was still about 13 per cent higher than five years ago. Enrollment of men under age 25 rose less than half of 1 per cent in one year and was down a fraction of a per cent in five years.

Part-time enrollment increased by about 9 per cent in the last year, the census study indicates, while the number enrolled full-time remained unchanged.

College officials interested in planning ahead may note with some concern that kindergarten enrollment last fall showed the biggest drop ever recorded — down 300,000 in one year, reflecting a decline in births five years earlier.

Since 1970, says the Census Bureau, the number of children enrolled in elementary schools has declined by 4.7 million.[28]

As this trend continues, it is likely that basic academic job security will change, and that attitudes will also. Professors will learn from experience, as others have, that adult learners are in many ways as capable as youth, and better motivated; but in any case better than no learners.

But attitudinal change is also occurring from pressures within academia. Strong leadership (like that, for example, of Dr. Patricia Cross, former President of the American Asociation for Higher Education) is bringing a message to academia that change is needed, is imminent, and should be accomplished with the full participation of the academic community.

The Third Assumption: experimental innovation and institutional change will continue in a primitive trial-and-error approach to change without theoretical underpinning.

Assumption three is not necessarily valid. The day of tinkering, instead of carefully planned and executed innovation based on relevant theory and instituted under professional guidance, is nearly over. Scholarship in adult, continuing, and non-traditional learning is coming into its own. Graduate programs of quality are guiding more students to Ph.D.s in this field than ever before. A growing roster of specialists in non-traditional learning are working in many countries, in national and international organizations, to exchange research, information and assistance. Extension, community college and other non-traditional learning leaders are freeing themselves of past notions of primary loyalty to higher education, and forging professional and political links with the needs, issues, and causes of the people – the continuing learners – whom they were intended to serve.

The battle, as Harrington says, has not yet been won. But neither has it yet been lost. The new urgency regarding learning, so natural for man the learner, is being met in many and diverse ways, although usually without an adequate theoretical base. Even that, however, may change as non-traditional learning at all ages and levels contributes to a better understanding of its lifespan dimensions.

II

Learning at the Back Door

Jonathan Swift, in 1704, said a few choice and satirical words about in-stitutionalized learning: "For to enter the palace of Learning at the Great Gate, requires an expense of time and forms; therefore men of much haste and little ceremony are content to get in by the back door."[1]

Swift's words seem to have anticipated today's world-wide yearning for learning — a yearning that has compelled millions of men and women, of much haste and little ceremony, to try to get into the palace of learning by the only gate available to them — the back door.

Bogdonov-Belski, a nineteenth-century Russian painter, depicted the plight of the millions who have not had front door learning opportunity (Frontispiece 1, p. ii). Entitled "School Door," the painting shows a ragged peasant boy looking into the world he was not allowed to enter. Just as in Jonathan Swift's time, adult education, continuing education, non-traditional–distant–independent learning, are still largely back door op-portunities to learn, in spite of the improvements that have occurred in education since 1704.

This is all the more astonishing in view of the substantial progress that has been made in the generation, collection, and conservation of knowl-edge. It is the *diffusion* of knowledge that has lagged behind the needs of the world. Diffusion of knowledge is a function that is shared by many societal and cultural institutions, but chief among them are the systems of education that are intended to serve the people who need to learn. For various reasons these systems have failed to progress in the diffusion of knowledge, at least to the same extent they have in the generation, collection, and preservation of knowledge, and in the democratization of schooling.

Sir James Mackintosh in 1791 argued that "diffused knowledge immortalizes itself."[2] That may seem an exaggeration today, but considering the elite character of education in 1791, and the greatly increased need for knowledge by all people today (a need which is still only partly satisfied through our front and back door learning enterprises) perhaps the comment is guilty only of high-flown phraseology.

In *The Ascent of Man*, that remarkable television series (and book) that fascinated millions of viewers and readers in many countries, Jacob Bronowski remarked that the long childhood of man will come to an end only when the importance of man *as a learner* is perceived, and when we learn what knowledge really is in terms of improving the lives of people.[3] Bronowski's comments show great insight. Very likely the diffusion of knowledge has been hobbled because of most people's narrow view of the nature of knowledge and their curious myopia about the most important characteristics of *homo sapiens* — his extraordinary and lifelong dependence upon learning for survival, and his astonishing capacity to learn. These characteristics separate man from every other animal.

To be sure, poets, philosophers, and savants have long pointed out that man differs from the lower animals, and survives, because he is a tool maker, an upright communicator, adaptive to changing conditions, an organizer of social conventions and institutions to assist in the long nurturing necessary to improve the chance of survival, and the possessor of a large brain and complex neurological system.

René Dubos called man "So Human an Animal." He noted, "We recognize him by his voice, his facial expressions, and the way he walks — and even more by his creative responses to surroundings and events. . . . Man makes himself through enlightened choices that enhance his humanness."[4]

Back Door Learners

In this light, Jonathan Swift's reference to back door learning — which describes the education of most of the people in the world throughout their lives — falls into perspective. Back door learners have been a largely unacknowledged source of the vitality, energy, creativity, and survivability of human existence on this Earth.

The fact that probably one-twentieth of all the humans who have ever lived are still alive[5] makes us newly aware of the significance of recent world population growth, of the effects of improved health care and nutrition, of the consequences of substituting mechanical, electrical, and chemical energy for human work, of the generation of knowledge to sustain industrialization and the democratization of society, and of the increase in learning — of all kinds — for the improvement of life and survivability.

Human learning preceded institutions, and proceeds with or without institutional sanction and guidance. Back door learners, of course, sometimes make use of institutions — or of institutionalized processes — but with a difference. Initiative and motivation reside with them, not the schools.

It is still widely assumed that back door learners are narrow learners, confined and imprisoned in petty pursuits for selfish advancements. Yet we also know of philosophers, scientists, writers, musicians, artists, and statesmen who had little formal education but were avid back door learners (for example, Eric Hoffer). Today we would classify such learners as independent, distance, non-traditional, and lifespan learners, making their own ways in learning by using libraries, historical societies, open schools and universities, university extension, and external and other alternative modes of learning to augment their own resources.

Frontispiece 2, page iii, a pen and ink drawing by Mike Smith, symbolizes "Learning's Open Door" that learners at the back door have always had to create for themselves. The concerns of a learner are suggested, as well as the richness of access to resources that modern communications provide, linking the learner with the entire world.

Different Perceptions of Man and of Learning

How one perceives man determines the role and importance attached to learning.

For example, Joseph Campbell, a widely known writer with a societal/mechanistic view of man, writes: "In his life-form the individual is necessarily only a fraction and distortion of the total image of man. . . . The totality — the fulness of man — is not in the separate member, but in the body of society as a whole; the individual can only be an organ."[6] This statement implies little initiative, value judgment, or free choice (except as a distortion) in individuals. With such a view, learning could only be perceived as primarily mechanistic, the other-determined behaviorism of a Skinner.

Joseph Wood Krutch, however, presents a different view of man:

If . . . everything which has been or ever will be was not fixed and inevitable from the dawn of creation [which Krutch had previously asserted] then it must be because of either a random element in the universe or because an effective freedom to choose exists somewhere. And there seems no more likely place where it might reside than in man himself. If he is to use this freedom actually to move the world . . . then he must have some point outside the physically and mentally determined on which to rest his lever. That fulcrum cannot be anything but "values" deliberately chosen.[7]

A comment by Dubos carries this individualistic view further: "The most dominant characteristic of Western culture has been the search . . . for ways to convert the universal characteristics of mankind into a great diversity of individual experience."[8]

Here we have man the individual, with values and power to move the world. From this view we could only derive an individual/developmental concept of learning.

But there are views that fall between those cited. Martin Buber, the theologian-philosopher who proposed the personalized "I-Thou" relationship with God and the world, noted that "the fundamental fact of human existence is neither the individual as such nor the aggregate as such."[9] While this is a sort of middle view, Buber insists on active roles for people in their I-Thou relationship with the aggregate and with God.

Albert Schweitzer put the problem in the form of a question: "What road [from the history of thought] can best indicate our future search for a world-view in which the individual can find inwardness and strength, and mankind progress and peace?"[10] This middle view is pregnant regarding concepts of learning for both individual and society.

Back door, self-motivated learning spreads along the same continuum, and implies the varied views of man, as does front door learning, and with probably the same statistical proportions. How did back door, self-motivated learning become important in America?

The Early Twentieth Century

In pre-industrial America most workers were engaged in farming and handicrafts.[11] Until the twentieth century, whether a person was literate, the product of regular schooling, or "self-made" was of little practical importance. However, in 1914 Thorstein Veblen pointed out that the educational emphasis of the machine age fell "rather more decidedly on general intelligence and information" than, as before, on apprentice training or the efforts of self-education.[12] In the fifty-five years between the Morrill Act of 1862 (establishing the college land grant system for the development of agricultural and mechanical arts) and the Smith-Hughes Act of 1917 (providing matching grants to states for vocational education and teacher training), a profound shift in education had taken place as a result of basic changes in American life.

America was being transformed from a predominately rural to a predominately urban setting. Torn with conflicts of interests and clashes of purpose, expanding industrialization brought urban growth and a labor class which began to outnumber the small independent farmers of rural America. The mainstays of American democracy, freedom of opportunity and competition, seemed threatened as large corporations realized financial and political power through monopoly. The faith in individualism — which had been strengthened by America's abundance and its relative freedom from social and religious intolerance — seemed to be weakening. Urban growth threatened the traditional democratic and egalitarian ideals of the earlier rural society and diminished the individualism which had made democracy viable.

The Smith-Lever Act of 1914 (establishing the Cooperative Extension Service for direct transfer of information to farmers) and the Smith-Hughes Act represented a new trend in American social and economic theory: society itself would begin to take responsibility for encouraging individual development. Government would be used to restore freedoms and opportunities curbed by the rapidity of change and the narrow focus of industrial development. The liberal doctrines of democracy would be revitalized by abandoning laissez faire economics and placing restraints on competition and private property. It was clear that the determinants of educational change in the twentieth century would be the politics of social, economic, and technical power.[13]

The Rise of University Extension
in the United States

As the century began, educational opportunity for children and youth was still uneven, but by 1918 all forty-eight states had enacted compulsory education laws. Yet the adults whose youth had been spent in westward migration, farming, and apprenticeship had little formal education. If they were to participate fully in the social and economic benefits which the industrial era seemed to promise, they would have to learn as adults, on a part-time basis, preparing themselves while working. As back door learners, they would have to find resources for learning where they could. Immigrant families, with educational deficits reaching back to their countries of origin, had to combine working and learning to survive, and later, if successful, to prosper.

Early America was not without opportunity to learn, even for the poor, the illiterate, the immigrants, the Westward seekers. Religious schools, the Sunday School Society, the New England (later the American) Tract Society, parish libraries, Franklin's subscription library, the mechanical and mercantile libraries, school district libraries, and the public libraries which emerged in the mid-nineteenth century as the "people's university" — all catered to learners whose needs could not be met in schools. For example, the Redwood Library of Newport, Rhode Island, in 1874 stated its goal to be "a library whereunto the curious and impatient Enquirer after Resolution of Doubts, and the bewildered immigrant, might freely repair for Discovery and Demonstration . . . true knowledge and satisfaction."

Another uniquely American institution, Chautauqua, originally a summer camp for Sunday School teachers, became Chautauqua University in 1886, and spread its influence throughout the country under the tents of its famous traveling Chautauqua. The Ethical Culture Society and various Philosophical Societies reinforced the emphasis on literacy, reading, and discussion as the tools by which a person could get an education. Even so, the mobility, the unstable conditions of frontier life, the remoteness of settlements from the resources and amenities of civilization, made opportunity inaccessible to many. But there were precedents for the concern and involvement of American institutions (including universities) in extending opportunities to learners beyond the campus.

The concept of "extension" appeared in Britain in the 1870s, to be replaced by the preferred concept of "extramural education," which survived there. But the extension idea found its way to the United States, where it was compatible with earlier precedents. Farsighted educators on both sides of the Atlantic perceived the need for extending university-level instruction to adults. Although not a figure in the extension movement itself, Alfred North Whitehead, the British mathematician-philosopher, had laid a solid philosophical base for the reform of all education. Whitehead (1861–1947) protested against dead knowledge, the teaching of inert ideas "received into the mind without being utilized, or tested, or thrown into fresh combinations."[14] Whitehead's views were not ignored in the United States, where many of his proposals had particular poignancy. "If education is not useful," he asked, what is it?"[15] Whitehead pointed out that education's nearest analogue "is the assimilation of food by a living organism,"[16] an apt analogy for a nation that would later perceive education as the surest means for social and economic mobility as well as self-development. Whitehead's belief that *life* is the only valid subject matter for education,[17] and that theory and practice must be taught in close proximity, found ready acceptance in America, his home after 1924.

But Whitehead was not alone. His contemporary, John Dewey (1859–1952), whose theories of progressive education were largely developed by 1916, clearly reinforced Whitehead and the pragmatic view of man and learning expressed by the American philosopher-psychologist William James (1842–1910). Another contemporary, sociologist Lester Frank Ward (1841–1913), influenced American education by advocating a problem-solving focus for American universities. This rational base for educational change contributed to the evolution of a phenomenon noted later by Meiklejohn[18] and Shannon and Schoenfeld[19] — that there is a symbiotic relationship between the practical aspirations of the American people for a more abundant life and the development of higher learning.

The humanist tradition, carried over from Britain, and identified in America with William Rainey Harper, Charles R. Van Hise, and others, nourished the concept of extension, which expressed an idealistic belief in the perfectibility of man. Harper had established extension as a major division in Rockefeller's new University of Chicago (1892), but efforts to create extension within the established universities met with opposition from faculties dominated by elitist views. In Wisconsin, where far-sighted university presidents (including Van Hise) had glimpsed the importance of the university's reaching out to farmers, teachers, businessmen, and workers, the first attempts to form an extension did not succeed, but in 1906 university extension became a reality and produced a model for the state university. William H. Lighty and Louis Reber organized the Wisconsin Extension Division, and carried their message to other universities.

But the self-directed and self-motivated learners who sought learning through university extension soon found that this, too, was a back door. From its inception, extension faced the slings and arrows of academics who were suspicious of any attempt to democratize higher education. In addition, the academic and managerial aspects of extension were different from standard career lines in the universities. A prominent dean, E. A. Birge, in 1915 stated that extension work was an academic "sideline" and that anyone "who entered and stayed in was almost bound to forfeit academic promotion."[20] But a British academic, Richard Moulton, told the National University Extension Association (NUEA) in the year of its founding that he objected "to the view that the extension movement is a by-product of university activity. On the contrary it is an essential product of the function of universities."[21]

Concern for academic respectability was a continuing theme in extension work, expressed regularly and sometimes bitterly in the Proceedings of the NUEA. To some extent the problem of standards and respectability was the product of a shift in extension purpose that occurred about 1915, when extension was changing from a movement that extended intellectual disciplines (the British model) to a service organization which also developed programs for groups according to utilitarian principles. These two thrusts were frequently in conflict, and their effect was to keep extension essentially a back door to the learning so jealously and patronizingly guarded by universities.

Expanded Communications and Technology

The early twentieth century witnessed the annihilation of the space-time-economic boundaries that had traditionally constrained the opportunity to learn. High-speed presses, inexpensive duplication devices, the telegraph, telephone, silent motion pictures, lantern slides, the phonograph, and radio did much to lessen the isolation of Americans from one another and the world. The automobile replaced the horse and buggy and even the train as the vehicle for circuit-riding teachers who fanned out into the countryside to reach extension students.

The techniques of World War I training carried over into peacetime. "If you need to be convinced as to the usefuness of visual instruction in the winning of the war," extension was told, "all you have to do is think of the methods of training that have been used."[22] Motion pictures, slides, and records joined print in extension's programs for distant learners.

William H. Lighty found in radio, greatly developed during the war, an ideal means for reaching distant learners. "Until the last three years," said Lighty in 1923, "educational institutions and the general public has [shown] little interest in radio communication. Within less than that brief period 600 radio stations have been put into operation."[23] Lighty conducted a vigorous campaign to encourage NUEA institutions to make use of radio, and so helped create public educational radio for the nation.

Diversity, Anti-utilitarianism, and Cooperation

In 1924 the growing diversity of extension programs caused Dean Louis Reber to remark, "In the time that has been given to this paper it is impossible to do more than hint at the field and scope of university extension."[24] This diversity was partly responsible for extension's shift away from its earlier utilitarian/vocational emphasis. Another reason was that other agencies began to take over work pioneered by extension. States and cities established vocational and continuation schools, industries launched training programs, private and proprietary schools multiplied, the Carnegie Corporation declared its interest in adult education. A measure of the success of extension, these events were also reason for change.

The number of agencies interested in extension education increased. Cooperation with other organizations became necessary, as an extension worker indicated in explaining cooperation between public libraries and extension. "We aim to place at the disposal of each individual just the material to meet his needs at the time when he is interested in the subject."[25] The task of extension had become too large for a single agency, and cooperative adaptation was necessary for further growth.

In all the cooperative adaptation since the 1920s, and despite the millions of successful self-motivated learners who have pursued learning with the resourceful help of university extension, extension and its various offshoots still retained their back door characteristic and utility.

But the phenomenon of the self-directed, self-motivated, independent, and often distant learner was well established in the United States. In the decades to follow, the Great Depression, World War II, the G.I. Bill (which did more than anything else to democratize continuing education), and the heady post-war years of increased aspirations for all, generated new institutions to meet the needs of independently learning adults: alternative schools and programs, open schools and universities, increased use of radio, television, and the telephone as media for learning, junior colleges and community colleges, and vocational-technical schools and colleges.

Many of the new institutions offered front door learning to adults on a part-time or full-time basis, though scornfully regarded by established universities.

The 1960s and early 1970s were marked by an innovative thrust in education that blended idealism, practicality, and scientific rationalism, and was in some ways reminiscent of the growth of education in the early twentieth century. Television had become the great leveler of American society, with commercial entertainment at the lowest level. But again, public television and radio offered an alternative for self-motivated learners.

The disillusionment that followed the Vietnam War and Watergate raised critical questions about accountability in a democratic society. The great problems of the seventies — health, peaceful coexistence, pollution, energy, the equal rights of minorities and majorities, responsible governance — began to be perceived as human behavioral problems. Disenchantment spread to institutional education with a sharp insistence that education, if it can't be resourceful enough or innovative enough to teach the ways to solve problems, must then accept some responsibility for their continuation. While some in education cried "unfair" at this new accountability, others noted that the emerging attitude towards learning was consistent with the view of man as maker of his world, and a confirmation of the traditional faith in education that has characterized America.

From Whitehead and Dewey to the seventies, the American people have never wavered in their basic belief that education makes an important difference in a society in which people are free to set their own goals, individually and collectively, and is the only consistent route to survival and self-determination. Nevertheless, at all levels criticism increased respecting institutionalized education. As parental controls weakened, and the family unit suffered erosions of some of its traditional functions as they were transferred to professionals and institutions, the family continued under siege as the basic cultural unit. Technology, blamed for much that is wrong in society, was also hailed as potentially a means of enriching the quality of life.

The Educational Experience Has Left Its Mark

Back door learners began to hope that their needs and accomplishments would some day be recognized, and the number of part-time, distant, independent learners increased sharply so that many leaders in education and government saw signs that we were on the threshold of a "learning society." Indeed, the courts, under new and old legislation, began to interpret opportunity for education as a personal right because it was so essential to self-development and survival.

Isaac Asimov, commenting on the significance of self-education and University Extension, said recently,

> . . . I have to educate myself. . . . the pleasure of learning new things has not diminished with the years. . . . And I think that's the way it is with everyone. . . . I think that right now the greatest institution in favor of the survival of the human species is University Extension — an institution which is dedicated to teaching mature people, people who are not "going to school," anything that they want to know. . . . any course that interests them — not necessarily one which they can use to make a living, but something which can fill them up inside; something which can make them feel better; something which will make them happier; something which will make it possible for them to be fuller human beings. . . . The ideal function of University Extension is to increase the joy of humanity and to serve as a nucleus around which the further development of the techniques of education, by means of technological advances as yet only in their infancy, can develop.[26]

Man, so long in his in-school activities confined and other-directed, and in his back door learning put down and ignored, is never more the celebrated *homo sapiens* than as learner, doer, maker of himself and his world. A former British Prime Minister, George Canning, in an address entitled *The King's Message*, said, "I called the New World into existence to redress the balance of the old."[27] The new era of learning we may be entering gives hope of redressing ancient educational wrongs, of diffusing front door learning opportunity to people where they are, of recognizing that people do possess the capacity to learn in response to their own needs and aspirations. It gives hope that people can learn in self-motivated, self-directed modes, and that, despite the vast machinery for the control and direction of teaching, learners will still learn for themselves what they need to survive and improve their lives.

Bailyn, looking back on education in the formation of American society, put it this way: "What was recognized even before the Revolution as typical American individualism, optimism and enterprise resulted also from the processes of education which tended to isolate the individual, to propel him away from simple acceptance of a pre-determined social role, and to nourish his distrust of authority."[28] Learning at the back door has been an important part of the American educational experience, and it has left its mark.

The Environment for Non-Traditional Learning

Non-traditional learning has left its mark in another way. Learning at the back door had to be carried out wherever learners faced problems, a need to know, or wherever they could find materials or assistance. They learned at home, on the job, in offices, on farms, in libraries, at cultural events and community projects, and in church-related activities — almost anywhere, in fact, except in schools. The growing importance of schooling and the increasing professionalization of instruction widened first the social gap, and later the economic gap, between those whose education was received in schools and those who had to go the "self-made" route.

And yet (except for the lack of credentials) the non-traditional learning accomplished was almost awe-inspiring. In agriculture, mechanical, industrial, and business development, in music, politics, the arts, in writing, communications, in invention and its application, non-traditional learning usually preceded the establishment of formal schools as the country expanded westward. It maintained, for those who could not go to school, a steady and persistent drumbeat for self-improvement that helped to transform a wilderness into a productive society. Literacy was an accepted social goal in America's schools because it was first the personal goal of thousands of immigrants and uneducated who, lacking much in the way of schooling, saw reading and writing as necessary tools for self-development and urged their children and communities to set high priorities for it. As America grew, the preachers, printers, and small town teachers prodded school and non-school learners alike to make something of themselves and their country.[29]

The assault on ignorance went beyond the question of basic literacy to larger social, moral, and cultural issues, as well as to practical and technical matters. Laubach and Mujahid explain this in a comment that echoes

Paolo Freire: "The process of learning the basic communications skills sensitizes the learners to an awareness of, and possible solutions to, their problems."[30]

Non-traditional learning, in the everyday environments of life, work, leisure, and community participation, raises an interesting question: If people can and do learn in a variety of places, where, then, is the environment for learning? People learn in groups, with or without a teacher; they learn alone, on their own; in conversations with others; while reading, seeing, feeling, smelling, and hearing things; while thinking. Except for school-type learning, learning seems not to be characterized by an exclusive place, time, or other environmental condition.

Learners placed in schools and provided with teachers do not always learn, or learn what they have been sent to learn. Nor do they always learn with efficiency and dispatch, or remember learnings long enough to pass a test, or remember learnings after a test has been passed.

If learning occurs outside the environment of the school, and does not always occur within it, then we must question the assumption (a given in our culture) that specified place, time, and environmental conditions are essential for learning. If learning can and does occur anywhere, any time, under apparently random environmental conditions, then perhaps some of the effort we put into creating special environments for learning may not be necessary.

The truism that man is the product of his environment thrives in street folklore. Yet this truism leaves much unsaid, and, on examination, appears to cloud the issue rather than clarify it. It is said that Winston Churchill once remarked in reviewing some new public buildings, "We shape our buildings, and they shape us." This comes closer to reality, for it recognizes the complexity of the relationship between man and environment, and acknowledges that man is creative and adaptive, and not merely passive.

The teaching-learning environment is especially the victim of cultural myth and misunderstanding. Ask nearly anyone to describe a teaching-learning environment, and he will say "school." Ask a teacher the same question, and he will very likely indicate that in the school building it is the place where the teacher and the learner carry on their work together. Ask a school board member about a new building design, and he is likely to tell you that the building is intended to bring pupils and teachers together in an environment that facilitates teaching and learning.

Now, these responses are not wrong, any more than the first truism is; they are just incomplete. However, they are appallingly misleading, because of the narrow and restrictive conceptions about teaching and learning which they perpetuate: that teaching and learning always occur together, in an institutionalized relationship, fixed in a place-time environment which teacher and learner share together. None of these assumptions fits reality. More teaching and learning go on — throughout life — outside the classroom than in; yet the myth persists.[31]

The ancient reasons for placing some learners in a separate place for teaching and learning reflected the contexts of earlier times: learning was related to power and magic; it was available only to the elite few; as a source of power over the future, it had to be protected; it could only be communicated (before writing and printing were developed) by verbal and gestural communication. In a world that lacked extensive information storage and retrieval technology, a learned person had to be at the center of teaching and learning as the recipient and conveyor of the tribal wisdom, which went from generation to generation in the oral mode.

In the context of lifespan learning, we must ask, where is the teaching-learning environment? Is it in "school," or is that a piece of folklore that has outlived its truthfulness? Is the lifespan learning environment the person and his *surround*,[32] not restricted in space and time? In one sense we have returned to the earliest concept of the teaching-learning environment — man interacting with nature, learning and teaching wherever, whenever there was need, without the interposition of institutionalization.

In a succession of different places, times, and circumstances learners learn, and achieve some degree of unity, coherence, and meaningful application of their learnings to their lives. What gives the succession of learning environments continuity and validity is the learner himself. Throughout the many changes of scene for learning, it is the learner that enables the different lifespan learnings to be blended together in the shaping of his own unique maturity.

The learner takes with him the essential environment for learning wherever, whenever he learns. In the unique way of every learner, he provides his own continuing "environment" in response to changing times, places, and situations. In fact, the learner and his surround are the basic environment for learning. Put the other way around, learning is a phenomenon that occurs only where the learner is.

Technology and the Learning Environment

This perception throws light on the relationship of technology to learning. Technology is the means whereby the individual brings into his surround and under his control those resources that are desirable and/or necessary to enrich, guide, and assist his development through successive stages of learning and maturation within the larger culture and value system.

The teacher, too, has his environment. When learner and teacher are together, they share to a certain extent the same surround. But their envi-

ronments are not the same because the essential element in the environment is the self of the person — learner, or teacher — whether alone or sharing some part of the surround with another.

Technology — the means for bringing things, ideas, even the presence of
other persons, into the surround — alters the surround just as a teacher in
a classroom might. For example, the television set is means; the channel
selector gives control, but the program brought in becomes — for the time
being at least — part of the surround for learning. Technology (print or
electronic telecommunications) is not alien to learning any more than a
teacher or a classroom is.

In traditional institutional learning situations (the classroom within the
school) the teacher or some more remote authority has control over the
environment. Space-time–bound concepts of teaching and learning specify place and chronology; thus, they specify environment. Learners have
minimal control, although "open" schools have introduced some element
of choice or option for learners.

Outside traditional institutionalized learning, learners have some control over their environments, with options of space and time as well. The
poor and seriously deprived learners, it will be argued, do not control
their environments, even out of school. It may be pointed out, however,
that away from school they have more options than in, and more leeway
— if they choose to use it — than in school.

Most Americans, in creating their own environments, have books,
magazines, newspapers, radio, television, disc or tape playback, and
photoprojection equipment: technology that may be used to bring into
the surround enrichment, stimulation, and guidance. Even persons in
lower socioeconomic strata possess such technology, though books as
such reach the smallest proportion of our society (not more than 20–25
percent, as compared with upwards of 80 percent for radio and television,
and somewhat less for the disc/tape and photoprojection equipment). In
some respects, at least, the surround of the learner outside school is not
only more closely under his control, but is richer in communication resources, hence richer in potential for learning, than the classroom.

What is brought into the surround through technology is another question. The problem of exercising responsibility of choice, at a high quality
level, is part of the debate over accepting the options offered by technology. It seems apparent, however, that learning materials communicated
by technology will be more effective if they are developed around realistic
perceptions of the learner as the center of the environment for learning in
the changing succession of surrounds that characterizes lifespan learning.

Back door or front door, the important element in the learning environment is the learner; in an important way, the learner is the environment
for learning.

III
Teaching, Learning, Schooling, and Knowledge

Teaching and learning, the two basic and essential activities of educational systems, are usually thought of as connected real-time activities, inseparable in space as well as time. The conventional concepts of teaching and learning (derived primarily from the Greeks and little changed in hundreds of years) deserve careful scrutiny. Instruction was first face-to-face. It had to be. To communicate in those early days, one had to be within hearing distance. The teacher talked to the learner. For learning to occur, the learner and the teacher had to be chained in a space-time relationship; they had to occupy the same space at the same time.

The Platonic model (learners at the feet of the master, interacting voicebox-to-voicebox, earpan-to-earpan, eyeball-to-eyeball) has provided the conventional continuous loop communication for nearly all institutional education. The limitations on communication in Plato's time have thus placed upon educational systems an extraordinary and outmoded constraint still dominant throughout the world. What other human endeavor can boast the retention of so ancient a model for communication?

The invention of writing was perceived by Plato as a threat to proper learning. Similarly, educators since Plato have looked with a mixture of fear, disdain, and suspicion at communication improvements which have revolutionized most of human activity, but have left institutionalized education relatively unchanged. The invention of writing, printing, efficient postal services, photography, the telephone, voice recording, radio, television, the computer, laser beams, holography, and the telecommunications satellite have significance for education that (except for writing and printing) has been largely unperceived, unaccepted, and unrealized. And writing and printing are losing some of their effectiveness because their essential corollary, reading, has apparently been downgraded in the schools in favor of an emphasis on speech.

Writing was the first invention to break space-time barriers to learning. Persons who could read could learn from a teacher who was in another place, even one who had lived at another time. But writing and reading were skills enjoyed by only a small elite, and schools were still characterized by teaching-*hyphen*-learning: the two acts chained together in space and time.

The invention of printing spread books — and learning — throughout the literate world. Tutors at the medieval University of Oxford had in their libraries books from Paris, from Amsterdam, from scholars and teachers wherever they lived, and from other times. But the tutors still taught their learners in a chained space-time relationship.

The invention and spread of modern postal services linked scholars together throughout the world for learning from each other in two-way communication. But scholar-teachers still taught their students in the chained space-time relationship. The early universities had their origins in church-related activities — the training of priests, for example. The young cleric was expected to withdraw from society, to abandon the reality of everyday life, to submit himself to the regimentation of the institution. As education was extended to wealthy, privileged, and powerful lay persons who were to be gentlemen, to state officials, managers, military, and professional people, the stress on the learner's removal from regular life for education continued. The university continued as a cloistered retreat.

The modern university has retained some vestiges of this medievalism, operating primarily at its convenience — setting requirements and schedules for the learner. In qualifying for certification in many professions, the applicant is still really a supplicant in that the criteria by which he is judged include not simply his ability, knowledge, experience, and skill, but in addition a medieval mystique of having passed successfully through a particular regimen related to the "laying on of hands."

Conventional Teaching and Old Mystiques

Conventional teaching and learning, therefore, make use of concepts of learning and teaching that have preserved the old mystiques, that have maintained space-time barriers to learning. The invention of modern means of communication based on electronics (tapes, discs, telephone, radio, television, the computer) has shattered the rationale for chained space-time teaching and learning; yet the practice still persists as though there were no alternatives today, just as there were none a thousand years ago. It is indeed true that teachers tend to teach as they were taught, and learners tend to learn as they are told.

The personal, eyeball-to-eyeball instruction of Plato and Socrates was a necessity; there was no alternative. We have long admired and tried to cling to the values of the great Greek teachers — adaptation to individuals, high learner participation, direct sense involvement, the role of teacher as thinker and mentor, and direct evaluation of progress or achievement. What we seem to have clung to, however, is chiefly form, i.e., keeping teacher and learner together in the same place and time, and mystique — the mystical values of the particular means, discipline, or order.

The space concept, of course, expanded: from one person, to a small group, to large lecture sections. The mystique has primarily rooted us to the time-space relationship. In much of conventional education, we don't adapt well to individuals (except as we approach the Greek and medieval situation of small seminar or person-to-person graduate teaching). We provide low-level participation. We do not often involve the learner in the use of direct sense impressions. The teacher is often not the thinker or mentor but an impersonal conveyor-belt for information.

We don't evaluate directly for achievement, but indirectly through an elaborate schema of credits, grades, prerequisites, prescriptions, and prohibitions.

Some will dismiss the space-time mystique as an unimportant aspect of schooling, on the grounds that it affects only the means of instruction, whereas needs, learners, content, and ends are the important things. Means, however, are the agents or vehicles of instruction. They often determine the success or failure of an instructional system built on needs, learners, contents, and ends. Selecting or employing compatible means is or should be part of the instructional rationale reflecting the societal contexts in which education is deemed to be important. When societal contexts change significantly, the rationale for instruction changes also, including, if necessary, change of means.

Changed Societal Contexts

What has happened in society to confront traditional education with demand for change? The societal contexts within which the traditional space-time–bound, teaching-learning rationale and means were compatible have changed. Consider, we have experienced

a. a population "explosion."

b. a knowledge "explosion."

c. an increase in complexity of all aspects of living.

d. an increase in educational requirements for almost all jobs.

e. an acceleration of rate-of-change in nearly all occupations, particularly as related to job-knowledge technology.

f. an increase in probability that substantial numbers of workers of nearly all classes must face periods of personal obsolescence during their lifetimes — obsolescence which will not be removed without personal retraining or re-education.

g. an increased mobility of almost all citizens — an advantage in following certain job or educational opportunities, but a disadvantage in that the mobile seeker of opportunity often is a disenfranchised citizen who has lost his roots in a community, who may now become a person without strong social, religious, political, economic, or educational ties to a "place" or a culture.

h. an increase in the number of learner groups that must be served by education, as a result of social, economic, and technologic changes that have in recent years brought to women greater freedom from home and family duties than ever before, and to some men, periods free from the necessity of gainful employment.

i. in addition, minority groups, members of sub-cultures within our society, have special needs that may not be met in conventional instruction, but who cannot become useful members of society without adequate education.

The changed contexts for education have presented us with new categories of learners, new needs, new subject matter, and new educational purposes. Few would disagree that the rationale for teaching and learning in the latter part of the twentieth century must derive from these, rather than earlier societal contexts. It is clear that the present task of education is to educate nearly all of our citizens beyond the high school level; to recognize that education is no longer terminal, and that for substantial numbers education must be continuous throughout life; to cope with the rapidity of change that is one of the fruits of the knowledge explosion; to adapt to the growth in population and in the mobility of the population; to bring all of our citizens to a useful role in society. These are only the more obvious factors that signal to us that we are living, teaching, and learning in a different society, in a different context, from that in which our standard institutional models were created.

Because the needs and contexts for learning have changed so radically, new guidelines are needed for providing instruction to learners.

New Guidelines for Instruction

1. Instruction should be available any place where there are students — or even only one student — whether or not there are teachers at the same place at the same time.[1]
2. Instruction should place greater responsibility for learning on the student.
3. The instructional plan or system should free faculty members from custodial duties so that more of the teacher's and learner's time can be given to truly educational tasks.
4. The instructional system should offer learners wider choices (more opportunities) in subjects, formats, methodologies.
5. The instructional system should use, as appropriate, all the teaching media and methods that have been proven to be effective.
6. The instructional system should mix and combine media and methods so that each subject or unit within a subject is taught in the most effective way.
7. The media and technology employed should be "articulated" in design and use; that is, the different media or technologies should reinforce each other and the structure of the subject matter and teaching plan.
8. The instructional system should preserve and enhance opportunities for adaptation to differences among individual learners as well as among teachers.
9. The instructional system should evaluate student achievement not by raising barriers concerning the *place* where the student studies, the *rate* at which he studies, the *method* by which he studies, or even the *sequence* in which he studies, but instead by evaluating as directly as possible the achievement of learning goals.
10. The system should permit students to start, stop, and learn at their own paces, consistent with learner short- and long-range goals, situations, and characteristics.

Only the first of these guidelines (an instructional system that will operate any place, any time, even for one student) is radical in the sense that it is incompatible with conventional teaching. All of the others could be introduced within the present framework of teaching. Guideline 1 can be accomplished by use of technology; the others by a combination of technology and modern concepts of learner-oriented, individualized teaching and learning.

Institutional education, which has tended to have the characteristics of a closed system, limited to a particular time and place because of its mode of communication, can now be more open and responsive to divers learners as the contexts of a diverse society and the needs of learners require.

What Model for Teaching and Learning?

Plato, disciple of Socrates and teacher of Aristotle, gave such powerful and compelling form to his discourses that for hundreds of years educators have clung to a concept of teaching-learning as a real time-space, continuous, and interactive communications loop. It is now recognized that teaching and learning are separate acts vested in different persons, and that neither activity need be constrained to real time-place conditions. Teaching and learning can safely and effectively be carried on with no loss of interaction, through various communications means, even though teacher and learner are separated in space and time.

The teaching-learning classroom model that has dominated traditional education has caused new models to be ignored or resisted, despite the failure of traditional education to fit the contexts and needs of present times.

Because education and schooling have seemed synonymous in our society, few have thought of asking why we have schools, how they got to be as they are, or whether the classroom model—a cultural given—now meets the needs of society and all its learners.

The classroom model arose originally out of the context and needs of earlier societies:

There were few teachers of any degree of qualification, and learners had to be gathered where teachers were in order to use the only communications mode available—speech.

As many as possible of the available adults and older youths had to be used to carry on the labor-intensive work necessary for survival of the group; they could not be spared for teaching and child care.

Child care could be accomplished in schools while teaching was going on.

There was an acute shortage of books and other resources useful in teaching and learning.

It was more economical to carry on teaching in groups.

By putting learners together in classrooms with teachers and resources, the shortages could be minimized, the work force could be deployed as needed, more children would (it was hoped) have the opportunity to learn, costs would be minimized, and children could be kept safe while parents and older siblings tended to the intensive work of home, farm, shop, and community.[2]

Of the five reasons from the social and cultural context of earlier times for the creation and continuation of the classroom model, only one has any current validity: the need for child care. Despite the irrelevancy of most of the early reasons for creating classrooms, classroom instruction is still a major cultural artifact so pervasive that, as new societal contexts, needs, and technologies for teaching and learning come into being, their value and relevance to education are principally assessed according to how they can be accommodated to classroom schooling. They are not perceived as signals for the creation of new models for general, public, and adult education.

In any teaching-learning situation it is generally agreed (figure 1) that there are four essential elements:

1. A Teacher
2. A Learner or Learners
3. A Communications System or Mode
4. Something to be Taught/Learned

Figure 1. Essential Elements in a Teaching-Learning Situation

Now, if the communications system is a given, either because it is the only system available (think of Plato meeting learners in the Grove of Akadēmos) or is a cultural artifact acting as an imperative, then there are no options, and the communication must be face-to-face, eyeball-to-eyeball, earpan-to-earpan speech. Then, if for the five reasons given earlier a box is put around the four essential elements, we have (figure 2) a classroom:

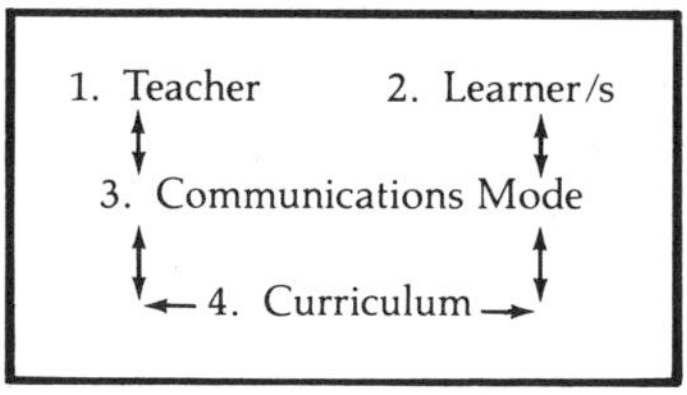

1. Teacher   2. Learner/s

3. Communications Mode

4. Curriculum

Figure 2. A Real Time-Space Teaching-Learning Situation: The Classroom

Each of the elements in the box is of course a subsystem of the total classroom system or model. Each subsystem is composed of all the elements and activities which make it up, and each of these is also a subsystem. A highly complex model thus evolves from the interactions of the four elements. A corps of specialists evolves a profession to oversee the operation of the system and to preserve its integrity. What was begun as a fortuitous and intelligent combining of the elements necessary to achieve teaching and learning in specific societal contexts became a general model that is still imposed on succeeding periods even though, as we have seen, the basic societal contexts and needs change and new options are available — which, if we were to start from scratch as Plato did, would produce different models.

Thinking back, now, to the ten guidelines for education discussed earlier, we recall that only one of the requirements is radical (a system that will operate any place, any time, even for only one student), and that the others are achievable within the present framework or model by using new technologies and modern concepts of learner- and learning-oriented instruction.

A teaching-learning system that must work any place, any time, for one learner or many, directly confronts the space-time-elite barriers of the classroom model. In fact, however, physical distance between teacher and learner has long been a problem in the classroom model. As classes became larger, and lectures replaced the dialogue that Plato conducted, the integrity of the model was breached. In many respects, only the illusion of being effectively face-to-face remains, as distance within the box lengthens between teacher and learners, and speech is amplified for ever more distant reception. Furthermore, "distance" is more than physical distance. There are social distance, cultural distance, and what has been called "psychic" distance, for want of a better term. All of these are present wherever teaching and learning are carried on.

Indeed, it seems that much of the fear or threat felt by classroom practitioners at the prospect of opening distance between teacher and learners has little to do with physical distance. Fear and threat are more likely the product of the presence and importance of social, cultural, and psychic distance in the classroom. Sensitive teachers intuitively perceive these distances. This intuition, subconscious and unrecognized, also probably underlies the persistent assumption that learning is an event dependent upon social interaction. That this assumption is a delusion, as pointed out by Gagne,[3] does not prevent its being used to reinforce the classroom model, which seems and indeed consciously attempts to confine learning to a social interaction space.

Of all the distance factors inherent in the classroom (social, cultural, psychic, and physical), only the factor of physical distance between teacher and learner is irrelevant to learning. Yet the practitioners of the model fear any relaxation of the confinement of teaching and learning to the box because they confuse physical distance with the other kinds of distance inherent in any teaching-learning arrangement.

Let us turn back to the classroom model to see what changes are needed to accommodate the one radically different element in the teaching-learning situation that permits operation of the system any time, any place, for one or many learners. Suppose we model the same four essentials of the teaching-learning situation this way (figure 3):

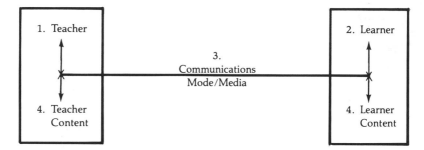

Figure 3. A Teaching-Learning Model to Accommodate Physical Distance

Note that the four essential elements of any teaching-learning situation are still present. Is this a new model? Yes, if the classroom model is identified solely by its single, unique characteristic — the confining of all the essential elements in a box defining the social space necessary for communication by speech. No, if a teaching and learning situation or system is defined according to the interaction of the four essential elements for teaching and learning. Figure 3 is in fact a more accurate representation of the actual workings of the old classroom model; it is a model for any teaching-learning situation, whether learning takes place in or outside the classroom.

What was earlier called a radical conceptual change (the any time, any place, single or multiple learners requirement) may now be seen for what it really is: a natural and logical consequence of the interaction of the four essential teaching-learning elements, for any learners, consistent with what we now know about learning as an idiosyncratic activity, the contexts of our times, and the purposes and capabilities of educational communications. Instead of a communications mode (speech) determining social space for learning (as in the classroom model) we have a model that leaves communications mode and learning space to the learner to select according to his situation and the options available to him. The availability of options implies institutional and teacher cooperation with the model in figure 3, something which has often been difficult to obtain because the model seems different from the cultural given, and hence threatens teacher self-concept.

Reluctance Regarding a New Model

Perhaps an important reason for the hostile or negative reactions of teachers to a different teaching-learning model has been their lack of involvement in design and decision-making regarding the new model. Uninvolved, they lack the opportunity to visualize themselves actively and successfully carrying out their teacher purposes and activities in any mode except that in which they were trained — the classroom. It is perhaps unreasonable to expect any professional to endorse change that appears to violate the concept of self built up through long years of training, preparation, and experience.

People do change self-concept to accommodate growth, maturation, and altered conditions, but such change has to be sought and learned. This kind of self-change represents growth in the professional self, from a conviction that the purposes and activities of the profession can be carried out as well or better in the new mode as in the old. Teaching within a new, even though better, teaching-learning model requires such an accommodation if it is to be done without threat, fear, hostility, or negative anxiety.

There is a lesson in learning here. Teachers have long been the object of books, articles, demonstrations, courses, seminars, workshops, and grants-in-aid intended to provide opportunity for involvement, design, and decision-making in the development of new models. Those who sought such experiences learned and applied. Those who spurned the opportunity or went reluctantly did not learn, just as students in schools do not learn that for which they are unprepared, that which seems irrelevant to their perception of reality, or that which threatens their self-concept. Teachers can be unwilling learners too, going through the outward forms of attending, listening, and giving back information to satisfy extrinsic pressures, but with essentially closed and unlearning minds because intrinsic motivation is lacking.

There are differences, however, between teachers as learners and their students as learners. Teachers, as adults and professionals, are not wholly dependent upon the continued approval or certification of those to whom they report. Even with outside pressures, teachers control their activities, and their futures, far more than their students do. Hence teachers can, and do, exercise some degree of self-determination respecting what they will learn, and whether they will apply new learnings to their teaching. The farther up the teacher goes in the teaching hierarchy, presumably the more autonomy the teacher has. Hence, as a teacher, a teacher can urge openness of mind upon students, stressing the element of trust (that the learnings are needed and relevant) to students. As a learner, however, a teacher can cling to self-interest and self-concept in the status quo, and block or delay needed change. Reluctance to change is more a matter of learning than it is a matter of professional politics. Without new learnings, old behaviors do not change. Changing immature, inappropriate behaviors is the basic purpose of all education, and the reason that teachers are empowered to teach others.

If teachers in a new mode must learn, adapt, accommodate, and mature in professional self-concept, what about learners? The learner who knows only one way of learning, who has been conditioned to be dependent upon a teacher for learning goals, activities, resources, and knowledge-of-results also needs to learn, adapt, accommodate, and mature in the processes of learning. This is not as serious a problem for learners in general, however, as for teachers learning different ways of teaching. Learners have not committed themselves to a professional model; they tend to be younger; they directly experience the reinforcement of the learning they undertake; they are familiar with, and have confidence in, technology; and they do not fear change so much because they have little investment in the status quo.

Accomplishing Learning

Learning is accomplished in three stages —
   A. *Acquisition* of Information
                    (from whatever communications or experience mode)
                    (according to coded capacity to receive information)
   B. *Transmutation* of Information
                    (internalizing; linking up with previous learnings, experience)
                    (This is where the reciprocal interplay between coded capacity and environmental stimuli combine in perceiving information, categorizing, organizing, interpreting; perceptions of self, values.)
   C. *Evaluation/Application* of Information
                    (according to coded capacity and environmental stimuli; values, convictions, perceptions of self and external reality)
Clearly, learning is idiosyncratic, active, can only be done by the

learner himself, and is not complete until the learning has passed through all three stages. The learner must do this for himself. In the old classroom model, learning was assumed to fit a space-time frame. A linear, sequential, cause-effect, time-controlled and determined relationship between teaching and learning was assumed. We know now that such a simple view of the teaching-learning relationship is fallacious, but because the classroom model required such a view, and did not provide opportunity for the study of any but captive and submissive learners, there has been little pressure to study learning in any other setting.

Classrooms impose a time constraint on learning that operates to discourage learning through all three stages. Consequently, teachers tend to assess learning only at the first stage — acquisition of information. We will have to extend our concern for learning through all stages of learning, in some ways an easier and more reachable goal in a non-traditional than in a time-sequenced classroom setting.

If teaching is not an event of social interaction that must be confined to a prescribed social space and communications mode, what is it? Here, though we reject the form, we may be able to return to the substance of the Platonic model, and consider teacher as critic, mentor, guide, adviser, problem-solver, thinker, and facilitator. In non-traditional instruction, the advance preparation of learning materials and the response needs of distant learners require such a change. The classroom model emphasized the first stage of learning, with teacher as information and lawgiver; it assumed passive learners and depended largely on extrinsic motivation. The new model will not work unless the teacher is seen as the developer of learners, preserving their integrity-responsibility for self-direction. It assumes intrinsic motivation in active learners, and an equal emphasis on all three stages of learning.

What Knowledge To Be Preserved, Taught, and Learned?

Jacob Bronowski pointed out that the long childhood of man will come to an end only when we perceive the importance of man as a learner, and free ourselves from older, prescribed notions of what knowledge is, and how it may be used to create a better society.[4]

Just over 120 years ago in the northwest territories of the United States, the Suquamish Indian tribe faced near extinction in its confrontation with the westward movement of white society. The chief of the tribe was a patriarch named Seattle. It was his responsibility to preserve, protect, interpret, assess, and disseminate the knowledge-store, the word-hoard, the meanings related to the quality of life and the survival of his people.

In his final negotiation with government agents forcing the Suquamish onto a reservation, Seattle said some notable things that lay ignored, as curious cultural irrelevancies, for over 100 years. He said,

> . . . if we do not sell, the white man may come with guns and take our land. How can you buy or sell the sky, the warmth of the land? The idea is strange to us. If we do not own the freshness of the air and the sparkle of the water, how can you buy them?
> . . . If we sell you land, you must remember that it is sacred, and you must teach your children that it is sacred, and that each ghostly reflection in the clear water of the lakes tells of events and memories in the life of my people.
> . . . If we sell you our land, you must remember and tell your children, that the rivers are our brothers, and yours, and you must henceforth give the rivers the kindness you would give any brother.
> . . . Teach your children what we have taught our children, that the earth is our mother. Whatever befalls the earth, befalls the sons of the earth. If men spit upon the ground, they spit upon themselves.
> . . . The earth does not belong to man; man belongs to the earth. . . . all things are connected. . . . Man did not weave the web of life; he is merely a strand in it. Whatever he does to the web, he does to himself.[5]

Chief Seattle's insights were not considered "knowledge" by the universities or the prevailing culture. His remarks were collected, stored, and ignored as unrelated and irrelevant to the needs of society: a striking instance of the immaturity of man's perception of what knowledge is.

Our perceptions of teaching, learning, schooling, and knowledge are all undergoing change. It is possible to delay change, to influence change, even (for those who can control their immediate activities) to deny change momentarily, but the trends towards change continue, with important implications for teaching, learning, schooling, and knowledge at all levels and in all methodologies.

Part Two

NON-TRADITIONAL LEARNING
AND ITS IMPLICATIONS

IV

Distance and Independent Learning

There are many names given to the wide variety of non traditional learning programs throughout the world. Undoubtedly the failure of traditional schooling to transcend the limitations of the place-time class-room,[1] the growing disillusionment with standard bureaucratic solutions to problems that peak and continue at the crisis level, and the global cultural disarray evoked by great social, economic, political, and technological change, have weakened the barriers that tend to prevent the acceptance of educational change.

But there are positive as well as negative reasons for the increase in non-traditional learning: the changed societal contexts in which education must serve individuals and groups, the growing need and demand for lifelong learning, the transition from education-perceived-as-a-privilege to education-as-a-right for survival and quality of life, the increase in the number and diversity of education consumers, and the availability and public acceptance of communications technology. These negative and positive factors have contributed to what Dieuzeide[2] has called a "Copernican" revolution in education – the conceptual shift from teaching to learning as the central concern of education, or at least of non-traditional learning.

The terminology of non-traditional learning programs obscures the similarities that exist among the programs and suggests a greater diversity than actually exists. In the exposition that follows, three major types of non-traditional learning programs will be examined: *distance, indepen-*

dent, and *open learning.* But even these three are not mutually exclusive. Distance and independent learning will be discussed in this chapter, and open learning in Chapter V.

Distance Learning

Whether called *Fernstudium,* teletuition, telemathetics, or education at a distance, the phenomenon of teachers linked with learners via various media over vast distances is a persistent and growing characteristic of education in the twentieth century.

Relatively little attention has been given to the study and significance of the education-at-a-distance phenomenon. In Marshall McLuhan's metaphor, educators have been driving into a new age of learning with their eyes on the rearview mirror. Furthermore, the drivers are gazing fixedly at a mirror image of schooling, not learning. No doubt they are aware of occasional peripheral impressions of such things as open learning, independent study, and mediated instruction, but since these are peripheral, they are largely dismissed before cortical perception can take place.

There is, of course, nothing new about education at a distance, except its growth and acceptance since the sixties, and the means now employed. Early man's symbolic speech was limited in effectiveness to the distance over which sound waves can travel. But drawing, and then writing, demolished man's time-bound existence; messages on the walls of caves could record and convey the meaning of an event long beyond the moment in which it occurred. Clay tablets, papyrus, and paper made messages mobile, and demolished man's space-bound existence. The tablets of Moses, the letters of St. Paul, the proclamations of Kings and Popes, the theories of Euclid, the maps of Magellan, the conventions of commerce, could circulate the known and unknown worlds. And even where the oral tradition persisted, the talking drums, the smoke signals, the traveling troubadours, the miracle plays, and itinerant preachers, teachers, and actors took messages to distant learners. In all developing societies there was and is stubborn pride in the self-made (meaning self-educated) person who achieved outside the space-time binds of formal schooling. There is nothing wholly new in the concept of education at a distance.

How is education at a distance defined? The names applied to things are important, for they not only acknowledge the existence of something, but either implicitly or explicitly they denote the attributes of the things named. Here there are problems, for the terms used to describe "education at a distance" are ambiguous and imprecise.

As any lexicographer knows, meaning is not only symbolized by a term itself, but is also defined by the term's usage. From the words that make up the term and a wide range of its usage, we can flesh out some meanings:

Education at a distance is teaching and learning, the imparting and/or acquiring of knowledge via methods used because teachers and learners are at a distance from each other. By logical extension, separated teacher and learner communicate by means of some medium or media, regardless (again by logical extension and usage) of the limitations of space and time, social and economic inequalities among learners, geographic isolation, and cultural differences.

This seems clear enough so far, but consider:

> Otto Peters of West Germany defined distance education as "a rationalized means for transmitting knowledge, skills and attitudes based upon divisions of labour, which involves the use of comprehensive technical means and the appropriate application of organization techniques through which the possibility of the reproduction of optimal learning materials takes place for a great number of learners without consideration of the place of domicile or prior education of participants."[3]
>
> However, the report of the Swedish Commission on Television and Radio in Education (TRU) pointed out that "'distance' cannot solely be defined in miles or kilometers. 'Distance' can also be a product of social or working conditions."[4]
>
> Heinz Schwalbe of Switzerland in a European paper remarked with dismay, "The definition of distance education is not uniform all over the world."[5]
>
> One reads, especially in European literature, that a wide range of teaching-learning activities previously identified by separate names — correspondence study, home study, open education, radio-television teaching, individualized mediated instruction — are now clustered under the term *distance education*, a term which Schwalbe, despite his dismay, says now includes "all teaching methods and media except face to face teaching."[6] Börje Holmberg of Sweden and West Germany writes, "The term 'distance education' . . . covers the various forms of study at all levels which are not under the immediate supervision of tutors present with their students . . . but which, nevertheless, benefit from the planning, guidance and tuition of a tutorial organization."[7] Holmberg adds that "the term distance education is not universally recognized. . . ."
>
> In the United States the 1976 College Entrance Examination Board and Educational Testing Service survey report retreats from the

problem of definition by using the term "non-traditional learning" instead of others in wide use. The report notes nevertheless that "non-traditional programs, learning experiences, or methods of instruction are *also* ambiguous terms," but bravely continues, "The report tends to view all programs, experiences and methods of instruction which are different from the typical, campus and classroom-bound, teacher-led, face-to-face, lecture or seminar-type of instruction as non-traditional." The report adds, "The ambiguity is unavoidable."[8]

While distance learning in Europe is by usage proposed as a generic term for a wide range of non-traditional teaching-learning activities, in many other countries these separate activities are still perceived largely as distinct programs without any generic relationship. Ambiguities multiply. It is only too evident that the problem of defining distance education is partly the widespread concurrent use of specific terms for "different, but similar" types of programs, terms which are imprecise and overlapping in meaning.

Nevertheless, there is a generic term that is more precise than either *distance education* or *non-traditional learning*,[9] the two catch-all (not really generic) terms so far proposed. The term, in addition, has significance respecting learning theory, and has historic continuity, at least in the United States.

Independent Learning

The persistent educational pattern in the long history of formal education has been the learner in the group — the dependent, physically present, non-autonomous learner, whose goals, activities, rewards, and punishments were dependent upon the policies and practices of ever-present teachers.

Correspondence study was the first formally structured method for *independent study*, a term now used in the United States as generic for the several kinds of distance and non-traditional learning systems that include correspondence study. Correspondence study makes use of older technologies (writing and print) and a nineteenth-century technology (reliable mail service) to link a teacher and learner separated in space and time.

As new technologies of communication became available, larger numbers of programs for independent learners emerged. Radio, television, programmed learning, the computer, telephone, and satellite made it possible for people distant or cut off from the regular schools to continue learning in ever larger numbers. In 1965 an American survey revealed that approximately 9 million American adults were carrying on independent study programs.[10] (This Johnstone-Rivera statistic was a serious understatement, particularly as independent learners not formally enrolled — probably another 15 million — were not included.) By 1970, it was estimated that approximately 40 million Americans of all ages were involved in some form of independent learning. Long ignored by the emphasis on formal group-based learning in schools, independent learning has re-emerged as an important method of learning.[11]

Independent study occurs both within (internal to) an institution, and without (external to) an institution. This duality of use is significant. The external and internal types of independent study had separate origins, but each had its roots in the British and American tutorial and extension movements of the late nineteenth and early twentieth centuries. In the United States, the two streams of independent study began at different times, the correspondence stream appearing about thirty years earlier than the honors or internal stream.

Since 1925 the two streams of independent study programs for internal and external learners have existed side-by-side in American institutions of higher education. Conceptually, independent study programs are linked together because, whether for internal or external students, they have much to contribute to each other, share to a considerable extent a common philosophical base, and employ similar media and techniques. They belong in a common category because in important ways they are more similar than different.[12]

A commonly accepted definition of independent study states:

Independent Study consists of various forms of teaching-learning arrangements in which teachers and learners carry out their essential tasks and responsibilities apart from one another, communicating in a variety of ways, for the purposes of freeing internal learners from inappropriate class pacings or patterns, of providing external learners with opportunities to continue learning in their own environments, and developing in all learners the capacity to carry on self-directed learning, the ultimate maturity required of the educated person. Independent Study programs offer learners varying degrees of freedom in the self-determination of goals and activities, and in starting, stopping and pacing individualized learning programs which are carried on to the greatest extent possible at the convenience of the learners.[13]

Moore noted in 1973 that teaching in "independent study is, paradoxically, both responsive and anticipatory." The independent learner is "independent, first, of other direction; he is autonomous. Second, he is independent of the space-time bondage made necessary only by a tradition of dependent or 'other directed' teaching. The greater his autonomy, the more 'distance' he can tolerate, and therefore the more he is independent."[14]

Note that the definition being developed emphasizes as conceptual elements the attributes of a logical universe or class of activities. It is not a definition according to the different means or techniques that may be employed in basically similar but differently named programs.

In 1967 MacDonald pointed out that the freedom sought for and by independent learners represents a hierarchy: First of all, independent learning should be self-pacing, that is, the independent learner should be free to pace his learning according to his circumstances and needs. Second, the learner should be free to follow any of several available channels for learning, and should not be confined to a single channel. Third, the learner should have freedom in the selection of goals and the activities he chooses to follow. This third freedom is the freedom of the learner to determine his own goals and activities because "morality in the schools" (the issue of whether schools serve the learner or the system) "is all a matter of beginnings. The concept of independent learning seems most provident for realizing a moral school."[15]

Gleason defined independent study as instructional systems that "make it possible for the learner to pursue the study of personally significant areas in an independent manner — freed of bonds of time, space, and prescription usually imposed by conventional instruction."[16] Dubin and Taveggia described two kinds of independent study, one including teacher guidance and direction, and the other carried on in the absence of a teacher.[17]

Dressel and Thompson observed that "independent study, interpreted as a capacity to be developed, comes close to being if it is not, indeed, the major goal of all education," and define independent study as "the student's self-directed pursuit of academic competence in as autonomous a manner as he is able to exercise."[18]

There is a fairly voluminous literature on the conceptual bases of independent learning. Authorities in philosophy, learning theory, media and technology, personality theory, psychology, phenomenology, social psychology, and cultural anthropology have noted links to independent learning. For example:

1. *The Philosophy of Education (John Dewey):*[19]
   Education is not an end in itself but a means to a larger end, and the individual has both the right and the responsibility to determine the purposes to which he gives his life.
2. *Psychology (Robert Gagne):*
   Although the class is the model for education in most schools, there is increasing emphasis on the centrality of the individual learner. The old single-stage model of learning . . . has been aban-

doned (for) the multi-stage model with the idea of an individual, idiosyncratic coding or mediation between the stimulus and response. . . . The multi-stage mediational learning concept exposes the delusion that learning is an event of social interaction.

3. *Behavioral Psychology (James MacDonald):*
 . . . The logical emphasis and outcomes of the behaviorists have been identified with independent learning. The modern version of reflective thinking gives emphasis to the mode of inquiry followed; and inquiry by denotation suggests independent learning.

4. *Psycho-Analytic Theory (Pauline Sears):*
 All learning is individual, and the goal of any specific learning is individual. When knowledge-seeking behavior is instigated by intrinsic motives there is greater success. . . .

5. *Socio-Anthropological Theory (Dorothy Lee):*
 In western society such beliefs or values as the integrity of the individual, belief in the equality of opportunity, the basic rights of every person for life, liberty, happiness — these undoubtedly have important influence on learning. In many cultures there is acceptance of the idea of independence of motivation, that motivation springs from within the individual . . . a reinforcement of the independence of motivation theory.

6. *Phenomenological Theory (Sidney Jourard):*
 Man always and solely learns for himself. We created the need for independent learning by the way we trained people for a role in a society that resists change.

7. *Educational Technology (Gerald Gleason):*
 The efficiency idiom in education finds a justification of independent learning because it is more efficient and of greater utility. . . .

8. *General Morality (James MacDonald):*
 Education must serve the person, not the system. Independent learning implies a moral good — the choice and freedom of the individual in realizing an education.[20]

Ambiguous and Disunifying Terminology

The terminology of non-traditional learning is disunifying and divisive, even for programs similar in purpose and developmental process. Some terms identify the medium used in communication: *radio-, television-, telephone-, satellite-, computer-,* or *correspondence study* (for example, the Chicago TV College). In fact, none of these terms is accurate, for each of these programs employs more than one medium, and signifies more than the system of diffusion that is named.

Two terms identify the *place* where the learning is supposed to occur:

(1) *home study* (but this is not accurate either since home study is widely employed in school-based programs); (2) *external studies* (less inaccurate but only because more general, and it excludes internal learners who can and do engage in independent learning).

Four terms identify the relatively *non-restrictive admissions require-ments* that characterize the programs: (1) *open university* or *open school,* such as the British Open University; (2) *University* or *school without walls;* (3) *free university* or *school* (such as the Free University of Iran); (4) and the *people's university* or *school* (such as Everyman's University in Israel).

Several programs operate under the name of the *authority which ac-credits* the learning — in the United States such programs as Empire State College, various Regents Degree programs, the University of Mid Amer-ica, The Community College of Vermont, and Minnesota Metro; else-where in the world, such programs as the Memorial University of New-foundland, Athabasca University of Alberta, Fernuniversität of West Germany, the University of the South Pacific, and the University of South Africa.

Several terms emphasize the *physical distance* between teacher and learner: programs called *teletuition, tele-enseignement, Fernunterricht* or *Fernstudium, telemathetics,* and, of course, *distance education* (although distance is a complex concept involving more than miles or kilometers).

Five terms are used to include all of the types of programs that are non-classroom-based: *distance education, non-traditional learning, indepen-dent study, out-of-school learning,* and *external studies* (although in usage the term often includes classes).

All of the terms in use originated out of the need to name *institutional* programs. The growing recognition of learning wholly under the control of learners (no institutional base) adds new terms, such as *self-directed learning, self-planning learners,* etc. Conceptually, these terms are consis-tent with such terms as *independent study, learning at a distance,* and *non-traditional learning.*

What is interesting about this disparity and ambiguity of terminology is that all of the terms cited signal an end to space-time barriers to learn-ing; they signal a separation of and concern for teaching and learning; they signal the use of a medium or media of communication to link teacher and learner; and they signal greater autonomy on the part of the learner as a desirable end. But the terms themselves (except for *open learning, independent study,* and *non-traditional learning*) are either quite restrictive (identifying a particular medium or technique) or are so general that it is difficult to define them. All of the programs described by these varied terms have striking and basic similarities to the other programs; thus there is no logical integrity in the present terminology used, and no universality with respect to the class of educational activity to which all obviously belong.

Furthermore — and this is the most curious aspect of all — the people who work within these separate but basically similar programs perceive themselves as in some way different from their colleagues in the other programs, as though the different labels represent genuinely different aims, methods, and programs in education.

As a result, not only are the programs fragmented from each other, struggling — even competing — for recognition, support, and survival, but also behind the deceptive and ambiguous labels all the programs are intended to do very nearly the same things for learning and learners.

Differences in point of view of those who use particular terms permit a looseness of interchange among terms that demonstrates how unrestrictive they are. For example, if an independent study program preserves distance between teacher and learner, some will call it *distance study.* Or if a distance study program permits learner autonomy, some will call it *independent study.* A program that is characterized by open admissions, with distance between teacher and an autonomous learner, could properly be called *open education, distance learning,* or *independent study* — depending upon the speaker's point of view.

Furthermore, whether the term used should modify study, learning, or education is not made clear by usage. It would seem that what is called a "study" (e.g., *independent study*) is a system or program. The Independent Study Division of the National University Extension Association implies, for example, that it is a division of university extensions that provides independent study programs. Referring to a kind of learning, however, puts the emphasis not on program characteristics, but on the kind of learning carried on by the learner, as in *independent learning.* And if the reference is to outcome or product (the result of study and learning) then the term *independent education* would properly be used. An international commission on terminology in non-traditional education is needed to recommend a terminology that would have broad acceptance.

For those in the field, which terminology to follow is a difficult choice. The terms chosen have frequently limited the users' perceptions of what they do; terms have often separated users from each other because of the focus on the different means employed, rather than the unifying ends that characterize the efforts of many innovators and developers of programs. The names applied to things are not always clear, rational, and unambiguous. Public acceptance of a term often seems to be independent of the precision and rationality that may be sought by scholars. In addition, the user's self-concept is involved in accepting or rejecting names.

Holmberg, of Sweden and West Germany, observes that "in the U.S.A. *independent study* is now the term preferred. It has the advantage that it emphasizes learning rather than either medium or distance, but does not seem very clear as it does not clarify what or whom the study is independent of."[21]

Moore and others, however, have pointed out that independent learners "are independent in two senses. . . . they are physically independent of the need to be resident on a campus, and they are independent of the control of their learning by pedagogues."[22] Independent learners are independent of the learning environment (including the teacher) supplied by the school to physically present learners.[23] But Moore's comprehensive analysis of learner independence makes it clear that the term is misleading if it suggests that "the student is a kind of Robinson Crusoe, cast away on an island of self-sufficiency, which is not the sense in which the term is used. The independent student is engaged in an educational programme, which by definition implies both a learner and a teacher or teachers in a transactional relationship."[24]

Moore proposes a new taxonomy for all teaching and learning required now by the Copernican transfer of the center of gravity of educational thinking and research, from the functions and activities of teachers (the "teacher-centered mentality") to the behaviors of learners (the "pupil-centered approach"). In this taxonomy, Moore refers to "distance, or Telemathic Teaching [as] a teaching programme in which, because of the physical separateness of learners and teachers, the interactions between them are conducted through print, mechanical or electronic devices." Distance is a function of two variables in the learner-teacher relationship: the extent of dialogue in their communication, and the extent of structure in the teaching program.

Hence Moore preserves the term *distance* to describe the (telemathic) teaching that supports learning at a distance. He employs the term *independent* to describe a learner who has matured emotionally so that he does not need emotional dependence on others, and can employ his independence in coping with problems. The learner's independence (autonomy) is a major characteristic of independent study, and a typology of teaching programs can be developed according to the degree of autonomy permitted by the teaching program.[25]

Field Dependence–Independence

Moore, following Witkin[26] and others, measured the psychological differentiation of "field dependence–independence" in students enrolled in distance and independent learning programs. (Field dependence–independence is a way of classifying people by cognitive style, although the differences seem to transcend cognition itself. Field-dependent or field-independent learners differ in how they find it most natural to learn. The field-independent learner follows a strategy of analyzing, breaking a complex situation into its components. The field-dependent learner reacts to a situation as a whole. Field-independent learners are active, self-motivated, better at problem solving when the solution requires analysis and restructuring of elements. Field-independent learners seek autonomy. The direction in growth for all learners is toward increasing differentiation or independence. Differences are also found in social and emotional characteristics. Each "style," field dependence or field independence, has advantages and disadvantages in specific situations.)

The Moore study[27] indicates that field independence could be used as a predictor of successful learner participation in distance teaching programs, but as distance is reduced, a more field-dependent learning style becomes desirable (or perhaps essential) in coping with teacher-structured programs.

As Knowles[28] and Rogers[29] have pointed out, individual maturation moves naturally and psychologically towards independence. This maturation can be frustrated by schooling which freezes the learner into patterns of dependence. A fully autonomous learner identifies a learning need when he finds a problem to be solved, a skill to be acquired, seeks information he does not have.

He is able to articulate his learning need in the form of a general goal, which is differentiated in several more specific objectives . . . with criteria for achievement. [He] gathers the information he desires, collects ideas, practises skills, works to resolve his problems, and achieves his goals, judges the appropriateness of skills, adequacy of problem solutions, the quality of ideas, and the knowledge acquired. He reaches conclusions, accepting or rejecting the material, and eventually decides the goals have been achieved, or abandons them.[30]

The term *independent* is thus more than a descriptor for a kind of non-traditional learning that makes use of distance teaching; it is a link with advanced learning and personality theory, and is generic to the entire range of learning programs which demonstrate the new emphasis on the learner and on learning.

Other-Directed Learning

The significance of independence in learning may perhaps be brought into clearer focus by examining dependence in learning. As indicated earlier, psychological and developmental evidence, from the birth of the human being on, clearly defines normal human growth as a long odyssey in search of self and independence. "The long childhood of man," as Bron-owski called it, is the process of learning what it is to have choices, con-ceive solutions to problems of survival, become civilized, take responsibil-ity for self, and become that which genes and environment make possible.

Learning is thus a part of the continuing "growing up" that lasts life-long. Much of the great literature of all societies concerns itself — in poetry, drama, epic stories, and legends — with the trauma, excitement, despair, and achievement of people who are struggling to become them-selves, facing obstacles, problems, dangers, and the agony of choice. In the end, the outcome turns on the maturity of self. "We have met the enemy," says Pogo, "and he is us."

Hence we are shocked when we perceive that the institutions and pro-cesses that we have invented and maintained to foster human growth and development — the traditional schools — frequently do the opposite. It has long been known that extended periods of institutionalization — in hospi-tals and prisons, for example — retard maturation. Schooling provides one of the longest periods of institutionalization that humans undergo in modern society. From kindergarten to graduation from high school is thirteen years; if the child begins his education with pre-school programs, the period extends to fourteen or fifteen years; with undergraduate tech-nical school or college it becomes eighteen or nineteen years; and with graduate school the total formal schooling reaches twenty to twenty-three years. From thirteen to twenty-three years is a long time to spend in other-directed, group-oriented activities if the goal of education is to lead to the maturation of self. The many years of schooling lead instead to de-pendencies, instrumental and emotional, which hamper maturation in learning and self-awareness. Dependent learners remain unskilled in the essential tasks of learning: identifying needs, setting goals, searching out resources, motivating study, and assessing progress and achievement.

Dependent learners continually need extrinsic proddings (rewards-punishments) because they have forgotten how to use the power of intrinsic motivation, and cannot any longer sense the pleasures of self-motivated learning. Dependent learners may acquire a store of information, but they are not likely to be good at problem solving, which requires curios-ity, persistence, and individually unique ways of processing information. Perhaps the dependencies fostered by traditional schooling contribute to the underdevelopment of learners and consequently to the waste of human potential.[31]

In his comprehensive indictment of the professional other-direction that prevails in our society, Christopher Lasch points out that "the history of modern society, from one point of view, is the assertion of social con-trol over activities once left to individuals or their families." Such assaults on the individual "have made people more and more dependent . . . and have thus eroded the capacity for self help and social invention."[32]

Toward a Blend

The schooling experience, however, need not emphasize and reinforce only dependence in learners; the new emphasis on learners and learning, contributed by burgeoning non-traditional programs, has the power to renew and invigorate education towards independence in learning and self-development. What is needed throughout the lifespan search for self and independence is a blend of learning experiences, some of which are traditional, and some of which are non-traditional. Each learner ought to have regular episodes throughout learning in which he gets experience in self-direction, self-motivation, and the evaluation of achievement. Distance, open, and independent learning are three kinds of non-traditional learning that could well supplement or even replace certain segments of regular schooling to fill an experiential void in growth towards independence in learning.

V

Open Learning

Non-traditional, distance, open, or independent learning innovations constitute not several different educational endeavors, but a single great new development in education. It has affected all levels of education, but is particularly visible at the post-secondary level.

Cyril Houle suggested in 1973 that America was entering a new era in higher education. The new conceptions regarding higher education, and the "bold suggestions" which grew from them, says Houle, "make it clear that a watershed has been reached."[1] But the watershed was not so much a product of self-critical higher education as it was a part of the general societal uncertainty respecting all conventional education. The effects of continued industrialization, the push for civil rights and full democratization, the unrest of youth in the sixties, political radicalism, changing needs and lifestyles, the yearning for some measure of control over personal destiny, disillusionment with institutional inflexibility, even a growing sense of the importance of education throughout life—all of these contributed to the eruption of concepts and innovations that have marked a watershed in all levels of American education, not only in higher education.

The non-traditional departures from the older courses followed by education seem to be based on these principles:

> The societal imperative of lifespan access to learning for all people requires institutions characterized by openness.

All learners, on the basis of needs, should have some degree of direction over the education they obtain for themselves, some right of autonomy of choice.

Different learners have different cognitive styles. In qualifying for educational opportunities, learners bring uniquenesses as well as similarities to group norms. Each of these is equally important. Hence, whether fully self-directed or in a transactional learning arrangement, learners should be encouraged to learn in ways that are natural, effective, and appropriate.

Wherever learners may live, however remote from instructional resources, whatever their socioeconomic condition, the ancient restrictions to access derived from a space-time-elite perception of learning can be overcome by various communications media.

Nor is this new era limited to the United States. It is evident throughout the world, strong in some countries, only faintly stirring in others. While America had much to do with originating and sustaining this movement, innovation in the creation and implementation of institutional forms for this new concept of education is found throughout the world, especially where education for human development is recognized as a national imperative.

The success and recognition of open learning is a belated recognition of the need for and validity of the non-traditional means of learning that have been in existence for generations. University Extension, correspondence study, and radio and television education were the immediate seed beds from which open learning grew.

The trend towards open forms of learning, in the United States and elsewhere, cannot be separated from the extraordinary efforts in our times to create better learning situations out of which an improved human condition may in time evolve. But the open learning trend is also related to a number of other phenomena — social, economic, political, technological, demographic, and educational.

Learning is the act or process of acquiring knowledge or skill. When the adjective "open" is used to qualify "learning" we have put a name to a process of learning that is not enclosed or encumbered by barriers, that is accessible and available, not confined or concealed, and that implies a continuum of access and opportunity.

The term *open* has been given to so many experimental programs, at so many levels, that it is difficult to find a common definition that will describe — or be acceptable to — all the different enterprises that use the term. There are "open" schools at the preschool level, the primary-elementary and secondary levels, and in higher and continuing education. However, all the open schools have one principle in common: they are to a greater or lesser extent efforts to expand the freedoms of learners. Some of the open schools are open only in a spatial sense, with learners in school freer to move about in more individualized learning patterns; others provide freedoms in more significant dimensions — in admissions, in selection of courses, in adaptation of the curriculum to the individual, and freedoms in time as well as spatial aspects (i.e., learners permitted to start, stop, and proceed at their own pace and convenience). Still others approach the more important freedoms — learner goal selection, reaching the learner where he is, in his own environment and situation, on his own terms, and involving him in the evaluation of achievement of the goals that he has selected.[2]

Characteristics of Open Learning Systems
(United States)

If one were to create an institution congruent with this enlarged definition and to accomplish its implied goals, what characteristics would such an institution have? Ten characteristics of open learning systems were identified in a study carried out by the National Association of Educational Broadcasters for the U.S. National Institute of Education.

The ten systems characteristics identified were:

1. The system is capable of eliciting, interpreting and analyzing learner goals and abilities at the entry point and throughout the student's participation with the instructional and learning program.

2. The system acknowledges that it embodies two separate but related programs — the instructional program embodied in the institutional system, and the learning program carried on by learners with the assistance of the system. [This item was omitted in the NAEB's final report.]

3. The system is capable of enabling learners to participate in the program of learning and instruction without imposing traditional academic entry requirements, without the pursuit of an academic degree or other certification as the exclusive reward.

4. The system requires formulation of learning objectives in such a way that they can serve as the basis for decisions in instructional design, including evaluation, and in such a way that they will not only be fully known to the students, but so that students can participate in decision-making.

5. As an operating principle, the system is capable, after reaching a critical minimum of aggregation, of accommodating increased numbers of learners without a commensurate increase in the unit cost of the basic learning experiences: i.e., costs must not be directly and rigidly volume sensitive. After reaching the necessary level of aggregation, unit costs should show a diminishing relationship to total systems costs.

6. The system makes it operationally possible for the methodologies of instruction and learning to employ sound, video, film, print and other communication-diffusion technologies as vehicles and options for mediating learning experiences.
7. The system uses testing and evaluation principally to diagnose and analyze the accomplishment of specified learning objectives, including the objective of self-directed rather than other-directed learning.
8. The system is able to tolerate distance between the instructional staff and resources, and the learner, and employs the distance factor as a positive element in the development of independence in learning.
9. The system accepts the learner and his "surround" as the environment for learning, and concentrates on enriching that environment instead of developing specialized teaching environments which intrude barriers of place, space, time and other-direction in learning.
10. The system seeks, obtains, and maintains the active cooperation of community and regional resources which can be important factors in enriching the learning environment, in diminishing learner dependence on a single resource, and in returning learning as a natural and continuing activity to the living space, the indigenous learning environment which includes living, working, recreating and learning . . . as an essential step towards the "learning society."[3]

Actual open learning systems (institutions) reveal considerable variation in the ways in which they do or do not exhibit the ten characteristics identified.

Put another way, "openness" is certainly not an absolute quality. First, there is a range of openness displayed by any one institution, which may be open with respect to some, but not other, characteristics. Second, if all institutions of higher education (including those called "open") were to be ranked on a scale from "closed" to "open," there would be a distribution that looks very much like a skewed bell-shaped curve. That is, there would be a few institutions at the extremes of "entirely closed" or "entirely open," a loose clustering of many institutions that exhibit some characteristics of openness, and a fairly extensive range between the institutions that mark the actual extremes on the scale. However, the differences revealed in the groupings are real, even though the criteria for measurement are still rough and somewhat primitive.[4]

Mackenzie et al. pointed out that the American concept of open learning embodied in the characteristics listed above "drew much of its inspiration . . . from the thinking and experimentation which, founded and encouraged by large grants from the major charitable foundations, had been exploring 'non-traditional' forms of post secondary education in the United States since 1960."[5]

Gould noted that "non-traditional study is more an attitude than a system. . . . This attitude puts the student first and the institution second. . . . it is not new; it is simply more prevalent. . . ."[6]

Faure's *Learning To Be* suggested that lifelong learning ought to be the concept which guides educational development in all countries, and that open learning has relevance at many educational levels and in many societal situations.[7]

Social institutions are created to operate within contexts that give them viability and relevance. When contexts change, as they now have, institutions lose viability and relevance for some portion of the society they are intended to serve. It is then necessary to adapt or modify institutions according to the new contexts, or, if that doesn't succeed, to create new institutions.

Since World War II there has been an accelerated adaptation and modification of institutions to fit new contexts. These contextual changes are the root of the turmoil and disarray in education in the past two decades. Present contexts supply the practical, quantifiable elements that make up the reality in which education exists. The concept and characteristics of open learning seem to have a high degree of congruence with the needs-requirements for learning within the new societal contexts.

On the other hand, conventional institutions, created in other times, other contexts, and on the models of even older institutions, seem to exhibit ever poorer congruence.[8]

We know that any institution must meet, reasonably well, the expectations and aspirations of its patrons or clients if it is to continue to enjoy that gentle rain of public or private subsidy which is essential for its survival. The ideological tendencies of the times, however unquantifiable, constitute a shift of context. Studies of the attitudes of youth in the sixties and seventies (e.g.: the Rockefeller Report of 1971, by David Yankelovich, Inc., and Ginott, "Between Parent and Teenager," *Fortune* 1969; in Sweden the SIFO (Swedish Institute of Public Opinion Research) Studies of 1969–72 and the studies of Clas Westrill) give important leads in understanding the ideological shifts that enabled open learning institutions to achieve acceptance.

For example, youth seemed to be saying: "Do not study to reach a position; study what is worthwhile and self-developing." "Say goodbye to marks and merits. Make yourself a worthy person."

Over 50 percent of the U.S. youth wanted a change in the education system — especially in the universities. They attacked the rigidity of the school system; they wanted it to adapt better to present-day society. They also wanted more democracy in the schools, and a decentralization of education.

Youth began to see life as a series of short pulls; the new *ars vivendi* was the creation of a tolerable life pattern out of unsequential and scattered contributions, experiences, learnings somehow brought together to form continually evolving meanings. This was a fresh perspective on lifespan learning.

Surveys of older citizens showed somewhat different attitudes, but a surprising agreement in attitudes towards the changes needed in schools, and strong desires for a more open and democratic learning system, acceptance of technology in learning, and perceptions of learning needs (for retraining/new career lines/coping/fulfillment) that are way ahead of present programming in post-secondary and continuing education. The surveys of the period identified a strong desire—almost a demand—for the creation of the "moral" school, one that serves learners more than it serves itself.[9]

In addition, technological development and extended exposure to the mass media have already convinced millions of people they can learn as well from mediated instruction as in conventional classrooms. The consistent yield of "no significant difference" in comparative studies of instruction methods backs them up.[10]

The adjective "open" was not formally applied to any school or university until 1969. It was in that year that Queen Elizabeth II granted a charter to a new British university. The concept of openness, however, which the Open University was created to implement on a national scale, was not new. The roots of the concept go back at least to the beginning of the twentieth century. It is clearly grafted to the British and American concepts of university extension and independent study.[11] This may be one of the reasons the open learning phenomenon—in so short a time—has won so remarkable a degree of acceptance in the face of much initial institutional hostility and contemptuous disregard, and has spread so rapidly. The seeds for open learning were in every region that had had experience with university extension, extramural, or independent study.

Relationship to Independent Learning

In the western world, for approximately eighty years (1850–1930) correspondence study was the only formal system of teaching and learning that enabled learners—wherever they were, and whatever their condition—to overcome the formidable barriers of space, time, social place, and economic status in the pursuit of learning. Correspondence study first appeared in a proprietary school format, and later became a major program in the spread of University Extension. Extension also pursued other instructional formats: Farmer's Institutes, Lyceum lectures, and class instruction offered off campus by itinerant teachers. The lecture tradition, established by Chautauqua, the Lyceum system, library societies, and literary and cultural societies, also enjoyed great popularity. Wright notes that "the zeal for self improvement which ran through Americans like a virus in the nineteenth century manifested itself in an exaggerated devotion to the lecture platform as an agency of intellectual and spiritual uplift."[12]

The schools of frontier America had provided a cultural center for their communities.

> The present-day city-dweller has no conception of the place the school occupied in the social life of rural districts. There literary societies met; there the people met for discussion and debate; there came the spellbinding lecturer or itinerant "professor" with his electric machine and demonstration of scientific wonders. When a raw Western town could boast a college, the populace of the surrounding country flocked to its "attractions." Lyceum programs were part of the college's contribution to general education.[13]

The veneration of education, which increased as the country pushed ever westward and became more remote from the settled urbanities of the East, contributed the rich soil in the seed bed from which educational innovation would grow. But with the coming of correspondence study, a person could pursue an education at the elementary, secondary, or collegiate level. He could go beyond occasional inspiration at a lecture, to a course of study, and even earn high school or college credits, or advance himself in a career. This he could do wherever he lived, at his initiative, and without having to wait for someone to visit his town with a lecture. The appearance of correspondence study marked an earlier "watershed" in American education, not realized as such for perhaps seventy years. By 1930, radio linked to education began to increase the learning options available to learners, and today correspondence is only one of a number of means for learning apart from conventional schooling.

It is curious that during that eighty-year period when correspondence study had an almost absolute monopoly as the only alternative to traditional learning, there was almost no interest in correspondence study as a method of learning. From the beginning there are fairly lucid accounts of the process of administering teaching by correspondence, but very little of substantive inquiry about the learners, the teachers, and teaching and learning by this method. Even William Rainey Harper and William H. Lighty, representative as they were of a turn-of-the-century interest of American universities in an alternate method of "extending to the people" opportunities for learning that conventionally went only to an elite few, contributed little to correspondence study as a novel method of teaching and learning.[14]

Yet during this same period the American psychologist-philosopher

William James published his best known works, Sigmund Freud published his most famous treatises, and John Dewey, contemporary with Freud and James, revitalized American schooling with his concept of "progressive" education. Except that correspondence study did not penetrate the concerns of professional education, the period was one of lively development in education and psychology.

The educationists of the time completely overlooked one of the most important educational trends of the period — the rise and development of correspondence study as an alternate to regular schooling.

After nearly a century, correspondence study is only just now beginning to be taken seriously as an important methodology and alternative. Indeed, many of the most innovative applications of correspondence study — in open learning systems, for example — are being undertaken by people who are unaware of their historical debt to correspondence study, and frequently proceed as though their applications are *de novo*. There is, as Mackenzie et al. noted, a reluctance in academia to accept or acknowledge thoughts, modes, or practices that emerged outside the established hierarchy, no matter how useful and appropriate.[15]

Nevertheless, correspondence study was the first method to emerge in the direction of independence, and away from continuing dependence in learning. As a phenomenon within the independent study category, it now has a more secure identity and a significant relationship to mainstream educational theory and activity. It is an important ingredient in most open learning systems, as are the other media systems for teaching and learning, especially radio and television.

Open learning, a worldwide trend, signals the application and employment of independent learning concepts and practices, the beginning of its liberation from ancient restrictions imposed in other times and contexts, and its admission (even though begrudged) into the educational mainstream. More attention has been given to open learning in the last decade than has been given to independent study in its various forms in the past 100 years; yet the symbiotic relationship of the two is clearly evident. Open institutions which have been ignorant of, or have chosen to ignore, this relationship, have been forced to reinvent at great cost in time and subsidy, practices and procedures that were already known and refined into highly developed specialties, and which were readily available to them.

Basic Questions

The appeal of open learning, worldwide, has encouraged numerous education authorities, states, and nations to create open learning institutions. The diversity of situations in which open learning systems have appeared, in widely different regions, cultures, and economies, suggests that the open learning concept has wide acceptance, and that it can flourish under a great variety of conditions.

Creating an open learning system or institution requires facing a number of complex issues, all of which should be thoroughly studied before a decision is made. The issues can be placed in the form of questions before the board, commission, ministry, or agency responsible for policy decisions. The questions themselves may seem simple — deceptively so, perhaps — but they can be used to probe the farthest reaches of educational purpose, policy, structure, and finance.[16] The questions that follow are phrased respecting the creation of open universities, but they can be quickly modified to suit other open institutions as well.

1. An open university or other educational institution must have some kind of curriculum; is it known what is desired and needed by potential students?

The curriculum question forces attention in two directions: the actual desires/needs of the learners, and the suitability, availability, and accessibility of curricula in institutions already in existence. The question cannot properly be answered without initiating a needs survey, or reference to surveys already completed, and an assessment of how well needs are being met by traditional institutions. This is a good way to begin the inquiry into the need for, and feasibility of, a new open institution.

2. Have the target populations been defined as to location, numbers, needs, attitudes towards an innovative university, characteristics, situations? Has a probability sampling been surveyed?

The needs survey is refined to yield other information essential in planning and decision-making. Attitudes (receptivity) of learners towards a non-traditional institution are studied, for these have an important bearing on enrollment and persistence.

3. Is it clear just what the new institution is to do that is different from what other institutions now do? What are the mission and objectives?

From a consideration of needs, desires, and attitudes of targeted populations, and an assessment of the current learning opportunities through traditional approaches, the unique mission and objectives of the new institution can be approached.

4. Where are the content and subject matter resources that will be needed to create the learning materials and experiences the institution will provide? Are they accessible (i.e., can they be readily and continuously engaged) for the development and maintenance of the teaching-learning program?

The focus shifts here to the academic resources that will be needed to create a new institution, and the availability of these resources for intensive employment in creating and maintaining the institution.

5. How will policy (purposes, admissions, fees, curriculum, development, diffusion, access, evaluation, rewards, maintenance) be determined, and by whom? An open institution implies a learner-oriented approach; how will learners have impact on the formation of policy?

This question opens the large issues of education for full exploration: Who shall be educated? To what levels? By whom? At whose expense? By what methodologies? These are properly public issues, so how such policies are decided, and by whom, is important. Learner impact on policy is an essential issue that must be faced early.

6. What is the attitude of content specialists (professors, researchers, professionals, and intellectual leaders) towards "openness" in a teaching institution? If there is reluctance or open hostility, what strategies will be employed to win at least minimal support, or to neutralize opposition?

As the central concept of the new institution emerges, it is important to assess the degree of support or opposition the institution will receive from the power blocs that can aid, impede, or destroy the institution. Strategies for winning support must be developed for power blocs, political forces, and the general public.

7. Will the institution be a teaching and learning institution? A learning institution? A teaching and learning and examining institution? Or an examining institution?

Educational institutions are powerful cultural artifacts that condition the thinking and accepting modes of people. Existing institutions are the givens of conventional thought about teaching and learning. Options in the design of the new institution hence may not be immediately apparent. The needs, desires, resources, policies, and attitudes towards innovation may suggest an other-than-conventional perception of the teaching-learning functions. Models for unconventional approaches do exist and can be studied. Few authorities, for example, consider the advantages of creating a university that is primarily an examining institution because the cultural artifacts persistently link teaching and learning. Yet the University of London has, since 1836, provided a prestigious model of an examining university whose degrees are accepted worldwide.

The current withdrawal of the University of London from its historic role of examining external students for internal degrees leaves a serious void in the world's non-traditional educational systems. It would seem that the option of developing an examining university ought to be considered by authorities pondering the creation of new, non-traditional universities.

8. How will rewards (credits, degrees, certification) be determined, and by whom validated? Will there be open acceptance of your learners in other institutions? How can accreditation be made reasonably secure for the learner?

The academic and professional controls of curricula and rewards are the powers used to prop up and sustain educational institutions, and particularly traditional institutions. Such controls are necessary, and arose originally to preserve the integrity of institutions for the professions, the public, and the learners. However, when power is exercised almost without challenge, it tends to fall back upon protectionism. The public and the learners, not represented adequately in the control of education, may be locked into an educational status quo that no longer serves societal needs.

New institutions, which arise largely because old institutions are unresponsive to need, may be allowed to develop according to the "cut them off at the pass" strategy of protectionism. At the pass, learners with their rewards (credits, diplomas, certificates, degrees) may find they have been outmaneuvered: the status quo academics and professionals, through the legal associations that control accreditation and entrance into professions and graduate study, declare the curricula, the learning methodology, and the rewards granted inferior, because different from those in standard institutions.

This impasse need not occur if the planning process involves persons of integrity from all the academic and professional groups whose approval is needed for the full acceptance of credits, diplomas, certificates, and degrees. The aim should be to create an institution of the highest integrity, for only this kind serves the public and learners best. But this does not mean bartering control to those who place narrow protectionism above learner, public, or national needs.

9. Through what communications media will the learners learn? What diffusion technology will have to be employed? What access systems will be required to link directly with learners?

If the new institution is being created to serve learners physically distant from the faculty, how will they communicate with each other? Human beings receive information through five senses by seeing, hearing, feeling, smelling, and tasting. Two senses are dominant in communication, sight and hearing. The classroom is a cultural artifact that confines teaching and learning to a place and time determined by the communication mode of speech. It involves both seeing and hearing. Reading employs sight for sighted persons, touch for blind persons, or may be conveyed by sound (as when one person reads to another or a person listens to a recorded message). Electronic media have now revolutionized communications, diffusing visual and auditory messages to the most remote places. Writing and printing never were confined to a place; indeed, their purpose was to spread communications to the most distant. Writing and speech (via telephone, recordings, cable, or broadcast media) can provide two-way communication between persons no matter how distant from each other. Computer services link persons to vast stores of information at the press of a button.

All this is obvious and well accepted in the world outside academia. Yet to spread learning opportunity and access it is now necessary to employ communications technologies in teaching and learning, activities primarily under the guidance and control of academia. Which technologies? How will access be provided? Where will academics be found who are willing to learn to use media? How are mediated courses planned, designed, and produced?

10. What level of aggregation (volume of enrollment) will the institution seek? (This is very important in costing out any institution.) Will the funding commitment extend beyond the initiation phase? (The initiation phase implies high risk, high unit cost, but relatively low overall cost if level of aggregation is low.) Is the funding commitment shaky beyond the early phase, dependent upon "success"? If so, policy and design strategies must avoid the build-by-accretion theory.

The volume of enrollment sought upon opening the new institution has significance in many obvious ways. Not so obvious, however, is its significance in the complex area of unit cost analysis, as a basis for further growth. It is commonly assumed (on the analogy of the classroom artifact) that an institution can start small and grow big as it succeeds. However, the classroom paradigm is a false analogue in non-traditional learning systems.

The starting costs for mediated teaching and learning tend to be large. Hence, if a small enrollment is sought, the unit costs are high — so high that those hostile to the new institution can endanger it by attacking its high unit costs.

The volume or aggregation sought for the new institution must be carefully determined by computing costs as accurately as possible, and then deciding what number of students (divided into instructional costs) will produce a unit cost somewhat below that of traditional education. That number becomes the target aggregation. Growth thereafter is accompanied by further reductions in unit costs until major curricular changes require new infusions of starting capital. If starting capital can be amortized over a period of years (something academic institutions find it difficult to do) then the dangers of a small beginning may be somewhat minimized.

11. What funding will the institution require? Over how long a period and at what level of subsidy? What will be the source of funding? Will the institution have to seek funding, or will some other agency undertake this responsibility?

The funding needs of the institution require a full exploration of all the costs: unit costs, maintenance costs (keeping the instructional system up-to-date and at peak efficiency), media and development costs, student services costs, etc. Fee policies will have determined the level of continuing subsidy required.

12. What collaborations with established institutions are desirable and feasible?

No institution exists in a vacuum. A new institution should carefully plan its relationships to other institutions and seek collaborations where these are in its, the public's, and the learners' interests.

13. Should the new institution seek an independent status with full development of academic processes, tenure, governance, etc.? Or should it seek a public service–public utility status, drawing staff and other resources for its creative, developmental, and teaching-examining-accrediting functions from other institutions on an ad hoc basis?

If collaborations are not possible without bartering away essential controls for the achievement of a unique mission, then it may be desirable for the new institution to seek full independence, or a special "public utility" status, without full faculty governance, but with faculty seconded (i.e., borrowed) from other institutions for specific developmental and instructional processes. There is an advantage in the latter route that is not readily apparent: the creative process tends to exhaust faculty innovation in two or three years. Renewing innovation may require, in some instances, extensive renewal of staff.[17]

14. What preparation and training will academic, administrative, and service staff need to create and maintain the institution? What training/development process will be followed? What preparation will learners need to make efficient and successful use of the institution in learning?

It is unlikely that academic, administrative, and service staff personnel available to the new institution will be trained and competent to design, develop, and operate a non-traditional, open institution. Nor will learners be able immediately to know what the new institution is like, how it conducts instruction, and the methods they will be expected to use to learn within this new format.

The fourteen preliminary questions touch on only the major problem areas, and there are many others that must be confronted. The process of searching out these fourteen, however, will most likely bring out the others.

What has been called non-traditional, distance, independent, or open learning is not simply a variant of traditional academic education, but in many ways is the opposite of it.[18] The different names given to the different forms of non-traditional learning are merely a reflection of the different facets of the watershed of change noted by Houle. The implications of change send far-reaching ripples through the education establishment.

VI

The Implications of Non-Traditional Learning

Non-traditional learning already serves substantial numbers of learners in the world. By being available to learners as an alternative to traditional schoolroom learning, non-traditional learning is changing the total system of education. If a local, state, or national system of education is truly a system, then when any part of that system is altered, the change produces consequences in other parts of the system, and in the system as a whole. Institutions choosing to offer non-traditional programs, and learners choosing to enroll in them or to follow entirely self-directed learning, introduce alterations in the expected operations of the traditional system. Comparisons are made, advantages and disadvantages are discussed. An option or alternative never before considered becomes viable. Non-traditional learning becomes part of the reality of education for others.

Some of the effects of any introduced change can be anticipated (indeed, that's the reason for introducing change), but only an extended period of use or operation of a social system will yield specific information on the actual effects of change. Thus, at the present time only the implications of independent learning can be suggested. In the sections that follow, the implications of independent learning for learners, teachers, and certain educational institutions will be examined.

Implications for Learners

Perhaps the most important implication of the recognition and acceptance of non-traditional learning, for learners, is the restoration of learning as a natural, individual human act, not dependent upon schooling. Over the past generations the power, prestige, and importance of learning were gradually attached to schooling, and only the formal evidences of learning that were accumulated in schools were viewed as noteworthy enough to deserve reward and recognition.

Self-Initiated Learning

Self-initiated learning, no matter how successful, was inevitably suspect and denigrated. But self-initiated learning did not stop, for learning continued to be the natural coping and problem-solving activity of humans. Hence, while schooling with its standard lock-step, other-directed, and social reward features captured all the prestige, a legend and subtradition of "self-made" men and women, who learned what they needed to know largely without the benefit of schooling, grew up alongside. In that curiously perverse way in which social custom sometimes grows, society can admire the accomplishments of the self-made man or woman, even though it will not acknowledge the learning each has accomplished.

Mass and universal schooling has had to aim at the average learner. The very bright, the late bloomer, and the dull could not be well served, and found themselves out-of-step. Miller pointed out that

> Being out-of-step is a difficult role in life. It is not a fashionable role. It calls to mind that dumb boy three years older than the rest of the class. Whatever happened to that fellow? The psychology of education which was dominant when most of today's teachers were students was one in which the bright student or the persistent student thrived and the other student had no recourse except to suffer. . . . There are many signs that education will be receiving a major overhaul in the coming decade. . . . The free school movement, the drop out of college movement, the "why go to college at all" movement all herald a loosening up of our former approach to education. Education as a "part of living" rather than as the "preparation for living" is likely to be a part of the future. The [new patterns of learning] may well fall heir to much of the enthusiasm which is likely to develop about "non-lock-step education." And if there should come to pass a change in society's notion as to "who education is really for," many of the psychological problems that face today's "out-of-step" student might disappear.[1]

What happens to out-of-step learners — the very bright, the unmotivated, the dilatory, the dull? They carry their learning deficits, including in many instances a dislike or distrust of schooling, into adulthood.

There, if they cope at all, they cope with the manifold problems of man in society by learning as needs arise, by themselves or with others, and using whatever resources they can find.

There is far more of self-initiated, independent, backdoor learning going on than is generally realized. Not many years ago it was commonly assumed by the general public, and especially by education professionals, that most people could not, would not, and did not learn very much outside of schools. Since about 1970, however, a clearer picture of the learning efforts of adults outside the formal schools is emerging. Tough summarizes current information by pointing out, "Adults spend a remarkable amount of time each year at their major efforts to learn. In fact, a typical learning effort requires 100 hours. And the typical adult conducts five of them a year: 500 hours altogether. Some of these learning projects rely on instructors and classes, but over 70% are self-planned and others rely on friends and peer groups."[2] Tough defined a major learning effort as "a highly deliberate effort to gain and retain certain definite knowledge and skill, or to change in some way. To be included, a series of related learning sessions [episodes in which the person's primary intention is to learn] must add up to at least seven hours."[3]

The phenomena reported by Tough and others were derived from surveys, some of which sampled all adults in a country, state, or city. Others sampled high school graduates, university professors, unemployed people, retirees, factory workers, union members, literacy classes, college administrators, extension agents, and suburban professional people. The surveys have been conducted in the United States, Canada, Ghana, Jamaica, and New Zealand — not the entire world, to be sure, but a culturally, geographically, and educationally diverse sampling which, so far, leads to the unexpected conclusion that the "basic picture is remarkably consistent from one population to another. The numbers change a little, but the general pattern remains constant."[4]

The evidence now accumulating indicates that whatever the motivation for learning — an intent to use or apply the sought-after knowledge or skill in meeting some real situation (most common), curiosity about things, and knowledge for its own sake (less common), or the earning of credit for some kind of certification (fairly rare) — over 80 percent of all learning projects were planned by the learner (73 percent), a friend (3 percent), or a group of peers (4 percent). Does this suggest that adults must retain in their learning that total, continuing, and irrevocable dependence upon professional educators that is implied in schooling? Of course not, for in the sample populations studied only about 20 percent of the learning projects were planned by a professional educator — for a group (10 percent), in a tutoring arrangement (7 percent), or with a programmed or mediated resource (3 percent).[5]

American adult learners surveyed by Penland studied (in this order) things related to personal development, home and family, hobbies and recreation, general education, job, religion, volunteer activity, public affairs, agriculture, and technology. They most often preferred learning at home, but also mentioned other places to learn, in this order: on the job, outdoors, in discussion groups, classrooms, library, and at public events. Penland's respondents said they chose to learn independently for these reasons (in rank order): to set their own pace for learning, to give their own structure to learning, to use their own style of learning, to keep learning strategy flexible, couldn't wait until a class was formed, didn't know of a class available in the subject sought, no time to engage in a group program, dislike of formal classroom situation, not enough money for class registration, transportation to class too difficult or expensive.[6]

Teachers, studied as learners (by Fair[7] and McCatty[8] in Canada, Kelley[9] and Miller[10] in the United States, Denys in Ghana[11]) reveal little difference from other adults in major learning efforts, chiefly self-planned and not for credit. The prevalence and persistence of non-traditional learning, allied in new ways with schooling, is an important feature of the changing American and world education scene.

In the past, for example, higher education students were largely full-time youth on campus. The open, independent learning trend implies that this will change. Part-time learners from youth through adulthood will become the new norm. The statistical average or mean age of students will increase gradually until it is about ten or more years higher than it is now. Flexible admission requirements — or no requirements at all — will open learning on the basis of need, motivation, maturity, and experience, and not on the basis of previous education or certification. As Woodall indicates, "Ideally, student selection should be largely self-selection."[12]

Part-time Learners

Between 1972 and 1974 part-time learners in American post-secondary education equalled and began to exceed in number the full-time learners who were generally assumed to be the consumers of higher education. This is a statistic of great significance. Not only are the new learners largely part-time, most of them do not live on campus. Current trends in American higher education suggest a new configuration of learners:

> Part time enrollments are currently increasing at a rate nearly four times as great as full time enrollments.

Enrollments of older students (older than 24) are also increasing nearly four times as fast as those of traditional college age.

In 1980, the archetypical college student is *no longer* a 19- or 20-year-old single male studying full time and living on campus: he or she is older, married and residing away from campus.[13]

Many of these new learners are distance learners with independent learning styles. Such learners are gradually being accorded more equal status with full-time conventional learners. More mature, they demand the right to determine their own goals, to participate in the development of curricular and course plans, and to be involved in the evaluation of their achievement. Non-traditional learning appeals at present largely to middle-class adults, with women attracted about as much as men. Whether institutions choose to offer or endorse non-traditional learning programs or not, the spin-offs from this phenomenon will be likely to have impact even on regular programs. Far-reaching questions about curricula for the new populations of learners will have to be faced, especially as open and independent learning institutions begin to attract those who are most in need of them: the minorities, the deprived, and the least-served segments of society.

The learners at the back door have been waiting a long time for improved opportunity and access, better counseling and guidance, teaching that welcomes a diversity of learning styles, courses and resources that let learners proceed at their own pace, recognition of the importance of relevance in learning to the lives and needs of learners. They now demand and expect equitable recognition of their achievement, knowledge, and skills — however, wherever, whenever learned. That these things may come to pass is one of the implications of non-traditional learning. When learners cannot find these humane and practical elements in the education offered by schools, they proceed to learn largely on their own. If non-traditional learning systems can free learners to pursue learning as a natural activity, lifelong as needed, the potential of non-traditional learning will be realized.

Implications for Teachers

The shift of emphasis in education that has been called *Copernican*, that is, the shift of gravity or emphasis from the inputs of schools and teachers to the outputs of learning and learners, has important implications for teachers. If the changes for learners suggested in the previous section come to be, teachers will be no less affected. The role of the teacher is changing from that of providing instruction to a class, to facilitating learning for individual learners whether in a class or not. The prospect of having to guide and enrich the learning of students who learn at different rates, by different styles, who may be physically distant, and who exercise a degree of autonomy over their learning, can be frightening to teachers trained in traditional classroom norms, techniques, and psychology.

In Chapter III the fact was mentioned that teachers have self-concepts too, and they will tend to reject a role which seems to violate the concept of self-as-teacher built up over many years of preparation, modeling, and experience. Yet the change will undoubtedly be made by many teachers without severe trauma, although others will suffer great frustration.

The role change requires learning on the part of teachers. The motivation for that learning is usually there, in the person whose aspirations to become a teacher evoked a steady supply of motivation to carry the neophyte through long years of preparatory learning, modeling, and practice. Tough, a researcher and classroom teacher quoted earlier, learned about adult independent learners through his research. He writes, "I have found my [classroom] methods changing dramatically as a result of listening to adults tell about the total panorama of their learning efforts. Their self-planned learning is so successful and enthusiastic that it naturally raises some implications for classroom teaching."[14]

Recently van Leunen wrote a short essay about "amateur" scholars — those qualified scholars who earn their living at something else, and practice scholarship as an avocation, writing their papers "unencumbered by academic protocol and precedence . . . unprovided with a captive audience [characterized by] the bland indifference of the professional reader who is paid to read." She adds, "Every writer should pray nightly for the grace of impatient readers; they are a prickly blessing, but worth praying for nevertheless."[15]

There is compensatory value in impatient readers, or — as Jonathan Swift called them in 1704 — impatient back door learners. Van Leunen celebrates the pleasures and the fulfillment that animate the interchange between the amateur scholar (in the British sense) and the audience seduced by good writing into attending to him. "Faced with such an audience, the professional scholar might chafe. . . . But at the end he would have a chance to taste the most intoxicating of stimulants, the knowledge that something he wrote was read, not by obligation, but by choice."[16] Van Leunen's paradigm aptly describes the pleasures and fulfillment that accompany a teacher role change that is successful: The teacher may find the independent learner less willing to submit to institutional or instructional protocol, but the genuine excitement and intrinsic pleasure of the more open learning is indeed an intoxicating stimulus — to teacher as well as learner. Even if the teacher is not compelled by rational processes to teach in the new ways, he will certainly find powerful emotional satisfaction in facilitating the learning of autonomous adults.

Teacher and Learner Self-Concept

Teacher self-concept generally includes seeing the self as someone who does good to learners: helps them to master a subject, helps them to mature as thinkers and learners, helps them to learn skills as well as concepts, helps them to apply values in learning and life, helps them to overcome hurdles at successive levels of learning, helps them to understand the uncertain and changing face of knowledge, helps them to become employable, helps them to a healthy perception of the present linked to past and future, helps them to develop positive self-concepts. The ends of teaching remain the same even if models and methodologies change, even if learners grow up, become more independent, and insist upon some control over the education they obtain for themselves.

Sensitive as he must be to his own self-concept, the teacher needs to appreciate that learners also have self-concepts. If learners do not have quite the same goals and motivation as the teacher, or as other learners, this is an important thing for the teacher to know. "Persons whose motivations are different," points out Frymier, "have very different kinds of self concepts, values, time perspectives, and personality structures, among other things." "Values," Frymier continues, "represent what people believe in: what they are committed to and what they cherish. Values are very close to the center of self . . . give direction to behavior. . . young people who are motivated to learn in school value the abstract, the aesthetic, and the general, whereas persons who are not motivated to learn in school tend to value the concrete and the particular."[17]

Self-concept is learned, and teachers are an important source of the reinforcement feedback that shapes the learner's self-concept. But learners, if attentively listened to, can help the teacher towards a healthy, positive self-concept. What seems to be needed is Carl Rogers' famous triad: accurate empathy, non-possessive warmth, and genuineness between teacher and learner.[18]

These qualities, exercised near at hand or over a physical distance, are unmistakably recognized and positively responded to by learners; so, too, by teachers whose learners perceive and respond to them as facilitators of learning, and not mere law-givers or transmitters of information.

New faculty roles, in which there is less teaching of the lecturing style and more individual counseling, are implied. Faculty may find themselves gently nudged towards the Platonic model, with teacher as mentor, guide, developer of learners, and problem solver, rather than information and law-giver. In addition, courses for distance, independent learners, using various media and technology in systems-designed formats, will occupy an increasing proportion of faculty time and talent. Faculty responding to the new openness will work more in teams, will share authority in certain activities with others, including learners.

The Academic Department

The academic department may come under extreme pressure because of the need for an interdisciplinary approach that will more often characterize course and materials development. In some cases the department may give way to a different structure, implying a change in academic governance. (This will be discussed more fully under *Implications for Institutions.*) Tenure and academic freedom may be viewed differently. In the case of tenure, there are implications that this much–sought-after status may be somewhat more restricted, but compensated for, perhaps, by alternate kinds of job security. More extensively used will be other grades of faculty personnel, of the specialist or adjunct type, drawn in from the community.

While there is no implication that academic freedom is likely to be modified in any way, the very openness of the learning process may provide a new dimension to academic freedom. Anyone in Britain, for example, can tune in on Open University courses via radio or television, can purchase O.U. course guides and materials in any bookstore, or get them in any library. Hence, the university's aims, courses, processes, materials, staff, and evaluations are continually under broader public scrutiny than those of any institution in the history of higher education. Until now, issues of academic freedom have been primarily campus affairs, adjudicated, as Taylor points out, under agreed upon procedures in a confined arena.[19] In open institutions with widely diffused programs, the arena for any dispute is no longer confined, and different procedures to protect academic freedom may have to be evolved. Certainly a high degree of faculty responsibility in controversial areas will be required.[20]

Quality control, once more or less exclusively the domain of academia, will be shared with others, including students. More objective means of quality control in research, teaching, counseling, curriculum design, materials development, assessment, and administration are likely to come into wider use, partly because of the design complexity of open institutions, partly because instruction and materials design will proceed along behavioral lines, and partly because of ideological tendencies.

Will the teacher be comfortable and secure in such a changed role? If not, he is likely to try to prevent the emergence and success of the changed teaching-learning arrangements that are becoming more common.

Implications for Institutions

The trend towards more open, distance, and independent learning has implications for both traditional and non-traditional institutions. The implications (in addition to those discussed earlier for learner and teacher) fall into these categories: Mission; Operations-Administration; Curriculum, Instruction, Learning, and Rewards; Diffusion, Access, and Communication; Faculty Governance, Renewal, and Creativity; and Institutional Funding and Support.

Mission

The implications of non-traditional learning are likely to be felt most strongly in a gradual reevaluation of the role and place of all formal education, but especially of post-secondary education. Post-secondary institutions are under greater scrutiny because they are relatively recent and optional additions to standard education, because post-secondary education is still developing in the United States and has not yet reached the "universal" stage (the point at which all persons of post-secondary school age would be able to attend a post-secondary institution if they chose to do so), and because of the erroneous assumption that the universal elementary and secondary schools prepare learners adequately to go in varied directions, after graduation, equally well. It is at the still developing post-secondary level that society attempts to do the tinkering and adjusting that may yet provide learners with lifespan learning opportunity and access. And it is at this level, consequently, that fundamental and value-laden questions are still asked. For example, What are the values of education? What are the purposes of education? Who shall be given access to the opportunities provided by education? On what grounds shall education be subsidized? How shall education be held accountable to society? and How shall education be organized, diffused, and governed?

These are philosophical questions that are periodically examined and reexamined. From that Athenian grove named after Akadēmos, the answers to these questions over the centuries have reflected the value contexts within which each society gave role, place, and power to education. The changed contexts of our society have caused old issues to erupt with new force and clarity.

The non-traditional learning trend raises questions affecting the mission of every post-secondary institution. The raising of questions will not impel every institution into non-traditional learning, nor should it. Institutions will make choices within the value contexts of that society (or part of society) which supports them. By making choices, institutions will also be selecting, though not necessarily determining, preferred consequences in their struggle for survival. Hence, the missions of post-secondary institutions are being reexamined.

It seems likely that whatever reevaluation takes place, the net outcome will be institutional missions towards a greater rather than a lesser diversity in post-secondary education. At the same time there may be greater (wider) "concept space" between different types of institutions and programs than has been the case in the past.

Some post-secondary institutions (such as universities) will choose or continue an institutional mission that makes knowledge an end in itself. This is a proper and important mission. The knowledge needs of society are increasing rather than diminishing. Institutions that choose to go this way, or continue this way, are likely to benefit from a sharpened, more specialized mission, which will provide them with more concept space — more separation from other types of institutions.

Some institutions, on the other hand, will choose a mission that makes knowledge a means to other social and humane ends. The mission of these institutions will be the application of knowledge. In the past, when institutions tried to serve both the knowledge-as-end mission and the knowledge-as-means mission, inevitably one or the other suffered. Reward systems, for example, have tended to be unitary even where there was a dual mission. It seems likely that both types of institutions or programs would benefit by widening the concept space between them. (When there is insufficient concept space between missions, usually the older, stronger, more traditional concept of mission remains dominant, and the second is subsumed under it.)

Non-traditional learning systems will find more ready acceptance in institutions with knowledge-as-means missions. Indeed, the non-traditional learning trend is fundamentally an eruption of knowledge-as-means as a mission, equal in importance to knowledge-as-end. There is a profound difference between the knowledge-as-end and the knowledge-as-means missions, a difference that has been obscured because past societal and value contexts have determined a unitary, hierarchical typology for the main business of higher education — knowledge. Knowledge for what, seems to be implied in the non-traditional learning trend. For itself? As a means to other ends? (Social, individual, economic, or whatever.) For both?

Dual Missions

Some institutions will continue to have dual missions with respect to knowledge. These may well be the institutions that have developed (or choose to develop) university extension. As mentioned earlier, the seeds for university sponsored non-traditional learning were sown in the extension movement of the late nineteenth and early twentieth centuries. For complex reasons, university extension reached a conceptual plateau in the forties and fifties, and while it has grown in size and significance since, there was not a fertile base in the university itself for the complete nurturing and maturing of the extension concept. There was, perhaps, insufficient concept space between the knowledge-as-end and knowledge-as-means missions of the university, and extension remained in a sub-priority position in the established hierarchy regarding the purpose of knowledge.

The non-traditional learning trend implies that institutions that follow a dual mission with respect to knowledge will be likely to increase the concept space between the knowledge-as-end and knowledge-as-means missions. This suggests equal priority for each mission, and greater autonomy and structural separation of the two functions. These changes with respect to mission are already going on. The situation is muddled, however, with respect to university extension. While greater separation (more concept space) seems to be succeeding in new non-traditional institutions, in extension there is an opposite movement to return credit non-traditional programs to on-campus residence, leaving non-credit programs to extension.

The motive regarding the return of extension credit programs to residence seems to be economic (fear of declining enrollments and the possibility of having to reduce residence department teaching staff). Returning credit, non-traditional programs to residence will succeed only if the mission of resident departments is enlarged; otherwise the concept space necessary for the development of non-traditional learning will be narrowed to the point where only traditional credit courses remain. University extension may be weakened in this process as it is foreclosed from credit course instruction. If so, non-traditional learners, and society as a whole, will (again) be the losers. Learning at the back door has its hazards, not only for non-traditional learners, but also for the institutions that serve such learners.[21]

In the shifting aspects of mission, there seems to be no implication that research will be directly affected. Those who are qualified and want to do research, either pure or applied, will carry on research according to institutional mission. Those who do not want to do research, or are not qualified, will not find themselves barred from achieving the upper ranks, at least in institutions or programs that are knowledge-as-means oriented.

What the non-traditional learning trend implies is a somewhat different view of the knowledge missions of higher education, with teaching, research (pure or applied), and public service proper and essential activities of each type of mission, whether knowledge-as-end, or knowledge-as-means. Institutions that combine both missions are likely to find that the problem of providing concept space between these missions is more difficult than separating the missions into different institutions or programs.

Open or independent study institutions at the higher education level face difficult questions of mission, although their origins were clearly on the side of knowledge-as-means. Form, as the saying goes, tends to follow function. Mission determines function, expressed in aims, objectives, structure, organization, and programs. Mission itself is an important basis for assessing institutions and holding them accountable to society.

Operations-Administration

This category includes administration, admissions, accreditation, inter-institutional relationships at local, regional, and national levels, interface with community, business, industry, and government agencies, and the determination of structure and organization necessary to accomplish function.

The non-traditional learning trend implies shifts from the conventional in all these spheres. Whichever knowledge mission an institution selects, it will still have options as to how its mission is to be achieved. Whether it chooses more, less, or no openness or learner independence, the institution must survive in a milieu that includes the reordering of educational priorities on the basis of increased learning needs throughout life for nearly all people. With only finite resources, some reallocation of educational dollars in the years ahead must be anticipated.

Institutions that move towards non-traditional programs will have to alter traditional admissions policies and accreditation processes, and adjust operations and administration to new or different priorities. Policy modification will not come easily, however, because of the diversity, ambiguity, and lack of hard comparative data on non-traditional programs. Cross comments on the diversity, "Programs flying under the non-traditional banner today range all the way from . . . a unidimensional program [a standard evening college for adults] — non-traditional only with respect to scheduling — to multidimensional non-traditional programs that are unconventional with respect to location, schedule, students, faculty, methods of instruction, and curricular content."[22]

Bowen, Edelstein, and Medsker point to the skepticism of decision makers regarding available evaluative data: "Part of this skepticism stems from the nature of non-traditional education itself — the great diversity of programs; unclear definitions of or agreement on purpose, mission, and goals; the fluid character of the issues; and the absence of a set of criteria that could be applied in an assessment of effectiveness."[23]

Operational characteristics will tend, inevitably, to become more specialized because the need to follow conventional institutional models as closely as possible will no longer be paramount.

Curriculum, Instruction, Learning, and Rewards

Curriculum, instruction, learning, and rewards have traditionally been under the control of the faculty. Non-traditional learning implies that institutions will become more learning- and learner-oriented. Institutions will evolve dual systems of teaching and learning; these two activities will be conceptually separate, as indeed they are in reality. Knowledge-as-end institutions will put the emphasis primarily on subject matter; knowledge-as-means institutions will emphasize learning as a problem-solving process in knowledge-applying situations. The rapidity with which knowledge is generated, and the inescapable implications of knowledge obsolescence, have already hastened this development.

The controls over curriculum and rewards (this implies the assessment of learning) will gradually be shared with others in the team process, including learners.

One of the ancient aims of education — helping the learner to become independent of "other-direction" in learning, so that he can take responsibility for learning throughout his life — will assume a new prominence. Efforts will be increased to diminish the dependencies of learners — especially in post-secondary education. Learning will be viewed by more and more people as a self-directed activity that must continue throughout life in many contexts and circumstances.

The present age and certification barriers that separate the education of infants, children, youth, and adults will become blurred. Stopping in and stopping out of educational institutions, as needs and situations change, will become more common. Situational learning will motivate many to take up learning again and again, using a variety of media, technology, and materials, no matter how distant from a source of instruction. Accreditation and the rewards of degrees and other diplomas will have nothing to do with the place where the student learned, how or in which sequence he learned, or at what pace, but only with *whether* he learned and can demonstrate the competencies and behaviors that were the objectives of the course.[24] Short seminars, vacation schools, and concentrated laboratory periods will bring faculty and students together periodically on a

face-to-face basis. More attention will be given to the "no significant difference" findings of past comparative studies of instruction methods,
which disprove the view that non-traditional approaches reduce instructional standards and quality of learning.

Extension and independent learning institutions will be more at home
in applying these concepts than more traditional institutions, and will
find their work more widely accepted.

Diffusion, Access, and Communication

Non-traditional learning implies more options and choices in learning.
Part-time learners in particular will take advantage of improved access to
learning opportunity diffused through various communications media.
Print, writing, television, radio, the telephone, the computer, graphics,
programmed systems, the satellite, tape systems, and the video disc will
find a place in the diffusion of instruction and learning resources. Learners will be able to communicate as freely or more so than at present. New
student bodies with different conceptual and communication patterns
will be attracted to non-traditional institutions only if the learners' needs
are better met than they were in traditional institutions. This may be
possible. As Salomon pointed out, "Media's ways of structuring and presenting information — that is, their symbol systems — are media's most important attributes when learning and cognition are considered. . . ."[25]

As already discovered in a world short of energy, there are many things
institutions can learn to do as well as, or better than, they could when it
was assumed that people must be physically transported to some place
where they can learn. The challenge to technology and its users is to communicate affective and cognitive meanings even more effectively and
humanely than at present; this, too, is an implication from the non-
traditional learning phenomenon.

Faculty Governance, Renewal, and Creativity

The development of new institutional models in post-secondary education has stimulated interest in whether the faculty of such institutions
should be permanent or temporary. What are likely to be the advantages
and disadvantages of permanent and temporary faculty for these new
institutions?

The term *permanent faculty* denotes a faculty recruited and employed
for long-term service, governed according to conventional principles,
and with controls over curriculum, methodology, degrees, and tenure in
the hands of subject matter departments or faculties. The term *temporary
faculty* denotes a faculty recruited and employed for short-term service

which (usually) does not imply concerns over rank, tenure, and promotion, or controls over curriculum, degrees, or other aspects of conventional faculty governance.

It is important to remember that the new non-traditional institutions came into existence because conventional institutions were unwilling, or (under their historic missions) unable, to respond to the societal needs that fueled the formation of the new institutions. That unwillingness or inability derived in large part from traditional faculty opposition. Hence it would seem prudent, in staffing the new institutions, to avoid the replication of traditional faculty power structures, which, in the future, could well lock in the new institution to its initial programs, and forestall future change.

In the earlier contexts, which the models for most post-secondary and higher education institutions were created to fit, social change was expected to be slow, clientele were the minority rich and powerful, there was little physical or social mobility, and the power conferred by knowledge was not expected to be applied directly to the solution of individual and societal problems. Other cultural and social institutions (the church and hereditary government) exercised power to maintain the status quo. Knowledge was sought chiefly as an end in itself. Learned teachers were expected to cloister themselves from practical affairs in much the same way as the priesthood. A powerful mystique arose about the "sanctity" of knowledge for itself, leading to truth. To protect this mystique against disbelievers and practical men who would intrude utilitarian concerns into the academic world, conventions arose placing control of this world almost completely in the hands of faculty. The architectonics of the university was intended to provide institutional endurance, to resist change brought by intrusion from the outside world. To do this, the permanence of a loyal faculty was essential.

Stability is one of the advantages of a permanent faculty, adherence to tradition another, and high scholarship perhaps a third, needed in the lonely pursuit of truth, with knowledge an end in itself.

The professions became rooted in the universities in a symbiotic manner. They needed the quality of the scholarly disciplines for their own development, and the faculty controls that could be exercised over neophyte learners for the protection of the professions, and indirectly the public, from false teaching and doctrine.

But the very strength and advantage of the permanent faculty have been its weakness and disadvantage in times of changed societal context. Post-secondary education is now becoming open to nearly all; populations are mobile; knowledge is valued as a means toward other social and individual ends; practical problems are increasingly referred to academics, who seek them, and the grants attached thereto, to provide a new reality for the pursuit and use of knowledge; clientele come in all stages of readiness, and the formal background of learners is not considered as important as is the evidence of potential for development. Traditional faculty controls of curriculum, rewards, and methodologies, even when legitimately exercised, have often stood in the way of needed change. The "morality" of schools, an issue in the sixties and seventies, was defined as education which serves not itself, but learners and society.[26]

Permanent faculties of traditional institutions were a major reason for the unresponsiveness of institutions to change. To be fair, some of the changes proposed seemed contrary to the inherent interests of established faculties, and to the historic missions of some institutions. The new non-traditional institutions had to consider alternatives to permanent faculty. Such consideration was forced on them, ironically, by the characteristics of conventional faculty governance.

Temporary faculty have been used by institutions over a long period of time; the concept is not new. In fact, the lower grades of academics (the apprenticeship period) have generally served a temporary trial period to assure the selection of only the best to the tenured ranks. But nearly 100 years ago, in the United States and some other nations undergoing rapid growth, democratization of government, and the industrialization of society, temporary faculty began to be employed for another reason: to care for the needs of back door learners who did not fit the traditional purposes and methods of universities. Adult and extension faculty were frequently placed in temporary positions where they had no voice in governance or control over programs. And when some of them eventually won job security, it was on the basis of a continuance of one aspect of temporary employment — exclusion from control over the curriculum, rewards, and methodology of programs.

Temporary, ad hoc faculty became the way of life for adult and extension programs, giving to program development and operations the flexibility that was essential to programs funded unevenly and inadequately through outside control. Rapid adaptation to changing societal needs was the hallmark of adult and extension programming. Knowledge was not an end but a means toward social and individual betterment, a profound shift from the knowledge concepts of traditional institutions.

Even after tenure and job security began to appear in University Extension, control, except over non-credit programs, continued to reside in regular faculties.[27] Temporary faculty are still employed in large numbers for adult and extension program development and operations because of the flexibility this system provides, and the creativity it makes available to the system. It is therefore not surprising that the debate over the issue of temporary or permanent faculty continues.

The non-traditional institution must be continually innovative and adaptive. Creativity thus becomes as important as quality in programming. Creativity is an on-and-off thing; it can be used up, burned out quickly. The creative exhaustion that is a frequent consequence of innovation at one stage of development may itself preclude further development and innovation at the next stage. Institutional rigidity, the academic rigor mortis of traditional institutions, may then appear in the new institutions. Permanent faculty who have lived through rapid change may desire a period of no change, consolidation of gains, a yearning for time to refill the wells of creativity, or a return to the respectable pursuit of knowledge as an end.

The advantages of permanent faculty, in fact, may not be fully achievable in the new institutions if flexibility, innovation, adaptability, and creativity are what is needed to keep the institutions going. On the other hand, the needs of the new institutions for reasonable stability and consistency of quality may not be fully achievable with temporary faculty.

A Possible Solution

There is a way to solve the problem of conflicting needs of faculty, institution, and society. Non-traditional institutions, created to meet needs that were not being met by traditional institutions, do not exist in a vacuum. The traditional institutions are still there, and functioning. The non-traditional phenomenon is, in effect, a specialized extension of the knowledge generating, preserving, and disseminating functions of the traditional institutions, with the emphasis on teaching and learning via technology, and the primary mission of knowledge as a means to other ends. The relationship of the new institutions to the old should therefore be symbiotic, each serving and being served by the other in order to meet broad societal needs.

If we conceive of all the institutions, old and new, knowledge-as-means and knowledge-as-end, as a *social system,* the symbiosis is evident. The old institutions need a means of renewing the vigor and effectiveness of teaching and learning without diminishing the quality and stability necessary to pursue knowledge as an end. The new institutions need flexibility in curriculum, methodology, and rewards, and consistency of innovation and creativity to disseminate knowledge as means. Both can achieve their (and society's) needs if they function in a system as reciprocal and interdependent units (symbiosis).

Faculties are the key to this relationship, and the mechanism to bring it about is a system of permanent faculty in the traditional institutions, seconded to temporary special assignments (one-to-three years) in the new institutions. Some permanent staff in the non-traditional institutions, such as the key administrators, non-faculty specialists, and the directors of curricula and educational technology and methodology, are of course needed to provide continuity, develop plans, oversee operations, and recruit and employ faculty from other institutions for specific developmental tasks.

The temporary developmental assignments offered by the new institutions should be prestige awards, with higher bonus-type salaries to compensate truly exceptional faculty of the highest quality. The extra compensation is needed not so much to attract quality faculty, as to recognize that the temporary assignments are likely to be more arduous than normal assignments, requiring extraordinary creative and cooperative efforts. The faculty so involved are likely to have to put aside for the duration the normal research and writing that promote their careers.

The internal governance of non-traditional institutions need not, and probably should not, be identical to that in traditional institutions. Subject matter departments should be replaced by larger curriculum units to encourage a knowledge-as-means, rather than knowledge-as-end, viewpoint, and to open teaching and learning to cross-disciplinary approaches. Needless to say, full control over curricula, rewards, methodology, and recruitment and hiring of staff should reside in the governance worked out by the non-traditional institution.

The traditional institutions would be served by the relationship, via their seconded faculty, to the new institutions. Quality in academic endeavors is largely the quality of specific individuals on a faculty; the secondment of selected and invited faculty will provide quality and experience to the non-traditional institutions. In return, the traditional institutions receive the recognition and involvement of prestigious faculty in a new educational innovation, in itself a learning experience, which, when the faculty member returns to his academic "home," will leaven the seconding institution and be a means of renewal there. This symbiotic relationship will strengthen all of the institutions in the system, without subverting the needs of faculty, institutions, or society at large.

Institutional Funding and Support

While caution concerning the finite limits of monetary support in the immediate future is well taken, in time the legal and financial bases of higher education will begin to reflect the growing public support of non-traditional learning. New kinds of institutions will require special or modified legislation. Private, nonprofit institutions will become eligible for certain kinds of federal, and even state, subsidy. Part-time learners, who have always been penalized by paying higher fees and receiving fewer rewards, will be treated on a more nearly equal basis with full-time learners. Adults, who in extension and adult education programs have usually had to pay close to 100 percent of costs for continuing learning, frequently without academic reward, will eventually be subsidized on a comparable basis with youth simply because it will become recognized that society is the co-beneficiary of any learning that improves a person's life, career, earning power, or coping power. It will make even more sense to subsidize adult learning, since any improvement in adult living, coping, and earning is immediately expressed in higher taxes paid on income, in less demand for welfare or assistance, or an improved community. Cookson found that adult education participation was as powerful as formal educational attainment in contributing to individual change and development toward modernity. He encourages educational planners to promote adult as well as childhood education because ". . . the stability of the social, political and economic order may depend to a much larger extent on the level of individual modernity exhibited by the adult than by the child."[28]

Industry, business, and government will continue the trend towards subsidizing workers who continue learning and can demonstrate improved competence. The elderly (as we note already) will be encouraged to continue learning under higher subsidy as a means of enriching life and understanding, and of increasing communication between learners of different ages to compensate for the social dangers inherent in shutting elderly people away from normal social intercourse, particularly with youth.

The implications of non-traditional learning discussed here will not become realities all at once and in every region, country, or institution. The diversity of political, economic, and educational processes will undoubtedly produce different mixes of change, models, applications, and developments. Yet the implications are there today in the range and complexity of institutional response[29,30] to the new contexts and guidelines for lifespan learning, and in the newly understood behaviors of self-directing adult learners.[31,32,33]

While the non-traditional learning implications suggested in this chapter have chiefly been identified with post-secondary education, it is plain that the changes and implications noted are spreading across the educational spectrum. Seventy percent of state Departments of Public Instruction in the United States already include, as statewide objectives for elementary and secondary education, the objective of preparing learners to carry on independent continuing learning when they leave school.[34] Perhaps an awareness of and potential for non-traditional learning, alongside of traditional learning and learning throughout the lifespan, may be possible.

Part Three

TECHNOLOGY AND SPECIAL PROCESSES IN NON-TRADITIONAL LEARNING SYSTEMS

VII
Technology and Non-Traditional Learning

To those who lived through Progressive Education in the 1930s — and a series of popular educational movements thereafter — there is both something the same and something different in the present emphasis on the use of technology in education. The progressive movement, sparked by educator-philosopher John Dewey, sought to free education from rigidities of form and concept derived from earlier periods. There was a strong effort to understand the whole learner, to recognize and respect his individuality, and to involve him in meaningful participation in the processes and activities of learning. Progressivism was in essence a liberating movement aimed at freeing the individual, through learning, from the restrictions that an unsympathetic social and educational system placed upon his development and fulfillment.

The rationale for the application of educational technology to education shares some of the aims (and some of the dedicated fervor) of the progressive movement. The arguments for a greater commitment of technology to education call up memories of the earlier progressivism: the improvement of opportunity, the improvement of instruction, the emphasis on independent learning, the freeing of the learner from external scheduling, the implicit assumption that unfettered learning will lead to individual fulfillment, to social and economic mobility, and to social betterment.

There are differences from progressivism, too. Progressivism was largely a movement among teachers and educators. Its opposition came from conservative forces in education, business, industry, and parent groups. Government did not overtly play a role for or against it. The arguments for the use of educational technology, on the other hand, are partly derived from business-industry models, with a large assist from government, and without learner or parent opposition.

Under the impact of dedicated (one is almost tempted to say zealous) leadership, educational technology is put forward as an approach to solving America's educational ills. Educational technology is a fast developing field, an interdisciplinary conglomerate with elements from behavioral psychology, social action philosophy, engineering, communications, audio-visual education, and cybernetics.

While progressive education had its greatest impact on elementary and secondary U.S. education, the interest in educational technology is noted at all levels of U.S. education, from pre-school to higher and continuing education.

The inclination towards educational technology is a legacy of the growing scientism that was in part an outgrowth of the progressive movement. While American business, industry, government, and science were developing technology, education tended to reject or ignore it. But social, political, economic, scientific, and international stresses produced problems in American education which have not yielded to solution through conventional means. Enrollment instability, the knowledge explosion, the hunger of industry for better educated workers, the decline of ruralism, the increase in individual mobility, the rapidity of change, the rise of automation, the equality ethic, the threat of vocational and professional obsolescence, the growing imperative of lifelong learning — all of these societal context changes have had notable impact on American education. The pressures of unsolved educational problems have thus joined with the pressures of an evolving technology to force radical consideration of educational technology at all levels. The educational world has been spinning down "the ringing grooves of change," on (some would say) a technological toboggan.

Educational technology has not made its way to prominence alone. It has had powerful advocates whose entrance, oblique or not, into the field of education has altered the traditional contexts and parameters of American education.

The first of the advocates of educational technology is business. There will be cynics who nod sagely and point to the profit motive, and it's a safe assumption that if the possibilities of sales and profit were not present, neither would there be business, poised to enter education through the door of educational technology. But that is not the whole story.

Education's rejection of technology and derogation of non-traditional learning created a void into which big business and big industry could move. Alone of almost all the areas of human endeavor, education has been singularly reluctant to keep pace with the development of technology, and singularly resistant to the radical notion that conventional educational means are insufficient, perhaps even unable, to serve society's needs in the last decades of the twentieth century. There is often dismay and suspicion in academia at the growing emphasis on technology, and particularly over the prominence of business interests in its promotion. In 1966 Ridgeway noted, "A new industry in education has been taking shape this past year through a series of mergers, principally involving electronics companies and publishing houses. Along the way, the electronics companies picked up smaller concerns that make films, design tests and programmed instruction materials, produce educational toys and cheap scientific instruments."[1]

Government also became an advocate of educational technology. After Sputnik there was a growing conviction that education in the United States was in need of an overhaul to meet the demands of the new space age. The National Defense Education Act of 1958 signalled the beginning of a new role for government in American education. Hailed by most educators, federal spending in education was intended to improve education, make research funds available, build new facilities. But government support caused dismay as well as delight, for a measure of government influence, if not control, was implied in the financial aid provided. The "Great Society" goals were seldom questioned, but the means were suspect. Ridgeway pointed out that the government was shepherding the new industry in education, and that federal monies from the poverty program and the U.S. Office of Education were priming industry for the development and testing of educational technology. The technology being pushed for education was not a series of single devices, but rather the technology of a systems approach in which every level, every aspect of education had its part.

The Elementary and Secondary Act and the Higher Education Act of 1965 illustrate the entrance of the federal government into education, with special emphasis on the application of technology to education. Again, a cynic might point out that of course the new education industry had enough lobby power to get funds written into the Acts for the purchase of their products. But it is also true that educators themselves, in failing to keep up with and apply technology to education, created the conditions that brought in these advocates.

A third advocate for educational technology was the big objective of American education. The Great Society could not be achieved unless all citizens found opportunities for fulfillment. This was the old American Dream restated. In an earlier America the lower schools, the vocational and technical schools, higher education, and university extension worked well in providing visible and viable channels of opportunity to fulfill the American Dream. The middle-class school philosophy succeeded remarkably well in providing social and economic mobility to nearly all citizens. By the 1960s, confidence in past successes was declining, for American society itself was changing. The big goals of the Great Society were an important advocate in the stress on educational technology.

In the schools themselves conditions existed that persistently gave emphasis to educational technology. Big enrollments had led to big schools; big schools had led to big management. Management in education was forced to become more professional, patterning itself after the management of industry and government. When schools were smaller, and the growth rate was moderate, the management of schools could still be conceived of as an extension of the function of the teacher or the professor. School administration-management was a somewhat looked-down-upon role that (it was thought) any reasonably successful teacher or professor could perform, but which was not at all as important as teaching or professing.

With rapid growth (bigness), however, administration-management became a major problem at all levels of education. The new administrator-managers were forced to search in other social structures (chiefly business-government) where there was greater experience in adapting to bigness and the new requirements for efficiency. Relatively sophisticated administrative systems began to appear, and the teacher or professor who had ignored educational technology found himself under a mild sort of pressure to pay it some heed. Indeed, the pressures for change derived from big enrollments, institutions, and management patterns seemed in some places at least to suggest that desperate plea in *Paradise Lost*: "Awake, arise, or be for ever fallen!"[2] The fact that these are Satan's words completes the analogy, for to many in academia, the infernal promptings to adopt educational technology must have seemed in origin at least as low as the devil.

America's concern for developing nations provided another advocate for educational technology. The mixture of idealism and practical politics that underlay American aid to developing countries confronted American educators with needs, problems, and opportunities that sometimes required a more intensive and purposeful use of technology. To design educational technology systems for use in developing countries, while ignoring the possibilities of such systems at home, was illogical; and so another source of pressure in favor of the wider consideration of educational technology was registered.

But the strongest advocate in the continuing effort to establish an appropriate place in education for technology has come from another and unexpected quarter: non-traditional, distance, and independent learning. Long thought to be inferior because it was different, non-traditional learning, with its different modes of interaction with teachers, and the various media employed, has become, if not respectable, at least a matter of interest to educators who, a few years ago, were scornful. As school enrollments declined, post-secondary and higher education institutions sought clientele that would enable them to maintain themselves. The new client groups are largely part-time learners, adults, employed, and resident in communities often remote from the institutions which now are beginning to help them learn. They must be reached wherever they are, when they have time for learning, and at their convenience. Ergo, educational technology.

Intelligence, Needs, and Opportunity to Learn

We now know that intelligence and needs are distributed randomly throughout the world, our global village. Yet schools are distributed discretely. As a result, opportunity to learn has been uneven and unequal. Educational opportunity has historically been related to power — social, economic, political, military. Dreams of universal education have rarely been implemented beyond elementary or secondary levels; and even where such opportunities have been made available, access to opportunity and the quality of opportunity have often been uneven.

The problem has been partly in our concept of teaching and learning as a chained space-time relationship. When Plato gathered his students at his feet and engaged in dialogue with them, the medium and technology — oral speech used for didactic purposes — were the only ones available. Students and teacher had to occupy the same space at the same time to communicate, participate, learn. Plato's enormous contributions to philosophy, to the organization of knowledge, and to learning enshrined his method. The invention of writing, printing, postal systems, and electronic communications systems should have shattered for all time the old space-time barriers to learning. But custom and reverence for the values believed inherent in the Platonic system rigidified the chained space-time relationship between teaching and learning. So the school (the place where opportunity to learn is provided by bringing learners and teachers together at the same time and place) continued to be our imperfect means of education. Schools are costly, involve land, buildings, facilities, and the nurturing of a complex academic structure, institutionalized environment and culture: They can only be provided discretely. Even when so provided, schools may at some later date be in the wrong place to serve society because society has changed, the birthrate has dropped, the population has moved, or the transportation patterns have been altered. Should we still try to solve educational problems, meet educational needs, with a technology (face-to-face teaching-learning) that was appropriate in Plato's time? We need to be reminded of Drake University President Paul Sharp's hard insistence that "Education . . . was created in the first place to be useful."[3]

It is quite true that it is immaterial whether teachers and learners are present at the same time, in the same place, for learning and teaching to take place. The technologies of the book, the postal service, the telegraph, the radio, the telephone, television, programmed learning, independent study, the computer, and the satellite have superseded the Platonic requirement that learners be physically at the feet of masters. Opportunity to learn need no longer be fettered by the discrete distribution of schools; opportunity to learn can indeed today be randomly distributed throughout the global village — just as intelligence and needs are.

Teaching and learning are separate acts, invested in separate persons. The communications between teacher and learner can occur across distances. Hence any person, no matter how poor, how remote, how socially disadvantaged, how physically handicapped, can be in communication with a teacher or many teachers — if he has an effective communication system. Technology can provide the means — the tools — to achieve learning towards social and humanistic ends.

Technology as Tools

It is intriguing to think of writing, radio, and television as "tools" of education. The metaphor, while it oversimplifies, does fulfill its function of suggesting a resemblance between, let's say, a shaper in the hands of a carpenter, and writing, radio, or television in the hands of an educator. The concept seems apt: the tool is used to effect a change on that which is worked upon.

There are, of course, numerous other tools used by educators: programmed materials and processes, teaching machines, books, kits, visuals of all kinds, audio materials, computers, laboratories, libraries, and many other kinds of structures: classrooms, auditoria, offices, carrels.

The educator, however, does not simply employ a tool as such. In using writing, radio, or television, he employs a process of teaching that in turn is used by the student as a process of learning. While the postal system, radio, television, and other devices or structures do exist as such, these tools are not used for systematic teaching unless they are part of a larger whole, and that whole is the instructional process.

The tool metaphor becomes less appropriate when one realizes that the tool itself (the radio, the classroom) does not alone produce the result in the learner; it is what the learner does that eventually produces changes in his behavior. To be sure, the invention and availability of tools have profound effects on the behavior of the tool users, and on the objects of their use. But in education, the use of tools and technology has lagged far behind invention and availability. Because teaching and learning are correctly perceived as being highly personal activities, educators have been reluctant to use tools and technologies that might depersonalize student-teacher relationships.

What educators have not perceived about the activities of teaching and learning is that these two functions can be separated from each other and still remain personal. Furthermore, teachers and students have been to some extent infatuated with what might be called the cult of personality in teaching. And here arises a curious paradox: the teacher often assumes that only he can properly teach the physically present student, yet if the student fails to learn, the teacher dismisses him as lazy or unqualified, his lack of achievement his own fault.

The student is perhaps no more understanding of the subtleties of teaching and learning. The student shows his concern with teacher personality by seeking out teachers of reputation (called taking the teacher and not the course), and then when achievement is unsatisfactory, he often blames his teacher for his failures.

To a considerable extent the misunderstandings of teachers and students regarding teaching and learning represent an inability — or unwillingness — to differentiate among the separate responsibilities and activities of the teacher and the student. Because our ideal has been teacher and learner at opposite ends of a log, we have assumed that what passes between the two must be immediate and continuous; that teacher and learner must be in some sense chained together in order that each may carry on his related but separate activity. It is not surprising, therefore, that conventional education almost alone in organized human activity has been largely unresponsive to tools and technology. As a result, opportunity for learning has been largely restricted to those learners who are able to submit themselves to this chained space-time relationship with a teacher. Non-traditional education, on the other hand, has been obliged to bring opportunities for learning to persons remote from centers of learning (and incapable of this chained relationship) and thus has been forced to experiment much more extensively with tools and technology.

The human and personal element in teaching and learning is thus basic to any consideration of technology in education.

Technology as Means

The continuing danger in a technologically oriented society and culture is that technology becomes an end in itself; i.e., there is sanction for doing something because you can do it, not because you ought to do it. Or a technology becomes pervasive not only because it fulfills the purpose that brought it into existence, but because it may fulfill, along the way, other unanticipated purposes. Profits, employment, taxation, political advantage, national pride — many reasons can lie behind a technology's growth. For example, on a total cost-benefit basis the automobile would seem undesirable because society can't afford the social, economic, and ecological costs of the cars that more and more individuals can afford to own. But building and selling autos creates employment, and "What is good for GM is good for the country"; the dynamic continues. Technology becomes an end as well as a means.

Yet technology usually originates as a means towards some useful or even humanistic end. It is one of the tasks of humanists, educators, and social scientists to resist the evolution of technology to ends, and insist that technology remain only a means. Joseph Wood Krutch observed that "'Know-how' has increased by leaps and bounds; 'Know why,' 'know what,' 'know whether or not,' all lag. . . . we might be wise just to call a halt in our search for the power *to do*, on a grander and grander scale the things we do not know whether or not we should do at all."[4]

On the other hand, technology makes available the means to equalize the opportunities to learn, and eventually through the wider spread of knowledge, to change society in humanistic ways. If humanists and educators abstain from participation in the use of technology in education, out of a vain hope that the technology will go away, technicians, broadcasters, salesmen, and engineers will fill the void, and technology may become the impersonal monster some now fear, partly because the humane goals of education will not have been used to guide the development of means.

Communication Technologies as Culture Diffusers

All technologies, regardless of what they are — a stirrup, a steam engine, a television, a sewing machine, a school — are also cultural artifacts that carry a message about the culture and society that produced them. The technologies that have been referred to in the collective "educational technology" under discussion are primarily communication technologies. The specific technologies or artifacts — books, records, audio and video tapes, radio, television, the computer, the satellite, writing, schools, graphics, photography, the telephone — were invented and intended to communicate messages of some kind. The messages were not invented with the technology; they are not "part of" the artifact itself. Yet the existence and use of the technology conveys a message or messages about the people who created the technology, and the society that uses it. The technology conveys the values and priorities that prevail, the kind of economy, the state of knowledge, and the historic-cultural roots from which it sprang. The technology even conveys the hopes and aspirations, as well as the fears and pleasures, of its creators and users.

Communication technologies, quite apart from their unintended and subliminal[5] cultural messages, are the tools for diffusing the intended or liminal messages of those who manage or use the communication device or medium. Inasmuch as communication is an essential element in the related activities of teaching and learning, communication technologies have a proper relevance to every aspect of education.

Our numerous communication technologies are extensions of what has been, and is. "What has been and is" is what we call our culture: our way of perceiving ourselves, the world around us, persons elsewhere, our relationships, our means of determining fairness and justice, our discoveries regarding what is true, beautiful, and good. Our culture also informs us regarding that which is ugly–beautiful, useful–useless, rewarding–not rewarding. It affirms our values, aspirations, priorities, and the role and usefulness of our technologies. In short, it expresses the ways of mankind that we have found useful or necessary for survival, and that we therefore prize and desire to pass on to successive generations.

When a new technology emerges, it emerges in the context of the culture of its creators or adaptors. Hence an emerging or existing technology is not value neutral; it is freighted with the aims and priorities of its creators, owners, controllers, or adaptors. For example, cable and satellite (like radio, television, computers, and other communication systems) serve the cultural values and aspirations of whatever society employs them. Hence an assessment of their ultimate use or application cannot be made (or ought not be made) without reference to the social-cultural context in which the technology emerges.

For example, *Society A* perceives radio, television, satellite, and cable as technologies to strengthen the supreme power of the state.

Society B perceives these technologies as means to serve society's needs for information, education, entertainment, and commerce.

Society C perceives these technologies as means to extend the rights of property to produce income for the owners — the commercial exploitation of the communication of entertainment and information.

There is, then, a range of cultural views regarding what satellite and cable are and what they communicate. The actual technology — the hardware — in each situation might be nearly identical; but socially, educationally, politically, economically, the *uses* of technology are widely different because of the cultural context surrounding the technological employment.

Consequently, what *Societies A* and *B* can "afford" in terms of media use may be beyond *Society C*; spending priorities derive from value systems, not merely from the absolute or relative wealth of the society.

In each society there are developers, users, and consumers of technology; but they are differently perceived. In *Society A*, the government would be the sole developer and user, and the consumers would be acted upon. In *Society B*, the government would not be the sole developer and user, and consumers would have a responsive role in determining user policy. In *Society C*, industry and business would be the primary developers and users, and consumers would have no true responsive role.

When technologies such as radio, television, satellite, film, and cable come into being via the communication/entertainment industries in the United States, they are seen as properties that have the potential of profit. Furthermore, the Federal Communications Commission does not have an educational or cultural mission or responsibility beyond the basic licensure criteria that Congress provided (1934): "the public interest, convenience and necessity." However, there were farsighted people who foresaw application of these technologies to education. These farsighted people were not only in education. General Sarnoff, for example, had great aspirations for fledgling television as a means of education for the public good, just as many educators did.

As efforts were made to plan for the educational use of radio, television, satellite, and cable, what happened?

> Because education was identified as something that happened in schools, the technologies were thought of as school aids.
>
> Because education was something that proceeded according to standard curricula, the technologies were conceived as media for school curricula.
>
> Because education was something that had previously developed goals and rewards, the technologies were conceived of as vehicles for conventional school goals and rewards.
>
> Because technology developers could see little profit in the use of technology for education, the technology developed in ways that largely excluded educators and the American needs in education from having any significant influence on technology.
>
> Because educators tended to perceive education and schooling as synonymous, few sought any role in influencing communication

technology or in employing it, and the profession generally resisted the adaptation of technology to teaching.

Here is an example of what happens when such perceptions prevail: the development of video disc technology came out of the communications entertainment complex — an extension of systems from which income could be derived from users and consumers. One of the industries developing the technology saw a possible use in education, with the video disc as competitor to the optical film projector in classrooms. Why was the educational use of the video disc limited to such a narrow concept? Probably because education and schooling seemed synonymous; and probably because the Federal Communications Commission (FCC), in regulating communications for the public interest, convenience, and necessity, did not perceive educational-social needs as bearing upon their communication responsibilities, or teachers and learners as part of their constituent publics.

What this means, of course, is that the strong cultural bias for schooling, and the lack of a broader social and educational representation on the FCC, predisposes the application of communications technology to narrow and conventional use in education. Education as schooling (despite some excellent but exceptional programs), nearly alone of all areas of human endeavor, has remained singularly aloof from the charms, powers, and benefits of communications technology. At the same time, in the larger sphere of education that lies outside of schooling, technology has had a greater impact, even though it is far indeed from reaching its potential.

Technology Communicating Beyond the Classroom

Children, youth, and adults now apparently spend more time linked, as McLuhan would put it, with electronic, mediated experiences than they do or ever did in school. The larger sphere of lifespan learning is outside of the schools. A society that fails to understand and exploit — throughout life — the intrinsic joys of learning, perceiving, understanding, accomplishing, coping, and caring may become decadent, and risk losing some of its social values — the cultural cement that binds us together, and gives us survival power. Schooling cannot do it alone.

It is interesting to note that educational television's greatest smash hit, "Sesame Street," exists in a non-school format. Similarly, many of the Peabody and other educational awards won by broadcasters are also in a non-school format, as are the BBC's great public education series, such as "Masterpiece Theatre."

The non-school format offers educational media the opportunity and the advantage of doing whatever is needed with respect to education and learning, and not merely extending and replicating conventional schooling. The intended pre-school audience of "Sesame Street," and the adult viewers of the other prize-winning programs mentioned, are outside the prescriptive boundaries of schooling. Programming for these consumer populations does not have to conform to conventional concepts of subject matter, teaching, and learning.

Additionally, our whole society hungers for values, for commonly shared beliefs, for the quietly savored pride and joy of being human, being American. The high value we place on rooting out evil through a determined exercise of freedom of speech to attack, expose, and bring down, is not, ultimately, enough. While as a people we have sometimes seemed inclined to turn our back on our Puritan heritage, nothing has been more Puritanical than the commitment of writers, producers, dramatists, entertainers, comedians, educators, politicians — practically all of us — to concentrate on exposing evils, great and small. This should unquestionably continue.

But what about our other great legacies from the cultures that have shaped the American people? Compassion, courage in adversity, trust, neighborliness, idealism, unselfish love, personal commitment? The upsurge of interest in the past, the nostalgia for a nonviolent, nonmaterial way of life, for enduring and ennobling values, is evident at all age levels. It is sometimes overlooked that such traits, behaviors, and attitudes are learned, just as are less desirable traits, behaviors, and attitudes. Hence, what is or is not on the tube (now our most important source of popular culture and education) makes a profound difference to the culture, health, and survivability of a society.

Hoffer pointed out that "Disintegrating values may have as dangerous a fallout as disintegrating atoms,"[6] and Quarton noted that the behavior of a person is dependent upon the models that are made available or denied to him: "Behavior is readily modified by supplying or withholding maps or models of how other individuals behave."[7] Media entertainment that stresses the bizarre, the violent, the inversion of values, replaces earlier cultural and behavior models with those purveyed. But an educational use of communications technology beyond the schools could help to restore and strengthen our popular culture.

In addition, we have been slow to perceive the importance of adult and continuing education. In the past, when generations lived together throughout their lives, the formal education that was provided to youth in schools was augmented throughout life by the elders of the society. One of the serious signs of cultural breakdown in our society is the separation of youth and age, with both groups deprived of the common cultural feeding roots they need in order to be, grow, know joy and reality, accept change, adapt, trust, care, love, and take unselfish responsibility. Public, popular education via technology could help meet the yearnings of people for such experiences, if the commercial media fail to do so.

The agencies that regulate communications and entertainment have a responsibility to set policies and regulate so that concern for the cultural development of a society has at least as much priority as property and profit. The violence, brutality, bad taste, and inverted morality of the commercial media may through sheer shock effect push ratings up, but this is hardly what an intelligent, compassionate, and caring people would regard as the public interest, convenience, and necessity.

Adult education is the area of greatest need and potential for educational technology. It reaches adults in the natural environment for learning —the home and community, where life problems must be faced. Adults are part-time learners, tuning in and tuning out as needs and self-motivation determine. They are not so much interested in subject matter per se, but in problem solving, and applications. They tend to be interdisciplinary in learning. They are more mature, have better perception of needs, manage their own time, make decisions, and discipline themselves independently. Hence in programs intended for adults there is greater freedom to innovate, and less need for academic or subject matter control. Adults will even spend money on learning opportunities.

Quite evidently, inadequate concepts of learners, learning, the learning environment, and the education process have frequently blunted the most sincere efforts in the use of telecommunications media. Media that reach across our society into communities and homes, that attract millions of self-actuated individuals in non-school, non-group settings, have nevertheless been focused primarily on in-school use. That there is a place for school use is unquestionable; but even school use does not have to be in the school. In fact, non-school use might begin to take education back into the home and community, as it does now in programs of open, distance, and independent learning.

The indifferent success of technology applied to the conventional learning concept and model should be seen as striking evidence that that route doesn't work. The general reluctance of teachers to employ technology is another signal that the standard classroom learning model is perceived by most teachers as complete and satisfactory without technology. Turning these two observations around suggests that the conventional learning concept/model is incongruous respecting learning via technology. On the other hand, the changed societal contexts and needs, the new guidelines for learning, and the integrity of the new learning model, which enables us to accommodate physical distance without violating the four essentials of teaching-learning, give us clear signals to proceed in using technology in learning systems beyond the classroom.

Problems that Impede Educational Technology

The problems associated with learning through technology are the product of ancient cultural givens about schooling, derived from early societal contexts and needs that are no longer relevant. There are other, related problems, the presence of which impedes the successful use of technology for learning. For example:

1. Media and technology are largely viewed as aids in support of conventionally conceived teaching and learning.
2. There is dependence upon conventional subject-matter–centered sources for software development.
3. There is a continuing perception of education as schooling.
4. There is a continuing emphasis on hardware over software in dollars appropriated and in design, development, and evaluation; there is an almost excessive concern with the *how* rather than the *what* and *why* of mediated teaching and learning.
5. No solution has been found to the very real psychological-philosophical problem of educators in the system who do not have intrinsic reasons for adopting technology.
6. It is difficult, if not impossible, to develop a consistent, long-range national policy for technology in education because communications technology is largely owner-controlled by communications/entertainment interests which have no interest in education or responsibility for it. Government regulatory agencies — which also unfortunately lack an educational mission — tend to follow a policy of virtual noninterference with private enterprise.
7. Educational interests have not been able to develop effective political strategies to equal and counterbalance the powerful communications/entertainment lobbies in the Congress, Executive, and regulatory agencies.
8. The political climate makes federal support for long-range development uncertain.
9. The prevalence of short-term research and experimental projects (the "think small and do it quickly" syndrome), which produce little of lasting impact.[8]
10. The difficulty of "putting it all together" as long as responsibility for education in government is separated from authority elsewhere

for communications policy, marketing control, copyright, distribution of materials — none of which has an educational mission.

11. The tradition in government, public service, schools, and service industries of doing things for people, making them dependent instead of helping people to do things for themselves with increased independence, self-reliance, and responsibility. The dependency-reinforcing concept always strengthens the established way of doing things, the status quo, and hence, most likely, the conventional.

12. Software developers have been fearful of the distance that the use of media places between teacher and learner, and have failed to perceive the utility and advantages of exploiting distance in such things as learner motivation, adaptation to individual differences, learner autonomy, and integration of learning and living in the real community, and exploring and discovering according to the role behaviors of learners rather than institutional roles. Distance implies freedom, independence, responsibility, and choice-making. Agencies accustomed to doing things for people sometimes see these concepts as undermining conventional institutional roles.

Some of these problems have been studied by Oettinger and Zapol,[9] Grayson,[10] and Berkman[11]. The problems mentioned above are all complex. For example, number five, the lack of intrinsic reasons for adopting technology:

A teacher decides to use or not to use technology according to his or her perception of how technology affects the concept of self as teacher. What questions go through the minds of teachers faced with choices respecting the use of technology? Here is the way they seem to run: What will happen to my role as teacher if technology brings in a surround not fully under my control? What will happen to my students' role and development when more options and choices are made accessible? What will happen to our relationship? Will I like or dislike that changed relationship and environment? Will I like or dislike the new activities that will necessarily replace some of the things I do now? Will I have to be trained or retrained to use the new technology? Do I want to be? Do I believe that the extra effort and trauma of change will make me a better teacher, and help my students learn more? Will it make my work easier or harder? What credit will I get for using technology? If the technology really works, will I be working myself out of a job? I know where my career line is now; where is the career line that strengthens pay and security for innovation and adoption of technology? If I am going to use technology, how do I check it out first, so I know it fits my and my students' needs? And if I want to use technology, how do I bring it in under my control? How do I have something to say about the content and quality of what comes in? How do I know what technology actually does to people under my charge? If I use technology, I seem to abandon the teaching models that I have followed; where will I find new models that help me to see that I am continuing to do good for my students and society? Who will pay for the technology — how can I get what I want and need without a hassle with administration, school board, and taxpayer?

The range of questions runs the gamut from the self-serving to the professional. It is too easy to blame teachers for failing to make use of the benefits of technology in teaching, denying thereby to students the benefits of technology in learning. The teachers' questions are relevant; and for the most part there have been few convincing answers, especially from the fabricators of the technology, the administrators of education, and policy-makers.

Uncertain Acceptance; Cautious Optimism

Despite the difficulties inherent in identifying significant roles for technology in education, and the complex problems that constrain development, there are grounds for cautious optimism. The employment of technology in schools has steadily increased in the past thirty years. Most modern elementary, middle, and secondary schools make use of instructional materials centers, which use various kinds of technology for the replication and diffusion of learning materials that otherwise would not reach learners. Most schools now have personnel who combine the skills of library and audiovisual services, not alone to help learners, but also to advise teachers on the planning and development of teaching units. In post-secondary and higher education there has been similar growth. The burgeoning continuing education phenomenon with adult, independent learners at a distance, learning in non-traditional ways, has provided a fresh assessment of technology in education.

Most professional associations now sustain interest or development units or divisions concerned with technology in education, and contribute to the growing professionalism of workers in this field. The National Institute of Education, troubled from the beginning by a skeptical Congress, and hampered by a lack of discretionary funds, has nevertheless managed to put some sizable grants for research and experimentation into education problem areas, including technology and non-traditional learning. Certain universities, particularly those with an historic concern for University Extension, have developed strong faculties and programs studying, teaching about, and employing technology in education.

Professional-level conferencing and the publication of regular journals not only nurtures the continuing development of specialists in technology for education, but spreads knowledge to others on the periphery. Teacher preparation curricula, at all levels, offer training and specialties in audio-visual technology and communications. The federal Educational Resources Information Center (ERIC) and clearinghouses serve researchers and students working in the area. Internationally, the same growth patterns can be noted.

The Public Broadcasting Service, National Public Radio, and the university and community stations that make up their networks are achieving new levels of local and national support and programming. Out-of-school learning via technology is already a major source of learning in the United States.

Learning via Technology

For most learners, learning via technology is not a new experience. Clay tablets, papyrus, paper-pen-and-ink, the hornbook, chalkboards, books, pictures, newspapers and magazines, the postal service, films, and records have been in use for generations. Most learners are familiar with some of these early technologies used to improve learning. Fewer have had direct experience with radio, television, electronic sound and visuals on tape, the telephone, computer, and the communications satellite, although these, too, have had wide use in learning in today's world.

What is different about learning via technology today is the scope of learnings facilitated by technology, the altered roles of teachers and learners, the changed environment for learning necessitated by technology, and the sophistication of the processes used in developing instruction that will be communicated by technology.

Learning via technology is not merely a matter of substituting technology for the classroom. As Moore pointed out, learning apart (physically separated) from a teacher by means of communications through print, mechanical, or electronic devices, implies a quite different concept of learning from that acquired in schools.[12] The person who learns through technology is not only physically distant from the teacher, using print, mechanical, or electronic media for communicating, he is also as a learner required to be both more responsible and more autonomous. The traditional learner dependency sets believed and practiced by teachers, and required of learners in schools, come apart when the teacher and learner are physically distant from each other.

As noted in Chapter III, the standard classroom model is composed of four essentials. (See figures 1 and 2.) Through controlled admissions and teaching requirements, schools could hold the teacher, learner, and communications mode (speech) relatively constant. The other essential (subject matter) was the chief variable.

However, if the communications mode is changed to accommodate physical distance between teacher and learner, a new variable is introduced. Learning via technology puts the teacher and learner in a different relationship, as indicated in figure 3. Teachers who design instruction for distance learners from a classroom view of learning often fail; learners who enroll in distance courses with an expectation of classroom-type learning often drop out. The factor of learner autonomy or independence is important to both teacher and learner in the new patterns of learning via technology.

The distinction between dependence and independence in learning is, however, not bipolar (between two extremes), but is best expressed on a scale or range. Moore identifies eight degrees in the range from autonomous to non-autonomous learning. He asks three questions in categorizing the autonomy of a learning program:

1. Is the selection of learning objectives made by the learner or the teacher?
2. Is the selection of learning resources (people, books, media) and their sequence and pace made by the teacher or the learner?
3. Are the method and criteria of evaluation decided by the teacher or the learner?[13]

Technology, per se, is not a determiner of learner autonomy. Technology, however, opens the doors to greater learner independence by permitting physical distance between teacher and learner. Learners not under the constant control and direction of teachers, in a different learning environment from the classroom, begin to exercise greater autonomy as a natural and maturing condition. Knowles has pointed out that growth towards learning independence is "in tune with our natural processes of psychological development."[14] All living things grow towards independence in order to survive. The basic purpose of schooling, as stated in numerous curriculum documents and commencement addresses, is the preparation of the learner for that time when school won't be there to teach him, and he'll have to proceed on his own. Unfortunately, school- and teacher-directed learning result in the conclusion that "most of us only know how to be taught; we haven't learned how to learn."[15]

Consequently, the new programs employing technology between separated teachers and learners — whether pre-structured with two-way communication with teachers — or self-initiated learning with teacher as facilitator — may frustrate the teachers and the learners. Knowles cautions that "students entering into these programs without having learned the skills of self-directed inquiry will experience anxiety, frustration, and often failure, and so will their teachers."[16] Yet the separation of teacher and learner, and the opening door to independence in learning, are fortuitous, for "people who take the initiative in learning (proactive learners) learn more things, and learn better than do people who sit at the feet of teachers waiting patiently to be taught (reactive learners). They enter into learning more purposefully and with greater motivation. They also tend to retain and make use of what they learn better and longer than do the reactive learners."[17] As pointed out earlier, the contexts and needs of our times are such as to require learnings of the self-directed type. Independence in learning can be stressed in any teaching-learning situation, but it is more likely to result from situations in which teacher and learner are separated, and which require for that reason greater initiative and autonomy on the part of the learner, and the use of some technology as the communications medium (the variable from the classroom model).

Learning via technology will, in the end, become a strong force in American education only if it serves learners better than conventional schooling. Since results are largely a matter of beginnings, it is prudent to begin with the learner as central to the use of technology in learning.

The use of technology can help shift the emphasis in education from the inputs of schools, teachers, and subject matter, to the outputs of learning and the learner. Schools, teachers, and subject matter are important, and technology will not replace them, but the accommodation to physical distance and the recognition of greater learner autonomy that are products of educational technology even in pre-structured courses, may make the learner more central.

Making the learner more central may unleash, for more individuals than ever before, the extraordinary power of developed humanness. The human being is more wonderful, miraculous, and incredible than any man-made system or technology. Through learning he can solve problems, cope, adapt, plan, analyze, and synthesize. He can apply in the present, extrapolate to the future, explore and understand the past. Capable of astonishingly high levels of skill, and subtle variations of feeling and emotionality, he can create in many spheres, extending sensation, feeling, imagery, and meaning to others. He links himself to all around him on three time scales, learning and communicating complex skills, ideas, and feelings. He has a strong and mysterious concept and awareness of self, yet can relate with empathy, compassion, and understanding to others. He can be aggressive and submissive, competitive and cooperative. All these marvelous human capacities are developed, refined, applied, and evaluated by learning through the lifespan. The "human technology" of body, brain, nervous system, musculature, organs, tissues, and cell and electrochemical structures and processes, is the wonder of the world. All man-made technologies pale beside the intricate technology of the human being.

To Use or Not to Use Technology

Lynn White, Professor of History at UCLA, once remarked that "technology opens new doors, it does not compel man to enter."[18] When the unproved tool, the new technology, is part of our environment, we have to cope with our own creation as well as with all the elements that were present before. This is not a new principle, yet it is often violated. In the twenties, an elderly gentleman bought an automobile. He was told how to start the engine, put the car in gear, and how to brake. He was not told how to drive. He roared down the village streets at full throttle, scattering chickens, horses, carts, and goods as he went. Clutching the wheel he shouted, "Whoa, dammit, whoa!" The old horse technology didn't suffice. He abandoned the car against an immovable object, and swore never to drive again. And he never did, because he would not learn the technology of use that becomes essential whenever a new technology is employed.

In the same way, technological tools cannot be used effectively in education unless educators and humanists are willing to learn the technology of use that teaching with technology requires. The technology of use that must be learned includes the special processes by which the tools of technology are adapted to educational use, in accordance with the humanistic principles that underly all education, but that have special relevance to non-traditional education. Technology is only a tool. The technology of use, therefore, ought to come from humanists as they learn how to use technology for teaching and learning.

The technology of use imposes constraints on teachers and learners. Each person, teacher or learner, has to understand the advantages and disadvantages of the media employed in educational communications. Where more than one medium is used, they must be employed in an articulated format, each reinforcing the other in a mix that produces the best communication possible.[19] The advance preparation of courses and materials, the sustaining of a vigorous multiple-path communication process among teacher, resources, and learner, the preparation of science kits for experimentation, programmed units, slide kits, cassettes, newspaper units — and all the processes for conducting market and need surveys, registration, monitoring progress, and evaluating learner achievement and system efficiency — have become highly sophisticated technologies in themselves. Specialists from other fields are usually brought in to help in these processes, and a team evolves in which each member has both specific and general responsibilities.

There is a danger, when work is divided among different specialists, that the overall purposes of the material or course being developed, and the needs and participation of the learner, may be overlooked. A carefully designed process, however, will turn the attention of the team to the basic centrality of the learner at every step. (Chapters VIII and IX deal with this problem in detail respecting instructional design, institution building, and evaluation.) The importance of educators as humanists in these processes cannot be overstated.

A humanist technology of use means accepting the learner as a person wherever he is; it means seeing the environment for learning as the learner and his surround wherever he is (not just the learner in school); it means respecting the learner and letting him take responsibility, experience failures and successes so he learns and accepts his own strengths and weaknesses, and doesn't blame others for failure, or envy them for their success, or assume success is solely the result of crooked machination. It means allowing options of short and long duration in learning, selected by learner self-determination. It means permitting more than one way of seeing and reacting to problems. It means teacher and learner satisfactions derived from an honest view of self and others; and it means the recognition of elements of trust and worthiness in self and others that bring people together in mutual caring, coping, and learning. It means reciprocal interdependence between teachers and learners.

The changing era of learning that we are now entering has been compared with that which burst upon man with the explosion of the first experimental atomic bomb. In this new era, technology has new functions with, for example, a "promise of a million-fold increase in man's capacity to handle information," according to Dr. Jerome B. Weisner, Dean of Science at the Massachusetts Institute of Technology. If that technological information capacity is to have significance for education, the central figure will have to be the learner, not technology.

Will technology dehumanize education? Not if those who enter the doors opened by technology take with them the humanism that prompted the new perception of the centrality of learners and learning that characterizes non-traditional learning and its technological systems. Perhaps a humanistic technology for learning will enable us to meet James Burke's ideal: "If we are to realize the immense potential of a society living in harmony with the systems and artefacts which it has created, we must learn — and learn soon — to use science and technology to enrich our intellectual lives."[20]

VIII

Instructional Design in Non-Traditional Teaching and Learning Systems

As Ely has pointed out, "Educational technology is one of the most misunderstood concepts in contemporary education. Since its roots are in the audiovisual movement and its manifestations are usually visible products, it is understandable that to some people educational technology is represented by media hardware and software. The products are only part of the picture; the other part is concerned with the *process* of educational technology."[1] In Chapter VII, reference was made to the "special processes" that are a part of educational technology. Instructional design is one of those special processes.

Instructional design is not inherently difficult. The problem with it is that it seems simple, to all publics and professionals alike. The solutions to teaching and learning problems appear self-evident to a wide variety of people, and a range of simplistic remedies results. How can teaching be improved, and learners rescued?

An Arthurian "Castle Perilous" Situation

Castle Perilous was an English castle in which a princess was imprisoned by an evil knight. King Arthur dispatched Sir Gareth to free her, and, in the action, Gareth fought four knights and won the fair lady's hand. Irrelevant to the problem of instructional design in non-traditional teaching and learning? Not at all. The Arthurian legends appear and reappear at different times because they are more than exciting tales of jousting in battle. Essentially, they are allegories recounting man's struggles with good and evil. They have a humane message not unlike that of Norbert Wiener's definition of cybernation, "the human use of human beings."

No area of endeavor has been more concerned with humane values than education, yet the best intentions of those who seek the improvement of instruction for improved learning are often thwarted. There is trouble at Castle Perilous. Indeed, in the mid 1960s the dedicated advocates of special processes for the improvement of instruction saw themselves as white knights doing battle with all the inadequacies of the educational system. The triumphs of early space travel seemed to assure a prestigious place for technology and systems development in the solution of all problems, and the disenchantment of learners seemed to imply public readiness for fundamental improvement in education.

Moir and others, reviewing the uses of television and other instructional technologies in Britain and the United States,[2] and Theobald,[3] discussing the relevance of cybernation to higher education, foresaw a new role for technology in education, and identified a major obstacle to its success. Obtaining the active interest and concern of educators in the application of the new technology to education was a basic problem. It still is.

Confused Ends and Means

Confusion of ends and means may be the root of the trouble. To create and adapt a technology, we have had to be concerned with the technology itself. We have had, in a sense, to fashion a means that would serve the other, larger ends of a multitude of teachers and learners — each individual, each unique, each pursuing in bright clarity or absolute fog some near or distant end. The need to make the technology work, to define and to extend competency in its use, has forced us into a means-concerning role that has threatened and sometimes alienated those whose ends we seek to achieve. In addition, the strong lobbies for hardware have consistently pushed school people into purchases for which they were not ready; this unreadiness of purpose has caused a scandalous waste of educational money in unused or misused hardware. Hence there has been a reinforcement, not only of the means-centered role mentioned above, but also of our identification with technology as an end in itself.

There may be some in media, broadcasting, audiovisual services, and technology who have made means into ends. If so, this may be one reason why we cannot reach our colleagues on a more significant level. Perhaps that is why there is trouble at Castle Perilous.

Educational technology is chiefly an adaptation to education of technologies drawn from other fields. It is to be hoped that what may in time result is a technology of education, an indigenous technology that includes what has been borrowed, but that through a synergistic process becomes a unique and specialized technology in itself. Education is a person-centered process; the elements that will eventually compose a technology of education must, then, go beyond the hardware and equipment (the means) to an inclusion of learner-person values, in special technology of use processes that place software above hardware, the teacher and the learner above software, and express primary concern with the ends of education.

Our borrowings from other fields have tended to take us further astray. The systems approach, for example, is an essential process in media and technology, a means by which we can design instructional systems more effectively than ever before. We borrowed this approach from engineering, but, in using it, failed somehow to give sufficient consideration to the fact that engineering goals and educational goals are different. We have taught the systems approach in a rational, abstracted way.

In fact, this approach, as suggested by Hoye,[4] is a clear, rational, but abstracted concept. Translating the abstractions of any systems approach into human activities is often a barrier to successful use of the system and the successful employment of educational technology. What we need, perhaps, is a plan for the human activity that implements the systems approach as a means, but emphasizes teacher-learner ends.

Preliminary to initiating a process aimed at designing instruction for non-traditional teaching and learning, the planners must define the objectives of the process itself and determine project staffing strategies. Defining the process objectives does not mean determining the outcomes of the process; the outcomes result from it, but are not known at the planning stage. Staffing strategy involves selecting personnel for leadership in the process and assigning responsibilities to them. With the preliminary planning completed, the major process begins.

The director of a sophisticated computerized information system recently expressed his frustrations in attempting to create a data information base on the instructional activities of his institution. In talking with many instructors, he could find no common elements in goals, activities, or evaluation on which to build a useful information system. This not uncommon situation is, of course, the reason that some institutions are giving increased attention to what has been called *instructional design*. The computer information specialist could find no design evident in the instructional activities of his institution because none had ever been built into it.

The Principles of Instructional Design

What is *instructional design*? The term has been in use since the early sixties, and those who use it seem to understand what it means; but nine years ago, the monumental *Encyclopedia of Education*[5] did not even index the term; nor, in 1976, did the more compact *Handbook on Contemporary Education.*[6]

That which is *instructional* is broadly intended to inform, instruct, guide, advise, develop, counsel, assist, manage, encourage, motivate, structure, and assess respecting the range of functions and activities carried on by teachers for the benefit of learners. The term *design* identifies purposeful conceptions or plans; planning to achieve a predetermined end, to devise or propose a specific function, to provide a framework for what comes after, to conceptualize a project or scheme in which the means to an end are specified.

Instructional Design seems to mean the purposeful planning of instructional functions and activities as means for achieving predetermined learning objectives for learners in an instructional system. This definition is, of course, unsatisfactory in several respects; but perhaps it will suffice for the moment.

The definition implies that education (teaching and learning) is a rational process, with purposes, roles, functions, and activities for teachers and learners; that the process can be learned, applied and evaluated; and that it is linked to general and specific theory and practice in teaching and learning.

Instructional design, first as a concept and then a process, came into being in response to the changed situations in which teachers and learners now carry out their different roles. Some of the reasons for the rise of instructional design are:

changed societal contexts in which schools function

expanded missions for many educational institutions, especially at the post-secondary level

evidence that conventional schooling is not very successful in producing learners capable of functioning adequately in our society, and carrying on continued learning

the rise of non-traditional learning systems

new client groups for education, and the increased mobility of all learners

consumerism in education, and new demands for accountability

the growth of scientism and specialization among educators

the upgrading of training to sophisticated levels

the application of cost-benefit assessment techniques to education the use of media and technology in education

the growing use of preprepared materials and systems in teaching and learning

coping with the factor of physical distance between teacher and learner in non-traditional education, and with the increased autonomy of learners

the persistence of differing philosophies and psychologies respecting learning — all the way from the cognitive developmental, to the romantic, to the behaviorist.

The pressures developed by these different factors affecting education underlie the need for instructional design. Superficially it may appear that instructional design is something new. In fact, it is the more sophisticated successor, in new social and educational contexts, of the "lesson plans" neophyte and in-service teachers were taught and expected to be able to use in an earlier day.

The principles on which instructional design is based would seem to include the following:

1. Instruction must be designed to fit the societal contexts within which education occurs.
2. There must be a consistent and appropriate philosophy and psychology of learning applied in the instructional endeavor.
3. Instruction must fit the age, development, socioeconomic, cultural, and linguistic needs and characteristics of target learners, and be directly sensitive and responsive to such individual learner characteristics as previous educational attainments, self-concept, and field dependence-independence in learning.
4. Instruction must assist learners to reach appropriate and relevant objectives, whether knowledge is an end in itself or a means to other ends.
5. Instruction must interest learners intrinsically in achieving their objectives or, minimally, a combination of extrinsic-intrinsic motivations.
6. Instruction must employ as many communications channels as possible in order to achieve the greatest possible individual learner achievement.
7. Instruction must recruit and exploit the skills and resources of the institution and the community as a whole to assist the learner in self-development.
8. Instruction must include evaluation feedback to meet the needs of the learner as well as of the instructor respecting achievement and learner self-development.

9. Preprepared instructional units must be tested or piloted with adequate samples of the intended target learners, and revised or modified as needed.

The techniques on which instructional design is based were set forth, in part at least, by the Association for Educational Communication and Technology in 1972. A systems approach to instruction (which is another way of expressing the concept of instructional design) was defined as generally including these activities:

1. a needs assessment
2. the selection of a solution to the problems indicated by needs
3. the development of objectives for instruction
4. an analysis of tasks and content implied in the objectives
5. the selection of strategies for instruction
6. the determination of the sequence of instruction
7. the selection of media
8. the location or development of resources
9. piloting the resources and materials
10. revising the resources and materials
11. recycling from continuous feedback[7]

The Application of Instructional Design

Suppose we employ a hypothetical situation that seems to require the application of instructional design. Let us assume that we have the responsibility for preparing the faculty at our post-secondary institution to serve an enlarged mission for the institution: we are not only going to serve students in conventional classroom instruction, but we are going to reach out beyond the classroom to learners in the larger community. There is administrative interest, and an expanded mission for the institution to include a larger clientele in continuing learning, partly because of declining enrollments in traditional programs.

Preliminary discussions with policy-making boards and administrators have made it clear that the institution is prepared to support, as an essential in achieving the broader mission of the university, the use of media and technology in the program of outreach beyond the campus. The faculty, however, is uncertain about the effect of the new program on traditional faculty roles, and quite unprepared to assess, realistically, the new requirements that seem to be implied for teaching staff. Media people, who see the situation as opportunity for expansion, are moving aggressively to secure for themselves central positions of power and control over the new programs. Extension, long denied the full support of the university in outreach, and required to carry out inferior roles in curriculum development and control over rewards for their successful learners, is furious because the expansion opportunities it has long sought now seem to be going to Johnnie-come-lately in communications. The School of Education, which might be expected to provide some leadership in the difficult period of transition, has been so committed to the support of conventional schooling and related research that it in fact has no faculty either competent to work in the new area, or willing to abandon school-related careers. As the implications of the new program become better known, faculty reactions become polarized, all the way from the converted enthusiasts who honestly see themselves as emerging Kenneth Clarks, Alistair Cookes, and Jacob Bronowskis, to the hostile and derisive who honestly see the new program as the death knell to all they hold dear in academia.

The president, sensitive to the polarized faculty and the jockeying for leadership by conflicting interests, decides that the wisest course is to bring in an outside expert to advise the institution on the process that should be undertaken. It's the safest course, at the moment, because the outside expert on a short-term consultancy can be ignored if need be: his recommendations can be thrown to various standing or ad hoc committees to be devoured until the internal power plays are resolved.

The outside expert sees the situation as an Arthurian "Castle Perilous" with needs and complications respecting both teaching and learning. Hence he devises an instructional design that will move the institution toward its new mission, and will also be a model for the development of the programs to follow.

The consultant brings the instructional design before the president, trustees, and various faculty groups in a presentation using a few slides, which the consultant explains as he goes along. He is employing and presenting what he regards as a humanized systems approach to instructional design. Here is his report:

There are three phases in this approach to instructional design.[8] The first phase is the Faculty Development Phase. It begins with an examination or determination of institutional mission and an assessment of faculty strengths in behavioral terms for the accomplishment of mission in the larger social sense.

Phase I: Faculty Development

The key to successful employment of the entire process is Phase I, yet this aspect of instructional design is most frequently left out. It is here that the educational concerns of the institution find early expression. It is here that the humanists, social scientists, scientists, and professional specialists of the institution—the content teachers, administrators, counselors, and librarians—provide the mix necessary to make substantive and process decisions respecting instruction for learning as an end rather than a means. The institution's media and technology personnel may or may not lead the process; that point was decided in the staffing strategies worked out earlier. Whether such personnel lead or not, however, they form a nucleus in the working group throughout the process.

Inquiry Regarding Mission, Learners,
Goals of Instruction

It is important to note that the process does not begin with a discussion of media and technology per se—a topic that quickly descends to a nuts and bolts level of significance. The intent in Phase I is just the opposite: to involve a total faculty in high-level inquiry, i.e., mission, philosophy, unmet learner needs, characteristics of learners, development of a rationale for instruction, and selection of instructional goals. Why? Ely makes it clear:

> The literature is replete with examples of media being introduced to solve a variety of educational problems only to discover after several years of time and considerable money invested that no significant improvements are visible. The generalization stemming from this experience is: *The introduction of educational technology and media are not as important as the development of appropriate contexts of use.*[9]

Such activities require time, patience, careful preparation, and commitment. As Silberman has pointed out, the school must be "a center of inquiry" in which all teachers are always learners, and in which learners are never objects.[10]

The process begins with a faculty development conference at which prepared position papers on the institutional mission, the needs and characteristics of target learners, and an analysis of faculty strengths available for accomplishing the mission are considered and debated. A rationale for applying media and technology — as a means of improving chances for success of the mission—is presented and debated. Out of this discussion, goals for instruction for identified learner groups emerge and are clarified. (See figure 4.)

The processes for reaching goals are agreed upon. The conference also may include short demonstrations of media and technology at appropriate points, but always as specified means for accomplishing some instructional objective. It is generally not productive at this point to divert participants from major concentration on ends and goals. *What* the institution should accomplish, for whom, in its instructional program is more important at this stage than *how* it should instruct.

Preliminary: Defined Objectives of Process and Staffing Strategies

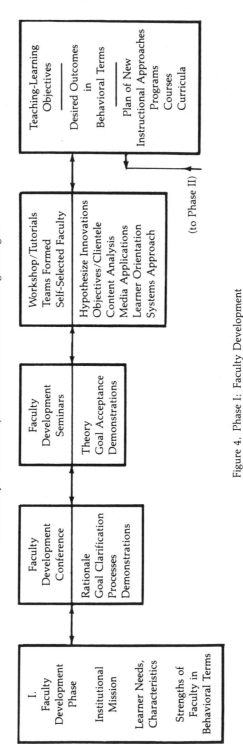

Figure 4. Phase I: Faculty Development

From the general faculty conference, the process then moves to faculty development seminars. In the general conference, new faculty leadership has emerged. Staffing strategies previously agreed upon enable these leaders to be employed in the seminars. It is important that strong faculty be prominent and responsible leaders in the seminars that follow. The seminars offer an opportunity for small faculty groups to probe instructional content, theory, and learner needs, and to move from goal clarification to goal acceptance, a very subtle and significant process itself. Again, demonstrations that are germane to the process and the debates should be included.

As the seminars come to an end, goals for instruction will have been accepted, along with a body of theory about instruction. A series of workshops and tutorials is then made available to faculty members who have elected to go the rest of the way in designing non-traditional instruction. In the workshops, faculty begin to hypothesize the innovations that they wish to make, to erect specific teaching objectives for particular learners, to make content analyses and selections, and to consider specific media and technology for application in a learner-oriented instructional program constructed through a systems approach, a term with which they now feel more comfortable.

At the end of Phase I, the institution can be expected to have achieved the acceptance of teaching and learning objectives, worked out desired instructional and learning outcomes in behavioral terms, and formed a definite plan of new instructional approaches. But there is often a remarkable bonus at this point: the waves set up by the process have reached far beyond instruction per se to affect concepts of courses and curricula. Indeed, because Phase I is deliberately focused on large ends, with media and technology considered only as amenable means, the inquiry is generally far-ranging. Only when the academic house is put in order respecting mission, goals, objectives, and outcomes for clearly perceived social and learner needs should media and technology get attention. Phase I, then, is not only the process of initiating renewal in the institution; it is also the process of legitimatizing the means to be employed.

The process suggested here is flexible. It can be used with an entire faculty as an institutional project, or it can be used in a school, division, or department. An individual could go through the process by himself, if he were the only innovator. But if action requires the involvement of others, then they must also participate in the process. Potential learners or their surrogates (demographic studies, needs assessments) must be included. The process can be entered wherever the participants are ready to enter. If they are at the workshop level, they enter there. If participants discover that they are not in fact ready, the process can be reversed to reach back to the elements needed. Of course, the process works more smoothly when an accurate assessment of institutional readiness has been made; this is one of the likely outcomes of the beginning faculty conference.

Phase II: Software Development

If Phase I has been successful in defining mission, goals, objectives, and outcomes in a plan for applying media and technology to instruction, then Phase II, Software Development (see figure 5), begins immediately. As an outcome of Phase I, self-selected and group-sought faculty have emerged to take positions of leadership. Working with media, technology, and educational specialists of various kinds, faculty continue the workshops and tutorials in which hypothesized innovations first occurred. The workshop tutorials are now, however, tightly focused on the specific projects that emerged in the instructional plan at the end of Phase I.

Software (the activities, materials, and processes for teaching, learning, and evaluation to be communicated by the hardware) is planned, and development is launched before hardware considerations are begun. The initial part of Phase II is design: the creation of the total scheme for a specific course, course sequence, curriculum, or unit. The design includes all the elements that must be incorporated into the finished product to be communicated. Much consideration is given to the selection of media and the application of technology, before hardware is procured. From objectives and desired outcomes in behavioral terms come clues that signal needs for audio, visual, and other kinds of mediated instruction. From analyses of activities and content come other clues that identify the kinds of learning sought. From a study of learner profiles and their actual physical environments for learning come still other clues that focus instruction on learner needs, characteristics, and orientation.

The design features would be incomplete, however, without a realistic appraisal of the institution's total resources for instruction. Such appraisal would include the strengths of its faculty and of its ancillary services. Finally, the design must include specific provisions for evaluation and feedback, for both are essential (but often ignored) parts of the instructional system. In short, the design must incorporate and adapt all the means at the disposal of the institution for achieving the ends that were conceived in Phase I. Each element of the design, as well as the design as a whole, is tested by continual referral to the conclusions and agreements reached at the end of Phase I. If the design takes a different direction implying a change of objectives or outcomes, all involved must agree to the changes, to conserve the integrity and credibility of the project.

When the design has been completed, it is a good idea to convert it to a document which includes both a narrative of what is proposed and a

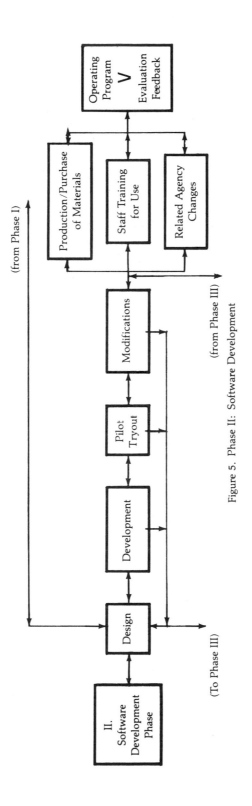

Figure 5. Phase II: Software Development

systems-based flow chart detailing each step of the projected development: Who is to do what, dates for beginning and completing units of work, points of coordination, review and decision-making (including approvals), and all the inputs from the resources to be employed.

Development may then begin; i.e., the persons or groups assigned responsibility go off to do their work. The project director orchestrates the activities from the design document. As the materials, activities, and processes emerge, considerations of media and technology become central. Decisions are made to use this medium or that, to employ this technology or that. From these decisions, the specifications for hardware are evolved. As soon as they are firm, Phase III (Hardware Procurement) may be launched to run concurrently with Phase II.

With completion of each segment of materials, activities, and processes, there should be a pilot tryout of the software, making use, if possible, of rented, manufacturer-loaned hardware or simulated means. The learners in the pilot tryout should be small samplings of the target learners. Modifications in the software should be made as required on evidence from the pilot tryout.

Phase III: Hardware Procurement

The hardware (the equipment and processes used to communicate the software) procurement phase is begun with the completion of the design and the start of software development in Phase II. That phase will have yielded the specifications necessary for selecting and procuring gear appropriate to the instructional goals. It is important to realize that hardware considerations should be subservient to those of software, which is designed to achieve agreed-upon goals. Selecting hardware first is usually a prelude to the disaster whereby means take precedence over ends.

There are some apparent exceptions to the principles cited. After a faculty member has been through the phases suggested, and he approaches a level of competence in the process, he can compress the process and work back and forth among the three levels almost simultaneously; yet he can preserve the order of priority according to the hierarchy of values and goals determined in Phase I and implemented in Phase II.

To suggest that hardware follows software (see figure 6) does not denigrate hardware. The three phases indicate priorities, a practical sequence of activities that will most efficiently achieve a marriage of software to hardware in reaching instructional goals. Hardware introduced at the wrong point often leads to failure. The hardware is not to blame; the process of planning and development is. Yet unused and misused hardware around the country (and the specialists who advocate technology) are the recipients of blame that often should be lodged elsewhere. When hard-

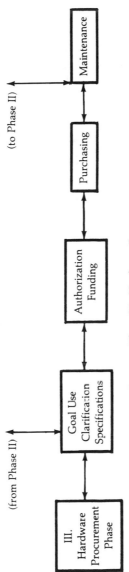

Figure 6. Phase III: Hardware Procurement

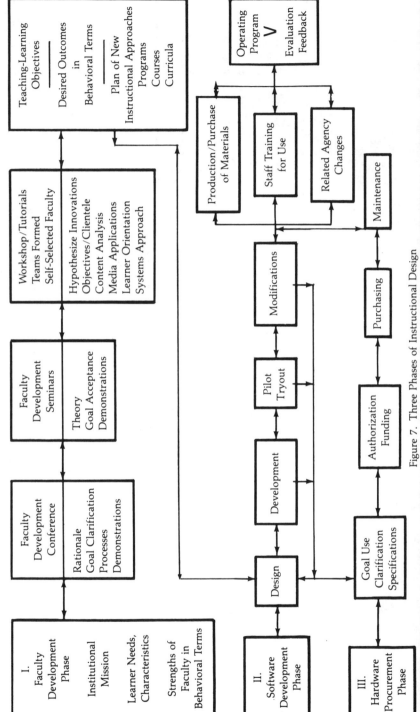

Figure 7. Three Phases of Instructional Design

ware is promoted and selected separately from software and the goals of education, means are in danger of becoming ends. Conversely, media and technology are most favorably employed when used as means to teacher-learner ends.

The marriage of software to hardware produces yet another bonus. Despite the prominence of McLuhan's views, there is still widespread disbelief or outright antagonism to his concept that "the medium is the message."[11] Yet anyone who has designed, developed, and produced a unit of mediated instruction will not ignore or mistake the meaning of that significant observation.

The total process of instructional design for the situation should now be reviewed (see figure 7). Phases II and III come together as materials are purchased or produced and as the staff are trained to use them, and any related agency changes are made as necessary in operating the new instructional program.

Evaluation and Feedback

A special word must be said about evaluation and feedback. The process suggested has been presented in linear form to suggest a sequence that is ideal. Evaluation (as noted earlier) has been part of the process from the beginning — not an "add-on" at the end, but an integral part of the entire process, and an integral part of the mediated instruction that the process creates. Hence, evaluation continues after the three-phased process ends, and feedback from learner evaluation, as well as from teacher evaluation, flows in reverse along the lines on the chart. If someone is there to receive feedback (as determined in the design), the process starts all over again at whatever point is appropriate.

So ended the report of the consultant to the mythical college.

The metaphorical Castle Perilous is any outmoded and unresponsive instructional system in which the institution, teacher, or learner is imprisoned. Instructional Design must give battle to four design problems: faculty development, software development, hardware procurement, and evaluation. The process suggested may be useful because it translates systems design principles into human activities, and emphasizes a hierarchy of institution-teacher-learner values and goals in organizing the human and technological means for non-traditional instruction and learning.

IX

Building and Evaluating
Non-Traditional Institutions
or Programs

In the previous chapter a special process for revamping an existing educational institution to serve non-traditional learners via technology was examined. In this chapter a special process for building and evaluating a non-traditional institution from scratch is presented. These special processes are part of educational technology, which "is a systematic way of designing, carrying out, and evaluating the total process of learning and teaching in terms of specific objectives. . . ."[1]

Until recently, non-traditional teaching and learning programs were almost entirely developed and evaluated according to the prescripts and canons of traditional education. Traditional education, of course, was there; it had visibility, prestige, professional acceptance, public support, constituents, and funding. Traditional education controlled curriculum and rewards. If there were to be any deviations allowed from the institutionalized norms, the deviations would have to be on the terms and under the control of traditional education.

In building the institution of University Extension, for example, the innovators and leaders had to convince the policy-makers, administrators, and the faculties of universities that the concept of extension fit the mission and general values of the university, that it would not harm the universities (i.e., would not compete for prestige or funding or students), that it would be under the control of the universities, and that it would not interfere with the main concerns of the universities, research and teaching resident students. At each stage of its development, Extension had to run this gamut.

As Sims, following Esman and Blase,[2] points out, there are three important aspects of institution building:

First there is the concept of an *institution* itself, with "those elements thought to be necessary and sufficient to explain the systemic behavior of an institution." These elements are the institution's leadership, its doctrine, its program, its resources and its internal structure. . . . Second there are the institution's *linkages* with other entities in the society external to itself. . . . four in number: 1) Linkage with external authorities who authorize the institution's existence and provide human and material resources; 2) linkage with other organizations which supply inputs and/or use outputs of the institution, or which are real or potential competitors in the society; 3) linkage with the sociocultural norms and operating rules and regulations in the society, since such norms and rules can inhibit or facilitate institution building; and 4) linkage with the "public in general." . . . Third there are the *transactions* between the institution and the other segments in the society external to itself. The institution carries on these transactions in order to 1) gain support and overcome resistance, 2) structure the environment, 3) exchange resources, and 4) transfer norms and values.[3]

The new non-traditional program or institution had to pay a quid pro quo for acceptance: institutional dependence rather than autonomy, inferior status as a substructure of the institution or the social hierarchy of institutions, and lower priority in the competition for funds and students.

Once established, non-traditional education — credit or non-credit off-campus classes, correspondence study, radio-television-telephone courses — was evaluated rather practically. The success of institution building was principally determined by the program's survival, the number of students enrolled, the simple criterion of generating enough income to meet budgetary requirements (frequently this meant returning money to the general fund of the university), of not getting in the way of the larger institution's recruiting of students and other support for research and residential teaching, and of not lowering the academic standards of the larger institution in reaching out to learners off campus.

Since the non-traditional programs (university extension, independent study, short courses and workshops, radio, telephone, and television courses) were conceived of as "extensions" of traditional on-campus programs, evaluation, when it finally came, had to be comparative. Courses and subject matter were the focus of traditional education, and a similar focus had to characterize non-traditional education. Evaluation compared the same on- and off-campus courses, with instruction as the chief variable. Such a comparison is difficult to make, meaningfully, because the comparison has to be in terms of the norms of residence instruction throughout.

Traditional residential instruction had evolved an elaborate process and vocabulary for evaluating student progress in courses: attendance requirements, library readings, laboratory, test and recitation grades, time-specified learning, and final examinations, all of which were based upon the assumption that the student was in residence, full time, and hence had no valid reason for not conforming to requirements. That many requirements were inappropriate to non-traditional learners was usually ignored. For example, the non-start, non-completion phenomenon that is characteristic of distance, independent, part-time learners (a proportion of learners will not begin or complete courses for reasons unknown to the school) was interpreted as learner failure, because that's the meaning generally accepted when resident full-time students "fail to complete." Non-traditional learners thus fell under constraints intended originally for learners of quite another age and circumstances.

The learner variable in the comparison of off- and on-campus courses was not studied until recently because course concepts, terminology, and processes were riveted to the care and guidance of the traditional learner. Few inferences from student data were drawn that could be applied to non-traditional institution building and evaluation. In fact, the prevailing wisdom asserted the importance of maintaining, to the greatest extent possible, the same course, subject matter, and instructional processes in non-traditional as traditional programs, despite inherent differences.

Traditional education has been the model which non-traditional teaching and learning has had to try to replicate, albeit with different instructional methods and students, in order to justify and maintain its existence. For example, lack of control in university extension over the credit-bearing curriculum and its rewards to students has generally kept non-traditional programs from competing with traditional education.

Nevertheless, non-traditional programs have survived in the United States since the late nineteenth century. In the 1960s, new types of non-traditional institutions began to employ systems design principles, and focused attention on the processes of development and evaluation that were thought to be more appropriate for open, distance, and independent learning.

The chartering of the British Open University in 1969 began a new era in the establishment of such institutions. The Open University included in its organization a research section responsible for the on-going study of the University, its processes, and learners. Furthermore, the Deutsches Institut für Fernstudien, the Fernuniversität, the Swedish TRU Commission, the University of Lund, and scholars in Finland, Australia, Norway,

Holland, Britain, France, Canada, and the United States began a systematic study of the phenomenon of non-traditional teaching and learning.[4] In the 1970s UNESCO, in cooperation with the International Council on Correspondence Education, funded research on the developmental processes of non-traditional institutions.[5] Erdos,[6] Perry,[7] Gooler,[8] Norman Mackenzie et al.,[9] Peters,[10] Holmberg,[11] and Kaiser[12] have described and analyzed non-traditional institution building and/or evaluation in frames of reference appropriate to these unique institutions.

Evaluating Non-Traditional Institution Building

Evaluation is frequently thought of as an add-on activity, after the institution has completed its work. The rationale for evaluation as an add-on to operations proceeds this way:

1. First we planned our work on the basis of needs which were assigned to us as our responsibility to meet.
2. Then we created the process to accomplish our work.
3. We got authorization, staff, and funds to proceed.
4. We did our work.
5. Now we must report to our superiors what we have accomplished, and ask for more subsidy so we can continue and grow.
6. What *have* we accomplished?

As an add-on, evaluation may be useful (and better than no evaluation at all), but the rationale is faulty and the consequences are hazardous. Consider, for example, the numerous examples you can think of in which institutional evaluation never occurs at all. The hazard, of course, is that the six-stage activity cited above is wholly operational; it does not include evaluation except, alas, as an add-on, an afterthought. Furthermore, personnel committed to operational stages that do not include evaluation develop a growing sense of anxiety about what they are accomplishing. If this anxiety is not reduced by actually doing an evaluation, it increases until it becomes fear of what may be revealed by a true evaluation. Even when such anxieties-cum-fears are groundless they inhibit the undertaking of an evaluation. What is usually required to break this barrier is a crisis of some sort:

1. an order from a superior
2. a new top administrator who wants to make it clear that he's not responsible for what went on before he took over, requiring an evaluation to stake out the grounds and goals of the new administration

3. problems of such magnitude that the survival of the operation is threatened
4. an opportunity for the program to grow dramatically if a case can be made on the basis of past performance

Summary Evaluation

Evaluation as an add-on is largely summative; that is, it is an activity undertaken at some point to set forth what has happened and what has been accomplished up to that point. It may be historical or sociological in focus; it may be narrowly directed towards management, cost-benefit ratios, completion studies, or other aspects; or it may be comprehensive in scope. An evaluation, however, is more than a summary of events or statistics; it is a careful appraisal of events and statistics leading to the formation of judgments respecting what has happened (good–bad, useful–not useful, authorized–not authorized), the identification of trends, and the elaboration of cause-effect relationships. An evaluation seeks the why as well as the what and how of things, and may well include recommendations for future action. It is highly analytical in nature, and depends not only on records of events and statistics, but also on generally accepted standards and criteria drawn from the professions. Comparative studies may be an important part of an evaluation if the persons concerned wish to know how the activity evaluated compares with similar activities conducted elsewhere.

Formal summative or add-on evaluations are generally carried out by persons who are separate from and neutral towards the activity evaluated. Objectivity on the part of the evaluators is essential. If the manager or staff of the activity conducts a summative evaluation, there is conflict of interest, and the evaluation is suspect. Summative evaluations by separate and neutral persons ought to be carried out periodically on a planned basis. The lack of periodic summative evaluation leaves the institution with insufficient information that is credible about what is happening, and increases its vulnerability. But even periodic summative evaluation does not meet the need for continuing knowledge of institutional results, especially during development.

Continuing Evaluation as a Function of Institution Building

The concept of continuing evaluation in institution building is important. It is, for example, an essential part of what has been called *systems design*, a process that has evolved specifically to guide project and institutional development. As such, evaluation becomes a function of institution building itself, organic and integral to development, not add-on or summative. In this context evaluation is sometimes called *formative* or *developmental* evaluation.[13]

Formative evaluation is a part of the process of institution building from the first step, and continues as an ongoing activity for the life of the institution. It does not replace summative evaluation, which should occur periodically, and which is separate and neutral. Formative evaluation is usually carried on by the regular staff; it is not necessarily neutral and separate. The people who conduct the formative evaluation are committed to the mission and objectives of the institution because they have participated in their development; they are responsible for building the institution, its programs, and services, and they are accountable for the consequences of design, strategy, programs, processes, and ultimate achievement. Responsibility and accountability require formative evaluation both for the self-interest and security of the people in the program, and for the survival of the institution itself.

Formative evaluation, viewed in this way, is a function of institution building. Formative evaluation in institution building is creative, developmental in focus. The institution being built is the issue of creative processes that derive their validity — always — from mission, broad objectives, and specific goals. This kind of evaluation continually throws inquiry respecting what is going on back to original questions:

> What are we committed to do? (Mission, objectives, goals)
> Why are we doing these things? (Social needs rationale)
> For whom are we doing these things? (Learner needs, demographic and market studies)
> How best can we accomplish what we are committed to do? (Method, process, staffing, funding)
> Is what is actually happening consonant with our mission, objectives, goals? (Responsibility)
> Why or why not? (Accountability)
> What decisions must we make now to improve the institution? (Continuing development, building)

Institutional Concept and Rationale

Formative or developmental evaluation is organic and integral to the building (and operation) of the institution. Consequently, formative evaluation begins with the conceptualization of the institution or program. In conceptualizing the program a theoretical model is being created, a prototype of the program (or institution) which will come to be through successive stages of development. The model is useful in making concrete and realistic the conceptual abstractions of institution building, and in guiding the development of the actual institution. The general concepts that precede the formation of the institution give the answers (or the direction in which to search for answers) to such basic questions as:

What will be unique about the non-traditional institution?

Why is the institution needed? How were these needs determined? Are they valid?

What is the authority for the institution?

What learners will be served, where are they, and what is their condition and situation?

What educational services shall be provided? How well do the services match with the needs? With characteristics of learners?

Who will develop these program services?

How will the services be brought to the learners?

What outcomes are expected?

These questions constitute an outline of, and rationale for, the institutional concept.

The Institutional Model and Evaluation

Given the institutional concept and rationale for a new approach to the education of non-traditional learners, including the overall objectives to be achieved, a model of the new institution can be projected. The model must define the "universe" within which the institution exists. All the elements that are now part of reality must be present in the model. In addition, as a response to the tensions inherent in development, the model system must picture the dynamics of activity, of movement, of things being done to achieve new objectives and to reduce the tensions through successful achievement. Hence the model has to portray also the new elements, activities, structures, measures, and modifications that were not present initially. A model will therefore include elements that are novel at the point of introduction in development. These new features, as soon as they are put into practice, become part of the system. So a model must not only represent things as they are, but also things as they will be.

A model system is also characterized by subparts, or subsystems. The subsystem (or submodel) must be as viable for its purposes as the overall model system. Each part of the system and subsystems must be tested for validity beforehand, as well as during its operation (comparing its representations with the reality of things at the start, and with changes introduced later). Any system implies a condition of equilibrium; that is, given the conditions, the objectives, the forces acting, the activities, there should be certain predictable outcomes. A change in any part of the system produces disequilibrium and requires change in the other parts of the system.

Alas, no human system actually operates so precisely. There may be errors in defining the "universe" within which the system operates because of unknown or unperceived elements not taken into account. There may be unperceived changes at some point, with consequent failure to make concurrent adjustments to other parts of the system. Predictability thus diminishes. Reliability falters. Validity fades.

The model system that follows includes a built-in formative evaluation or sensing element. If feedback warns the persons in charge of institutional or program development of something unanticipated, of a failure at any point, an immediate analysis of the system model in situ is called for. The system's equilibrium, which makes it reliable and outcomes reasonably predictable, must be restored. Consequently, an evaluation scheme that only comes into being to measure effect *after* institution building is an extravagance that human planners who care about their work cannot afford. Even success, evaluated after the fact, offers little enlightenment. Institution or program builders use formative evaluation to analyze what is going on, almost day-to-day, to make decisions on the basis of known realities, and continually to develop and refine the model system until it does achieve that reasonable equilibrium that assures reliability and predictability. Such an evaluation does not require control groups, since its purpose is not comparison with some presumed standard. However, operation of the model will eventually produce norms or standards that can be used in other kinds of evaluation or as part of periodic summative evaluations.[14]

Building an institutional model is therefore not a simple matter of putting together a project according to a pattern or template. It is a creative effort to achieve the thrust and counterthrust, the tension and countertension, the actions and reactions that the inventors of the model systems *hypothesize* are needed to produce the results desired. And since institution building is not carried on in order to prove or disprove the models, but rather to make advances in human organization and activity towards better education (in this case of non-traditional learners), the burden of the institution builders is to work creatively with the system to make it produce what is needed. Continuing evaluative feedback will make that kind of development possible, and will also contribute to later summative evaluation.

To suggest formative evaluation as a function of institution building it is necessary to provide a view of institution building. Hence the succeeding pages have a dual purpose: 1) a compact delineation of institution building as a process, and 2) an exposition of the role of formative evaluation within that process. While the presentation has general validity, it is specifically focused on the problems inherent in building a non-traditional institution serving distance learners.

A Conceptual Matrix

The matrix presented (figure 8) cites the various situation realities that must be considered in constructing and operating a distance institution. Each of the realities is, in fact, a variable, because in no specific place or region where such a program is established will the situation be exactly the same. However, the matrix is useful in modeling because (1) it identifies all the elements that must be dealt with, and (2) it provides a way for builders to "select the universe" that they wish to work within. For example, institution builders may wish to approach their test universe through the selection of target populations, through a subject or content focus, or through some other situational reality. The matrix enables the builder-designer to locate the approach that is closest to his situation — that fits his resources, the population that he regularly works with, etc. He can select the universe that is indigenous to him and thereby apply the special talent, expertise, resources, and experience that his situation offers.

The conceptual matrix suggested is not complete. Each institution builder must insert into the appropriate columns his mission, objectives, and the other items that describe his universe, and delete what is inappropriate to complete the conceptual matrix for his own institution. Vertical columns should itemize all the development concepts of the particular categories, spelled out in specifics. The first column (far left) will spell out mission and objectives. Hence by starting with a specific objective on the left, it is possible to follow horizontally through the succeeding columns to conceptualize the model or system that is being built to achieve that objective. Of course, it is not possible to get the grand design on one sheet of paper, as presented here. Laying out the entire model or design in detail, unique to a specific situation, may require an entire wall in your office.

Laying out the matrix may look like a boring chore. It isn't. It's an exciting, intensive effort, for here before your eyes and under your hands the institution begins to come into being. The matrix is dynamic, not static. It changes as your conceptualization matures, as the realities of your universe are perceived or altered, as mission and objectives are modified. If nothing else the matrix is useful as a series of check lists, but it will be more than that if it is employed thoughtfully.

The conceptual matrix is not at this point a system, model, or institution. The concepts fashioned in the matrix, however, are the basic ingredients of the next steps: modeling, testing, and operating. The modeling process suggested here consists of three essential elements — a systems development plan, an analysis of learner roles and behaviors, and a matrix for modeling.

Systems Development Plan

A systems development plan itemizes, in appropriate sequential order, the major tasks that must be completed in working towards a model system. For example,

Task 1. Concept
Task 2. Mission, objectives, goals
Task 3. Learner needs and role behaviors
Task 4. Resources required to achieve objectives with learners
Task 5. Communications media to be used
Task 6. Coordinations required
Task 7. Learner services
Task 8. Curriculum, courses, diplomas, degrees
Task 9. Continuing formative evaluation
Task 10. Staff required, regular and ad hoc
Task 11. Organization and structure
Task 12. Software and hardware
Task 13. Training: staff and learners
Task 14. Finance: fees and budget[15]

The order in which tasks are taken up is important. The aim of a systems development plan is to go from the concepts and generalizations of the conceptual matrix to quite specific plans that will be needed in the later stages, and to ensure that particular tasks (such as organization and structure, or finance and budgeting) are not considered until the institution builders know in considerable detail what the institution will be so that practical models that fit the requirements can be produced.

Modeling to Fit Learner Role Behaviors

To construct and test a model, and operate it as an institution, it is now necessary to conceive or visualize events as they are likely to occur in the universe described by the conceptual matrix. The institution builder "acts out" the events intellectually, and puts them on paper as a model of the institution and its behaviors. Modeling is thus a test of the completeness

	Target Populations	Subjects of Focus in Courses	Educational Process	Educational/ Other Resources	Linkages with Other Departments, Agencies
Objectives	Age Groupings	The Range of Content Offered in Curricular Units	Media: Print Other	Educational: University Extension; Residence Ad Hoc Instruction, Field staff	University Adminis-tration Unit Admin-istration Academic Depart-ment Ministry of Education Other Col-leges/Uni-versities Local Schools
Goals	Socio-cultural Groupings		Educational Package	Counseling Evaluation Libraries Media/Print Production	Technical Colleges Vocational Programs Educational Associa-tions Libraries
Purpose	Occupational Groupings		Practical Work	Postal Service	
Mission	Demographic Charac-teristics		Achievement Standards	Other: Space: Buildings Rooms Equipment Kits	
	Profiles		Exam Procedures		
	Market Surveys				

Figure 8. Conceptual Matrix for Non-Traditional Institutions/Programs
In building the institution model, variables such as these itemized here must be considered as parts of the "universe" being created. While each variable is conceptually separate, it has validity in the universe only because it is a part of the whole. Hence the variables must be studied and acted upon vertically and horizontally, separately and in relation to others according to mission, purpose, and objective.

142

Structure/Organization	Administration/Management	Training Development of Staff	Quality Control and Assessment	Financing
Design to accomplish Mission Objectives in each Situation	Conceptual Matrix Recruitment Counseling Registration	Course Writing Course Editing Production Instruction	Reporting Evaluation for Decision-Making Evaluation for Development and Institution Building	Government Bilateral Aid; Fees from Students Budgeting Cost/Benefit Ratio
Relationships to Faculty, Government, Ministry, Public, Private Schools	Records Student Services Transfers Accreditation Process Certification Reporting Quality Control Process Budgeting Evaluation/Assessment Employment Policies Staff Training/Development	Record Keeping Recruiting Counseling Management Other Media Liaison/Relationship with Other Agencies Population/Market Studies Evaluation/Quality Control Standard/Criteria Formats to be Used Time Allotted Rewards Standards Criteria	Persistence Completion Criteria/Standards Periodic Comprehensive Evaluation Conceptual Matrix	Unit Costs Risk Practices Report Points Control Points Approval Points Lead Time for Reports, Budgets Process: Internal External
Advisory Council Vertical/Lateral Work Flow, Authority Control Check Points Report Points				

and appropriateness of the concepts first sketchily drawn together in the matrix. It's not unusual to find that concepts that looked adequate are too fuzzy to act out; or that ideas that seemed realistic at the conceptual level are at odds with certain realities of the universe which are unchangeable givens in the situation; or that some concepts are in conflict with others. Hence modeling tests and improves the validity of the concepts upon which the institution is built. This is formative evaluation at work focusing inquiry on concepts and processes, and providing feedback to the institution builder of what is complete, what works, what is incomplete, what doesn't work. Voids in design or process may be found, signalling the need for decision-making, modification, or redesign.

Traditional institution modeling has generally focused on institutional roles, not on learner roles. If the institution has the mission simply of teaching learners who are required to attend school (the source of most of our concepts of teaching, learning, and the institutional models that have evolved), the roles of learners and their role behaviors are different from those found among non-traditional learners. In the traditional institution the learner is a given. The institution builder works out a model according to what the institution has to do from that point on, with captive learners. There is thus a tendency for the institution to become authoritarian, to deal with the learner as an object or supplicant, to fashion objectives, courses, and processes in the image of the institution and at its convenience.

The institution that seeks to encourage self-selected, non-captive distance learners must develop its model on other concepts and on the roles played by its learners. This is not an easy task if the distance learner program is a department or division within an otherwise conventional institution. In such cases the institution builder has to face pressures, and a climate engendered by educational theory and operating practice, that may be inimical to the concepts, purposes, roles, and processes that he is trying to model. Nevertheless the builder of a non-traditional program for distance, independent learners has no real choice. If he wants to build to serve those learners, he must be prepared in his modeling to deviate from the conventional.

Learner Roles and Role Behaviors

A learner role consists of functions performed by a person in particular situations or processes, such as learning. Role behaviors are the responses of the person to the functions carried out in the situations that make up the role. The learning roles and role behaviors of traditional and non-traditional learners are sharply different. For example:

The Traditional Learner Role/Situation	The Non-Traditional Learner Role/Situation
Learning is the principal occupation of the learner.	Learning is a subsidiary occupation of the learner.
Learning is required by law or custom, or impelled by avoidance mechanisms (e.g., the person goes to school or college to avoid some unpleasant consequence of not being a learner).	Learning is not required by law or custom. Avoidance mechanisms play little part because non-traditional learning does not confer a change of social or legal status on the learner. The learner volunteers for learning according to advantages that he perceives will affect his principal occupation or quality of life.
The learner is full-time.	The learner is part-time.
The learner is generally a young person without experience or responsibility beyond himself.	The learner is generally an older person (especially respecting age-grade norms) and has accumulated more life, work, and family experience and responsibilities extending beyond himself.
The learner is familiar with school and academic processes as continuing and largely uninterrupted full-time experiences.	The learner is less familiar with school and academic processes because his education has been interrupted by work, family, and other experiences.
The learner is close to the institution that provides learning opportunity and access.	The learner is physically distant from the institution that provides learning opportunity and access.
The learner is able and willing to defer, or suppress to an inferior level, other roles for the duration of learning (full employment, earning, family responsibilities, marriage, and parenthood).	The learner is not able, even if willing, to defer or suppress other roles (employment, earning, family responsibility, marriage, and parenthood) because these generally occurred earlier and take precedence.
The learner follows a largely prescribed curriculum based on long-range goals, with advice	The learner follows a largely self-determined curriculum towards short-range goals, modified by

The Traditional Learner Role/Situation *(Continued)*	The Non-Traditional Learner Role/Situation *(Continued)*
and counsel from professional staff.	opportunity and access, with advice chiefly from non-professionals, but perhaps occasional counsel from professionals.
Learning is evaluated by others according to normative standards.	Learning is evaluated largely by practical and personal standards and considerations, from a mix of short- and long-range goals extending beyond the learner to employment, family, parenthood, and other areas.
The learner's principal environment is the school or campus, with facilities provided to meet needs for study, access to resources, laboratory work, living and socializing, sports, recreation, health, and cultural development.	The learner's principal environments are the work place and the home, but also the other places where he carries out his learning functions such as the library. His principal environments are enriched by self-effort to provide the best facilities and accommodations possible for study, resource access, socializing, sports, recreation, health, and cultural development.
The learner communicates primarily through a learning-related network with his peers, evaluators, advisers, teachers, and social companions.	The learner communicates primarily through a work, social group, family, and community related network with his peers and others.
The learner's social, health, recreational, and leisure-time activities are coupled with his status as full-time learner in institutional programs intended to preserve this role.	The learner's social, health, recreational, and leisure-time activities are linked with his work, family, and peer groups, not with his part-time learner role.
The learner's costs are principally assumed by others (family, spouse, government, scholarships and grants) although sav-	The learner's costs are principally paid by himself. Stress frequently occurs because learning costs may be paid with money

The Traditional Learner Role/Situation *(Continued)*	The Non-Traditional Learner Role/Situation *(Continued)*
ings as well as part-time work may be required to help out.	diverted from first priority responsibilities in the family. The learner may be forced to take another job or to borrow to meet learning costs, and/or to forego high priority purchases that affect others as well as self.

The contrast in learner role/situations above provides useful clues in understanding the difficulties experienced by traditional institutions in serving non-traditional learners, and the difficulties of non-traditional learners at traditional institutions.

The non-traditional learner role behaviors that derive from the role/situations can be clustered in seven categories. These categories relate to the initiation, continuance, and/or suspension of non-traditional learning activities. They are important to the institution or program being developed to serve the non-traditional learner.

Role Behavior 1: The learner is passive with respect to learning because he thinks he is learned enough to survive and perceives no new learning needs.

Role Behavior 2: He is anxious because he thinks or fears that maybe he doesn't know enough, and begins to weigh whether and how he could learn general or specific things that would meet his needs better. His needs are only vaguely perceived but he is beginning to display goal-seeking behaviors.

Role Behavior 3: He casts about for leads that will put him in touch with learning opportunities to satisfy his needs in his situation. His needs are now more sharply perceived, and are being transmuted into learning goals. Anxiety increases, particularly if he fails to locate opportunity that is accessible to him.

Role Behavior 4: He acts on his goals, makes decisions among the possibilities open to him. He does something to enhance his learning, such as enroll in a learning program or begin one on his own. Whatever overt or covert action is taken to initiate purposeful learning, goals continue to undergo modification. If the action taken is formal, goals are modified according to institutional programs and accessibility. The learner displays learning- or knowledge-seeking behaviors.

Role Behavior 5: He becomes a student in a specific program. He begins learning.

Role Behavior 6: He persists (or does not persist) in learning.

Role Behavior 7: He reaches (or does not reach) his and/or the institution's goals. Anxiety is reduced if successful; increased if unsuccessful. Further goal modification.

These seven role behaviors are cyclical. For example, in Role Behavior 7, the learner whose needs and goals are in equilibrium will cease formal learning and return to Role Behavior 1. Or, if needs and goals are not in equilibrium, he will go back to Role Behavior 2 or 3. Similarly success or failure (for whatever reason) in Role Behaviors 3, 4, 5, and 6 will push the learner ahead to the next role, or will force him back to a preceding behavior. Role Behavior 1 is characterized by passivity respecting learning which, as needs are perceived and transmuted into goals, gradually phases into activity, first through goal-seeking behaviors, and then through learning- or knowledge-seeking behaviors. The dependency of the early roles is replaced (if the learning is successful and the institution's goals are met) by growing autonomy and independence. If the cycle of role behaviors described above is reasonably accurate for most learners (differences in socioeconomic, cultural, and educational background and geographic and situational circumstances naturally affect role behaviors) then the educational institution ought to focus on these role behaviors.

Teaching the Non-Traditional Learner — A Model Structure

The purpose of bringing learner and teacher "together" even at a distance from each other in the institution or program being developed and evaluated is to encourage, guide, and assess learning. In Chapter III, figure 2,[16] four essential elements in the classroom teaching-learning situation were presented. (The four essential elements are: teacher, learner, a communications mode, and a content.) In figure 3,[17] the four essential elements were rearranged to explain their relationship in distance learning arrangements. In Chapter IV and Chapter VI[18] reference was made to the Copernican revolution in education that underlies non-traditional learning: the learner, instead of the teacher or institution, is at the center of the teaching-learning arrangements.

If the learner is to be central in non-traditional learning, the four essential elements (teacher, learner, a communications mode, and content) must be planned and employed to meet learner independence and autonomy, characteristics of learners at the back door. The non-traditional learner role and role behaviors can be used to hypothesize a model for the non-traditional institution or program.

For example, figure 9 models the learner and the non-traditional institution or program in a distance teaching-learning arrangement. The model, built around learner role behaviors, depicts the learner in communication with a distance teaching institution serving the learner through a cyclical three-stage program.

		Activities of
	Two-Way	*Distance Institution*
Learner	*Communication*	*or Program*

Non-Traditional Role/Situation
Some Degree of Independence, Autonomy
Role Behaviors

1. Passive; No Sense of Learning Needs	Stage I	Public Information
		Recruitment/Admissions
2. Vaguely Perceived Learning Needs		Counseling
3. Needs Transmuted into Learning Goals		Goal Setting/Modification
		Available Curriculum Choices to Meet Learner Needs
		Enrollment
4. Action Towards Purposeful Learning; Selection of Institution/Program and *Content*	Stage II	Instruction for Learning
		Content Learning Tasks
		Assessment of Learning
5. Begins Learning Tasks		Goal Modification
6. Persists or Not in Learning		Persistence or Suspension of Learning Noted
		Counseling
7. Reaches or Does Not Reach Learning Goals	Stage III	Completion of Learning Tasks
		Examining
		Certifying
		Accrediting*
		Transferring*
		Counseling
		Goal Setting/Modification
		Employment Changes*

*in cooperation with other institutions, agencies

Figure 9. Model of Teaching-Learning Relationship Between Non-Traditional Learner and Distance Institution/Program with Three Stages of Institutional Activity to Mesh with Learner Role Behaviors

The vertical listing of learner role behaviors and the three-stage institutional activities suggests probable sequence. However, as the discussion that follows indicates, both the role behaviors and the institutional program activities are cyclical. Figure 10, much simplified, illustrates the cyclical nature of these behaviors and activities, and the centrality of the learner.

Figures 9 and 10 are idealized models. Few learners and institutions find it possible to relate needs and activities so neatly, and to keep the learner central. Nevertheless, the best teaching-learning situations approach this ideal. Most of the responsibility for achieving this ideal is the institution's. The cyclical movement of learner role behaviors and institutional activities is suggested in the following discussion of the three-stage institutional model.

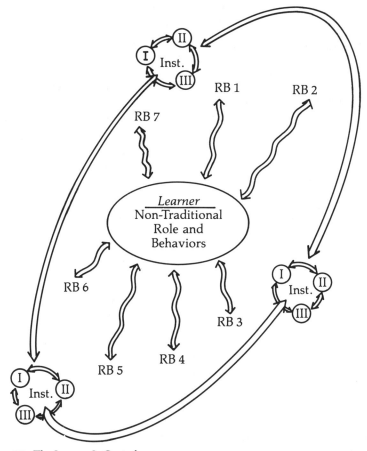

Figure 10. The Learner Is Central
Institutional activities orbit. Communications maintain interface of RB's and institutional activities.

↔ = communication
RB = Role Behavior
Inst. = three-stage institutional program

Stage I

Stage I is a subsystem designed to reach and serve the learner in Role Behavior 1, in which the learner is passive, and assumes that he knows what is necessary to survive, to meet his needs and goals. The learner does not perceive the coterminous relationship of ignorance and knowledge, and there is lack of goal-seeking and knowledge-seeking behaviors. The learner (or, from the point of view of the institution, the potential learner) may be neutral, friendly, or hostile to the institution, but that he needs a relationship to the institution for learning is presently inconceivable.

The subsystem to cope with learners in Role Behavior 1 is sometimes called "Public Information and Recruiting," but the activity should be broader than that. The purpose is to reach as many learners in Role Behavior 1 as possible, and help them advance through Behaviors 2, 3, and 4. Although learners in Role Behavior 1 may seem to represent an undifferentiated mass of people, the subsystem to reach and serve them must be discriminatory. Mass recruiting is generally unsatisfactory, as is mass public relations. The subsystem must be channeled to reach those who are most likely to respond to the opportunities made accessible. Communications formats must be of the kind to which such learners pay attention and respond. This may be difficult, for non-traditional, back door learners do not usually communicate through the networks common to institutions and front door learners. A special effort has to be made to penetrate non-traditional learner networks.

Although the long-range institutional and social objective may be to encourage purposeful learning through an enrollment in a course, the institutional Stage I enabling goal is more general: to get the person to examine his situation, concerns, needs, and goals, and discover that continued learning may contribute to the improvement of his and society's well-being.

Since it is well known that the more education one has, the more one perceives continuing needs for learning, the Stage I subsystem tends to build on what educational experience or awareness is already present among role behavior 1 learners.

Formative evaluation at this point focuses on what happens, the successes and failures, of this stage of the institution's model activity. The institution builders ought to be able to estimate how many learners in role behavior 1 must be reached in order to get an adequate yield of learners in Role Behavior 2, and so on. Demographic data as well as program data are needed. Who is to do these important tasks, what reports are needed, how often, and how they relate to decision-making all along the line must be carefully built into the subsystems.

The Stage I subsystem will also enable the institution to reach and serve learners in Role Behaviors 2, 3, and 4, not only as role behaviors change from efforts with Role Behavior 1 learners, but also because the communications effort will reach persons already in Role Behaviors 2 and 3.

The subsystem hence will have specific enabling objectives to guide activities with Role Behavior 2, 3, and 4 learners. At some point the general public information and recruitment activities will be replaced, for specific learners, with advising and counseling activities. Here again the institution builder must be able to estimate the number of learners in each role behavior that will yield, through the institution's activities, the learners required in successive stages so that the total system remains economically and academically sound. Formative evaluation at each stage and substage will analyze, pinpoint, and criticize in order to achieve the necessary flow of learners, and to generate the demographic data that are needed in order to design teaching-learning programs that will work.

Stage II

Stage II is the institutional subsystem that enables the institution to work with a learner who has enrolled in the learning program. Stage II is composed of two subsystems to accommodate Role Behavior 5 and 6 learners.

Role Behavior 5: the learner begins learning or does not begin
Role Behavior 6: the learner persists or does not persist

Each substage will accommodate branching. Essentially, branching in the system proposed is a reversal of progress to a previous learner role. For example, if a student who has progressed from role behavior 4 to role behavior 5 does not begin learning (the performance of learning tasks and the submission of evidence of learning) there may be many reasons, including a decision just to drop the whole thing. Perhaps 10 percent of the self-selected, non-captive distance learners who progress to role behavior 5 (are enrolled, obtain materials, pay fees and exhibit initial learning seeking behaviors) actually do not begin. They branch out, in effect, before starting. Ten percent of an enrollment is a high figure, and both for the learners and the institution it is eminently worthwhile to have a subsystem to cope with this phenomenon. Whether the subsystem retrieves (i.e., reverses the behavior regression) every learner or not (it won't) the counseling at this point can be very valuable in helping learners and in compiling data that can be used to construct profiles of learners that will help assess and modify all the subsystems. This is a function of formative evaluation.

There may be a tendency, as the systems are routinized, for a certain rigidity to creep in; for managers and staff people to shrug their shoulders over the non-start phenomenon because the learners who do progress through successive learning behaviors keep everybody busy. Furthermore, the nature of most institutions – and the people who staff them – is to focus on what appear to be institutional successes rather than failures. (Non-starts do not necessarily represent failure, but they may be categorized as failures by an unknowing public or institutional authority unless the program people research the phenomenon, work at improvement, and have the evidence to avert a misreading of the raw, superficial statistics.) This, again, is a function of formative evaluation.

The same observations may be made about learner branching in role behavior 6, persisting or not persisting in learning. Research has generally indicated that the learner who makes early responses to a learning task is more likely to persist; that a learner who persists through a third of a course is more likely to persist to the halfway mark; that a learner who passes the halfway mark is likely to complete the entire course. Again, there are many causes for lack of persistence, some completely outside the institution's responsibility, but some that may be directly the result of problems that have their origin in the instructional system itself.

Formative evaluation will probe learner progress to monitor what is going on, to sort out learners who cease for reasons external to the system, and those who are hung up for reasons that are the institution's responsibility. Profiles of learner persistence in each course are instituted and maintained; if a profile, for example, shows that a substantial proportion of learners in X course falter at lesson 7, this is an unmistakable signal that something unanticipated is happening at lesson 7. What is it? Why? What must be done to correct the situation? Who is responsible for modifying the lesson? For counseling the learner? When must all this be done?

Note that the total system (the stages and substages working together) are in effect a closed loop. Each successive stage is dependent for its success on the success of the preceding stage. For example, if there is a problem with lesson 7 in a course, and substantial attrition occurs at that point, the stages of the system that are to serve completing learners are endangered. Learners in sufficient numbers to support the later stages do not get that far. Objectives (both individual learner and social-institutional) are not achieved; unit costs escalate; a budget crisis may arise; the program may come up for review by higher authorities. Formative evaluation is intended to signal malfunctions early on, to pinpoint causes, and offer evidence on which decisions may be made for correction – before a crisis occurs.

If there is no built-in formative evaluation system to be used as a guide in institutional development, the academic or administrative staff frequently will not know where to look when trouble occurs. All that is known is that learner and social-institutional goals are not being met. In a complex system the trouble could be anywhere. A comprehensive, summative evaluation by a neutral outsider is time-consuming and expensive. The program could wither before appropriate remedial action can be taken; learner and institutional goals could be left unachieved.

Stage III

Stage III is a subsystem that works with learners in Role Behavior 7, reaching or not reaching completion. Learners close to completion, approaching final exams, winding up the submission of all learning exercises, are likely to complete. But some do not; and some who do complete are failures as a result of a poor examination, poor overall achievement, or other causes. Learner failure cannot be avoided. There are learners who are lazy, who fail to show requisite progress, who simply have failed to learn despite efforts made by others to help them achieve successfully. However, self-selected learners who have persisted to completion have exhibited a high level of motivation plus a willingness to invest energy and resources over a period of time. It would seem unrealistic to classify them as lazy, or uncooperative, or lacking in resourcefulness, or even lacking in capacity at the end of the course, in order to explain failure. Such causes for failure should have shown up earlier, been noted so that counseling and instruction could be modified accordingly, in order that an unqualified learner does not in fact approach the final stages unless he has reasonably good prospects for satisfactory completion. In a well designed course the risk of failure should diminish as the learner progresses even though it can never be completely eliminated. Hence the final examination is as much a test of the instructional system as it is of the learner.

Distance learners face one examination hazard that deserves careful study. Throughout a course of instruction, distance learners generally prepare their lessons in an open book, untimed format. This format works well, preserves freedom of choice, and is appropriate for non-captive learners. However, learners in this mode may not be prepared for conventional examinations that are supervised, timed, and exclude access to materials. Some distance learners find this switch of format disastrously upsetting. Yet for quality control and certification-accreditation reasons, the institution may require conventional examinations. The system must therefore anticipate the problems and prepare the learner to meet them. A mid-course conventional examination may be needed not only to check progress, but chiefly to give the learner experience in taking a final examination in a different format. Lessons may be designed to give practice in some of the skills important in taking examinations.

Formative evaluation of the system and subsystems will yield up evidence of "what is actually going on" so that the institution as well as the learners are prepared for eventualities and ready to make decisions that will improve performance and success.

But even successful achievement is not the end. Learning is lifespan in scope. With completion of any learning project, a new learning cycle is ready to begin. The institution should not abandon the successful learner any more than it abandons learners who have regressed in various roles throughout the process. The subsystem must cope with learner and societal needs at the end of a process as well as at the beginning. Examination, certification, accreditation, transfer, continuation, counseling towards new or continuing goals, employment changes — these are some of the activities that cluster when the learner in Role Behavior 7 achieves closure. Since a substantial proportion of the enrollments of educational institutions is composed of previously successful learners (the more you learn, the more you want to learn), an adequate subsystem for coping with successful learner needs is important to the development of the institution.

The tentative three-stage model (system and subsystems) suggested above is not yet complete. A system model is not complete unless it clearly indicates:

> what is to be done
> why
> how the work is performed (the various systems and subsystems in stages)
> who is responsible for what
> when things are scheduled to take place (sequence or order, including branching)
> mechanisms for sensing what is actually happening (continuous feedback analysis through formative evaluation)
> checkpoints for monitoring and developmental decision-making
> participatory relationships with learners, teachers, counselors, administration, and others as necessary or desirable

The institution builder who has progressed this far can now begin to flesh out his own model. Fleshing out (supplying in detail all that the model calls for) is likely to be successful because of the preliminary work already accomplished. Bringing together the results of previous steps (conceptual matrix, systems development, analysis of learner roles and behaviors, and tentative three-stage model with subsystems) may be made easier if a modeling matrix is followed.

Matrix for Modeling

A matrix as a guide in fleshing out the model is suggested in figure 11.

When the planning model is fleshed out, each subsystem can be modeled. It is desirable that the institution developers carry out this step to test the completeness, accuracy, and appropriateness of the total systems model. Following modeling, the systems and subsystems should be piloted, tried out. Here the sensing mechanisms are also tested, and the information yielded enables the institutional developers to modify and improve the model where needed. Full operation follows the piloting and modification.

The steps in institution building suggested here may seem more complex, burdensome, and unwieldy than building the institution itself. Experience shows that they are not. Ordinarily the theory and practice of institution building is assimilated over a long period of time. Here a "grand design" has been compressed into a single exposition, partly as a vehicle to suggest the place and role of formative evaluation in institution building.

Ends and Means

Formative evaluation systems design, and all the other concepts and practices discussed, are not ends in themselves. They are only means towards those larger institutional ends that animate social and institutional planners and builders. Their chief virtue is that they continually remind builders of the true ends of all institution building—the improvement of the lives of individuals in society, and thereby the improvement of society itself.

Mention has been made that in planning and building one has to cope not only with what is present as a given in any social or institutional situation, but also with what one has created to ameliorate conditions and meet needs. The consequences of intervention (in an individual, institutional, or social sense) are not always accurately foreseen, no matter how carefully the model has been designed and tested. Means that have been employed towards valid goals tend to become goals themselves; and valid goals when achieved tend to become means by which other goals may be realized. John Dewey noted this in pointing out, "In the continuous temporal process of organizing activities into a coordinated and coordinating unity, a constituent activity is both an ends and a means: an end insofar as it is temporally and relatively a close; a means insofar as it provides a condition to be taken into account in further activity." He also reminds us that "No human activity operates in a vacuum: it acts in the world and has materials upon which and through which it produces results. . . . That organization which is the 'final' value for each concrete situation of

Learner Role Behavior	Model Stages; Systems and Subsystems	Enabling Objectives	Responsibility (Institution)	Tasks, Problems Anticipated	Processes (Subsystems)	Responsibility (Learner)	Sensing Mechanisms	Checkpoints
1	Stage I Public Information Recruitment							
2	Goal Seeking Counseling Registration Goal Setting							
3	Adaptation of learner/ course goals							
4	Beginning learning Persisting							
5	Stage II Persisting Reaching Objectives Counseling							
6								
7	Stage III Examination Certification Accreditation Counseling Transfer Continuation New goals Employment changes							

Figure 11. A Planning Matrix for Modeling a Non-Traditional Teaching and Learning Institution

valuation thus forms a part of the existential conditions that have to be taken into account in further information of desires and interests or valuations."[19]

Formative evaluation has been suggested as a means that will aid in the building of non-traditional institutions, a process by which academic and administrative staff can monitor the institution's development, and through which the consequences of intervention in the universe that constitutes the institution may be more fully and accurately known.

All this is also implied in "Murphy's Law" and its subsequent amendments. Murphy's Law expresses the common man's observation of how things work out in a complicated world: "If anything can go wrong, it will." Apocryphal amendments to the law include, "If anything can go wrong, it will, when and where you least expect it"; and, "If anything can go wrong, it will, not only when and where you least expect it, but you will be the last to know."

The employment of formative evaluation as a function of institution building may help prevent the unwanted consequences that sometimes dog the activities of institution builders; and it may help create an institution that achieves its purposes so that non-traditional learners can achieve theirs.

Part Four

LEARNING FROM A LIFESPAN PERSPECTIVE:
ITS ENDS IN A LEARNING SOCIETY

X

Lifespan Learning

We are the victims as well as the beneficiaries of our cultural inheritances. The inheritance of language, and the system of thought it orders, enrich us but also constrain our thinking, speaking, and writing. Poincare pointed out, "We have to make use of language, which is necessarily made up of pre-conceived ideas."[1] Nietsche noted that "by the grammatical structure of a group of languages everything runs smoothly for one kind of philosophical system, whereas the way is as it were barred for certain other possibilities."[2]

If we think, speak, or write about education, schooling, teaching, and learning, we have to use the symbols (the words) that signal what it is we are thinking, speaking, or writing about. But these words already had "meanings" when we learned them. If a novel idea or modification in thought occurs, it has to be conveyed by symbols that were earlier defined in another way, and must now undergo alterations in meaning. Thus it is that new ideas are frequently rejected out of hand. The very symbols used seem to preclude any change from the culturally prescribed meaning: "You can't [think, say, write, do] that; that's not what [education, schooling, teaching, learning] are all about."

Nevertheless, changes in ideas do occur, though slowly and sometimes painfully. Among our current inheritances is the concept of our solar system with the sun at its center. Before this once radical idea could be accepted it was rejected as heresy, scorned by intellectuals, and derided by common people as dangerous lunacy. The words that Copernicus had to use in proposing and defending his novel idea were symbols freighted with cargoes of ancient meanings: that the earth was the center of the cosmos, and the sun the lamp supplied by a beneficent creator.

Thousands upon thousands of lonely speculations, discussions, and publications had to occur before the Polish astronomer's idea could begin to be accepted. Bloomfield states, "In the long run, anything which adds to the viability of language has also an indirect but more pervasive effect. Even acts of speech that do not prompt any particular immediate response, may change the predisposition of the hearer for further responses. . . . Education or culture, or whatever name we choose to give it, depends upon the repetition of a vast amount of speech."[3]

In the time of Copernicus the exchange of ideas was slow. Few people in the fifteenth and sixteenth centuries experienced the "vast amount" of discussion of ideas that is characteristic of people in society today, wired as they are to receive by telecommunications the almost minute-by-minute expressions of opinion and advocacy of ideas that now crowd the airways. Predisposition to further response, as Bloomfield puts it (and this would include the possibility of acceptance of change), still requires that vast amount of communication, but modern speed-of-light media accomplish this exposure in a much shorter period of time, bringing change or acceptance in a decade or so that required as much as two centuries in the time of Copernicus.

Hence the changed and changing concepts of education, schooling, teaching, and learning that are the themes of this book are the products in part of the improved communication of ideas made possible by technology. To alter the traditional meanings of such symbols as education, schooling, teaching, and learning, certain qualifying terms such as nontraditional, distance, and independent have been used to signal an intended shift of meaning from that conveyed by the basic symbol. In Chapter IV the irrational and disunifying confusion that terminology in the process of change introduces was exposed. One of the predispositions derived from vast amounts of publication today is a degree of tolerance for this confusion of terminology, as the threshold essential to eventual clarification.

The radical idea that the learners should be central to the teaching-learning situation (to education) has been compared[4] to the revolution in scientific thought introduced by Copernicus. And, as was the case with astronomy when freed from the restrictions of an older cosmology, placing the learner in the center of the educational firmament has led inexorably (despite the tyranny of words) to a reexamination of other aspects of education that must be modified when the centerpiece is changed.

A Patchwork Program

The educational system or apparatus was not created all at once; it evolved in successive stages as society evolved, and as learning needs were recognized and acted upon. Furthermore, it is still evolving. The system that now exists is a patchwork of programs primarily aimed, not at the education of learners throughout their lives, but at learners at successive ages: pre-school, elementary, secondary, higher, post-secondary, adult. It is generally agreed that there is poor linkage between all these chronologically determined programs, and also a degree of overlapping.

Yet, if we know anything, we know that learners even of the same age and immediate environment are uniquely different — in interests, concerns, motivation, and physical, mental, and emotional characteristics; in progression, achievement, and developmental growth and maturation. If we can conceive of the learner as central to education, then we are compelled by logic to conceive of the wholeness of education for each developing learner throughout his life. We become concerned, then, that while the separate levels of education in the system are designed as discrete units, the total system is essentially undesigned. The successive units, in effect, have been add-ons to what was there before. This was the consequence of evolving education step by step, piece by piece. Now it must be asked that the implications of a fragmented system be looked at carefully, vis a vis the developmental needs of learners during and throughout their lives.

New Vantage Points on Learning Lifelong

The rise of extension, adult, continuing, open, post-secondary, distance, post-experience, independent, and other kinds of non-traditional education, as supplements to the standard educations intended for children and youth, has begun to provide new vantage points from which the process of learning throughout life can be assessed. *Lifelong learning*, more and more accepted as a concept and a new societal imperative, is defined by the Lifelong Learning Project as "the process by which individuals continue to develop their knowledge, skills and interests throughout their lifetimes."[5] While this widely accepted definition focuses on the individual and learning throughout life, it reflects the continuing or add-on origin and purpose of programs supplementing the regular schools, as indicated in this further statement by the Lifelong Learning Project: "Lifelong learning implies that learning *continues after high school* and that learning and doing are not mutually exclusive activities to be parceled into separate periods of life. They interpenetrate not only in the adult years when learning is usually accompanied by work, but also earlier."[6] (Emphasis added.)

The accepted territory of lifelong learning is thus primarily the learning that occurs after the formal schools no longer serve the individual. Indeed, as Luke observes, "Adult education, (also called further education, century education, postsecondary education, recurrent education, continuing education, permanent education, *lifelong education*, or out-of-school education) involves *a return to organized learning activity* by individuals who because of age, employment, or family situations cannot conveniently be enrolled in the established school system."[7] (Emphasis added.)

The concept of lifelong education may be that of learning lifelong, but the terminology and the educational structures already in existence constrain it to an add-on function. This add-on function is presently important and necessary, but there is still an overriding need for a holistic perception of learning from birth to death. The Lifelong Learning Project recognizes this by pointing out that "the broadest view of lifelong learning is one that proposes reshaping both formal and informal learning opportunities so that they meet the needs of individuals and families at each stage of the life cycle."[8]

Emphasis on Child-Centered Learning

Perhaps one reason that it has been difficult to develop a cultural perception of lifelong learning (except as an add-on) is the prominence of educational theories developed by educators working with children and youth. The learning of children and youth has been the almost exclusive focus of educational thinking until recently. In the education of children and youth there were theories to be raised, teachers and other professionals to be prepared, schools to be administered, research to be conducted; there were funds available to do all these things. There were culturally significant constituent and advocacy groups to assist in the political struggle for educational dollars, and the possibility of careers in the study of learning among children and youth.

Great educational leaders that almost anyone can name — Thorndike, Dewey, Piaget, and others — arose to work where the need was clear and the opportunities to study children and youth were good. Piaget's theories of cognitive development, for example, derived from extensive work with children and youth. Widely respected, these theories have held such power among professional educators (the great majority of whom were prepared to work with children and youth) that the theories were sometimes accepted uncritically. Any evidence of inappropriateness of theory to, let us say, adult and lifelong learning, lay elsewhere than where the investigators and practitioners were — outside the realm of children, youth, and pedagogy, and hence unperceived. Knowles, the originator and long-time advocate of the need for andragogy (the psychology of adult learning) pointed out, ". . . our Western educational system has had only one model of assumptions about learners, the pedagogical model, and it has been ideologically committed to that model to such an extent that any questioning of that model was considered heresy."[9]

Piaget postulated four stages of cognitive development, culminating in the Formal Stage at ages twelve to fifteen years. Hence, if cognitive development reaches its peak at about age fifteen, what happens to learning thereafter can only be the "maintaining," at best, of the level of cognition reached in the middle or late teens. Piaget's theory seemed in some ways to affirm older culturally given assumptions that adults don't progress in learning development. As a result the emphasis was thrown back, again, to the learning of children and youth. However, as Long, McCrary, and Ackerman note,

> Piaget's theoretical and experimental positions concerning cognitive development have generated a vast amount of research concerning cognition among children, and more recently among adult subjects. The traditional position that favored the necessity of achieving formal operations [the fourth stage] and of maintaining formal operations capability across the life span has been brought into question by a number of investigators who have studied the cognition of adults of all ages. [There is] sufficient reason to question the traditional views that are heavily childhood centered.[10]

Despite continuing support for Piagetian Theory, as noted by Carlson,[11] there is a growing sense among many adult and lifelong learning educators of the inappropriateness — perhaps even the futility — of attempting to conceive and develop lifelong learning on a theoretical basis that posits only the learning capabilities of children and youth extended (maintained) into adulthood. Carlson believes that "democracy requires andragogy," and urges that "we infuse a deeper, more substantial meaning into andragogy — a philosophical and political meaning that supplements and enriches the learning theory that currently seems to support the concept."[12]

Adults as Learners

As suggested in the previous chapter,[13] adult non-traditional learners are in situations, and have role behaviors, characterized by independence, responsibility, and autonomy that contrast sharply with the situations and role behaviors of children and youth. McClusky has pointed out the dimensional differences of learning as an adult:

In a rapidly changing society an adult, to survive and develop, must continue to learn. What he learns, and how he does so, depends upon the stage he occupies in his life cycle and upon the suitability of the learning situation to the learning potentialities and learning handicaps he has at that state. . . . The strategies for learning (and for teaching) in the adult years require consideration for the individuality of adults, for their life commitments which may aid or obstruct learning, for their adult time perspective, for their transition through critical periods of life, for their acquired sets and roles which may aid or obstruct learning, and for their adult requirement that the learning be relevant to their problems.[14]

If the structure, content, and instruction of lifelong learning for adults is primarily an extension of concepts and systems assumed appropriate for children and youth, then in an important sense adult learners must be non-traditional, for they do not fit the traditional assumptions, concepts, and systems provided for them to learn by. Is this a reason so many adults, compelled to learn, have sought non-traditional methods or modes of learning? The adult learner is essentially non-traditional because he must learn and act at his own level, in his own situation, with independence, responsibility, and autonomy. This sets him apart, immediately, from the traditional learning systems provided. Being apart, or "out of step" as Miller called it,[15] is an aspect of being non-traditional as a learner. In the past it has meant entering at the back doors, instead of the front doors, of institutions.

The traditional cultural artifacts regarding learning that persist throughout our society tend to constrain our thinking about lifelong learning to that which is traditional. We may see the forward, continuing aspects implied in lifelong learning, but we usually do not see its implications backward in time for the education of children and youth. Frank Jessup, director of extramural studies at Britain's Oxford University, asked in lecture at the University of Wisconsin, "What would happen if we were to look seriously at the implications of the word 'lifelong' in our discussions of lifelong learning?"[16]

A Holistic View of Learning

Jessup was referring to the need to view all the learning that individuals accomplish during life to achieve a more holistic and planned approach to lifelong learning. If a person is going to learn beyond high school, for example, then curriculum planners at the high school or higher education levels do not need to feel compelled to require certain subjects "because this is the student's last chance to learn such-and-such." School curricula might begin to present content and activities more consistent with the present need, interest, motivation, and maturation levels of learners. If people continue to learn throughout life, activated by need and opportunity hand-in-hand, the lifelong learning curricula might be quite different, some subjects appearing earlier and others later, according to need and developmental patterns. In the present age-grade planning of education and the separation and fragmentation of successive structures of education, such a view of education is for most people difficult to conceive, and even more difficult to apply.

Part of the problem is that education is still thought of by most persons as schooling. Hence very little attention has been given to learners before they go to school, or after they leave school. If education or learning is only schooling, the arrogance of such inattention to human learners before and after schooling might be justified. However, Tough and others have begun to analyze the non-school learning of adults. Evidence is emerging that contradicts the myth that learning is only schooling,[17] and is beginning to fill in the after-schooling picture of learning. The picture of before-schooling learning has not yet emerged so clearly, although recent studies of infant learning have indicated that infants do learn and remember, and modify behavior as a result.[18]

Infants as Learners

Infants have been studied over a long period of time, but they have been studied largely from a normative point of view: what constitutes normal growth/behavior at a particular stage of growth. The infant as learner has only recently begun to excite the interest of investigators. Earlier studies of infants tended to emphasize the development of infants according to physical/mental growth norms, but without the important inference that learning was perhaps a critical element in the development that took place.

Klausmeier and Ripple, for example, define learning as "a process or operation inferred from relatively permanent changes in behavior that result from practice."[19] They point out that "contemporary learning theories are useful in analyzing individual and group behavior in school settings,"[20] and that "learning in school may be examined fruitfully in terms of a *system . . .* an array of components designed to accomplish a particular objective according to a plan [including] objective or purpose . . . design or arrangement of components . . . materials, equipment, space, personnel, and information . . . allocated within the system according to a plan."[21] This is classic educational psychology, but the symbols and sets of meaning employed constrain the phenomenon of learning only to those places and conditions specified, and continue the cultural bias that learning is schooling. Schaefer, writing about education, says:

A comprehensive definition of education includes "the act or process of rearing or bringing up . . . " and "the process of providing with knowledge, skill, competence or usually desirable qualities of behavior and character." . . . However, both popular and professional discussions of education usually assume a more restricted meaning, i.e., the activities of professional educators teaching the traditional subjects to school-age children in the schools . . . a description of formal or academic education.[22]

Whether one studies education or learning, the concepts and symbols employed begin with an a priori assumption that neither exists without intervention and management by professionals, although Schaefer does document important roles for parents in early child development.

Lipsitt concedes that "little is known of the possibly pervasive influences of early educational enrichment including that occurring in the first weeks and months of life."[23] He points out that "the normal newborn is not only equipped to receive sensory stimulation and react to it but has the capacity to make progressive and learned changes in response to repetitive stimulation. . . . newborns are capable of memory, of retaining and processing information, and many of their changes in behavior with experience can properly be designated as learning."[24]

Lipsitt has left the door open a notch for recognition of the infant as a (non-school) learner. Schaefer, in recommending the establishment of a new discipline — *Ur-education* (early, basic education) — to "supplement the current system of academic education,"[25] seems to be implying that infants and small children could profit from non-school learning: "If the evidence is convincing that intelligence and competence can be increased by early and continuing education, the development of a comprehensive system of education that would extend from birth through maturity is necessary."[26]

If the capacity for, and evidence of, non-school learning by infants and adults is now becoming recognized, the concept of human learning throughout life is strengthened. Does the infant have capacity to "learn"? Eccles states categorically that "the essential building of the brain with all its wonderful and various potentialities is complete soon after birth."[27] Furthermore, Eccles points out that "it must be recognized that each human individual has to be educated from babyhood to be able to participate even at the simplest level in the culture he was born into."[28] In what he calls "World 3" of the brain, Eccles identifies "the whole world of culture. It is the world that was created by man and that reciprocally made man. . . . It is the world of civilization and culture. Education is the means whereby each human being is brought into relation with World 3. In this manner he becomes immersed in it throughout life, participating in the heritage of mankind and so becoming fully human."[29]

Birth to Death Learning

The concept of human learning from birth to death seems well founded, despite the fragmentary and sometimes poorly connected age-determined schools that have evolved, and the add-on programs of continuing education. The Lifelong Learning Project has listed (figure 12) the sources of education and learning in the United States that outline our present lifelong learning apparatus:

	Usual Age of Students	Approximate Number of Participants (in millions)
I. *In the Schools*		
A. Pre-primary Education	1–4	10.0
B. Elementary and Secondary Education	5–17	42.0
C. College and University Undergraduate Education	18–21	9.5
D. Graduate and Professional Education	21–27	1.5
E. Public School Adult Education	16 and Older	1.8
F. Proprietary Schools	18 and Older	1.2
G. College and University Extension and Continuing Education	28 and Older	3.3
H. Community Education	All Ages	.5
II. *In Non-School Organizations*		
A. Private Industry		5.8
B. Professional Associations		5.5
C. Trade Unions		.6
D. Government Service		3.0
E. Federal Manpower Programs		1.7
F. Military Services		1.5
G. Agriculture Extension		12.0
H. City Recreation Departments		5.0
I. Community Organizations		7.4
J. Churches and Synagogues		3.3
K. Free Universities		.2
L. Parks and Forests		No Meaningful Estimate
III. *Individually Used Sources*		
A. Personal – at Hand		Virtually Everyone
B. Personal – at a Distance		Virtually Everyone
C. Travel		Virtually Everyone
D. Print Media		Virtually Everyone
E. Electronic Media		Virtually Everyone

Figure 12. Sources of Deliberate Education and Learning in the United States

The above summaries represent estimates based on data from a wide variety of surveys and from summary reports developed by the National Center for Education Statistics. From Richard E. Peterson, and Associates.[30]

The estimates above suggest that 69.8 million Americans are involved in school-type learning; that 46 million are involved in non-school learning. These estimates yield a learning force of 115.8 million Americans — not counting those in Category III, which would include "virtually everyone." The number of individual learners in Category III cannot presently be estimated with certainty. Tough and others have documented consistency in learning projects carried on independently by "average" adults in several countries (summarized in Chapter VI). The Educational Policy Center of Syracuse, New York, predicted a learning force of 149 million Americans by 1976.[31] It has been suggested that by the year 2000 about 75 percent of the adult population will be engaged in some type of purposeful (though not necessarily formal) learning activities.

The varied bases of available statistical data, unevenness of survey responses, and the voids respecting child and adult learning, make it impossible to conjure up reliable numbers of Americans engaged in individual learning. But it seems likely that the individual learners in Category III would probably outnumber those in formal school and non-school programs. We may be, as the Lifelong Learning Project suggests, on the threshold of a Learning Society, "composed of three elements: individuals who foster their own growth and development; local providers who collaborate in offering learning resources; and Federal, State and local governments which pursue policy strategies directed toward encouraging individual growth and enriching learning opportunities."[32]

It is indeed time that we try to conceptualize, unrestricted by past language and thinking, the varied dimensions, characteristics, and significance of learning as it occurs throughout the whole of life.

In searching for a way to assess the significance of learning activities throughout life, from a point of view different from that implied in conventional symbols, it is sometimes desirable to employ symbols that do not bias presentation and response. The consequence, of course, is still confusion in terminology, for the new symbol must make its way in the sea of symbols already there; but a fresh symbol may at least slightly ameliorate the problems of presentation and response by separating the new concept from others (providing more concept space).

Lifespan Learning

Because *lifelong learning* carries the implication of add-on learnings after the learner has left school, and there has been little attention given to the development of a holistic view of the sequence of learnings from birth to death, the term *lifespan learning* is suggested instead. Lifespan learning includes these concepts: (a) the idea that human beings learn throughout life from birth to death; (b) that their learning experiences are a blend of formal/informal, traditional/non-traditional; (c) that the sequence of learning experiences throughout life is jumbled, and not as integrated as it could be; (d) that the traditional views of learning as schooling should be supplanted by a more holistic concept of learning throughout life.

Why *lifespan* rather than *lifelong*? Lifelong learning seems nearly fixed in usage as learning after formal schooling. The second element in the compound (*long*) seems to throw the emphasis on learning that occurs after a long period of living. *Span*, on the other hand, symbolizes the inclusion of everything that is spanned. It means "a portion of time; especially the period of one's life on earth."[33] The term may be useful to throw the attention of educators and investigators towards the entire spectrum of learning.

Lifespan learning connotes all the learning that occurs during life, including that which is "natural" or self-motivated and directed; that which is intuitive or developmental; that which is other-directed and contrived; that which is purposeful, whether the learner pursues it, consciously or subconsciously, or whether it is other-directed from the outside.

This is indeed a wide net, bringing together learnings resulting from both intrinsic and extrinsic factors. The concept suggested is perhaps more philosophical than psychological. As Tyler has pointed out, the aim of psychologists for many years was prediction and control of behavior.

This purpose generated a self contained system that worked reasonably well as long as research efforts were confined within the boundaries of laboratories. The outcome of one experiment enabled one to predict what would happen if stimuli were manipulated in a certain way in the next one. Successful pre-conditions were considered to constitute a validation of the reasoning on which they were based.[34]

Psychological interest has begun to turn elsewhere, but the effect of decades of research and teaching from narrow concepts of learning will be with us for a long time.

Incomplete Learning Theory

In general, learning theories derived from experimental psychology are to some extent unsatisfactory because they do not adequately explain most of the learning that occurs in the lifetime of any learner. Most of the learning in any life is not acquired in schools, or in experimental laboratories, or in situations remotely comparable to those of caged experimental birds or animals. Yet most of the learning theories that underlie our concepts of what learning is, and how it occurs, have been derived chiefly from the study and observation of learners in schools and in laboratories, and of animals in cages.

The formalism that pervades schools, the compulsory element in much school attendance, the almost complete reliance on "other-directed" activities through the authority and intervention of the teacher, and the obvious removal of the school from the ongoing activities of daily life and work, form an unnatural setting for the study of learning. What we get from studies of learning in schools, it would seem, are theories about school-type learning. That this is recognized is at least partly implied by the concern expressed over "transfer."

Learning is broader than school-type learning. Any theory that does not explain all the learning behaviors in the population must be viewed with some skepticism. Conventional school-type learning theory is not without value, but it is incomplete.

If one looks at the "complete learner" at any stage of development, if one further looks at the lifetime of learner development stages, if "learning" is seen as inclusive of all purposive behavior modifications that enable the person to achieve needs satisfactions, then one begins to perceive that there are three kinds of learning that characterize lifespan learning. Lifespan learning focuses primarily on the learner, not on systems or institutions. Schools, teachers, the materials, media, and mechanisms of instruction are the means available, in uneven quantity and quality, for the provision of instruction. Learning and teaching are thus conceptually as well as operationally separated; they are different activities, invested as they are in different people.[35]

If the mystique embodied in the phrase *teaching-learning* (that is, the assumption that learning inevitably must follow teaching) is abandoned, then one is better able to view learning (as well as teaching) more perceptively. Learning may be seen for what it is (and indeed, what almost all philosophers and learning theorists have always said it is) — an idiosyncratic, personal, unique, and self-directed activity. No one has ever been able to learn anything for anyone else. Learning may also be seen for what it is not — an event of social interaction. Schooling experiences have so stressed social interaction, and social and instructional dynamics have so exclusively focused on the group, that an unwarranted assumption (learning as an event of social interaction) has almost become accepted as a "fact." Furthermore, teachers (who are motivated and trained in social interaction and intervention techniques) are threatened when they are confronted by any theory that seems to undermine their self-image. Hence, the irrationality of maintaining that learning is both idiosyncratic and social is simply not perceived. It is more comfortable to live with inconsistency than to face a fundamental reexamination of one's beliefs and purposes.

Learning is clearly idiosyncratic.[36] What about learners? They seem to range between *independent* and *dependent*. And while natural development seems to be towards independence, the effect of years of schooling on learners instead seems to move many from independence to dependence. There is ample evidence of this.[37] But if the aim of education is the nurturing of a person who is capable of self-direction, who is able to solve his problems, who continues to grow (through learning) in ability, maturity, wisdom, and self-fulfillment, then the cruel dilemma of our present educational systems becomes clear. Conventional schooling, regardless of intent, does not produce a preponderance of learners of this kind.

If we begin with different than usual assumptions about lifespan learning, we may be led to conclude that the kinds of learning in a person's lifetime represent an accommodation to two kinds of realities, the reality of the self in a succession of surrounds or situations, and the pseudo-reality of schooling, which in many societies occupies most of childhood and youth, and for many persons includes early adulthood. The three kinds of learning in the lifespan are not strictly sequential, and not hierarchical. Rather, they coexist, in different sequences and mixes throughout the lifespan. Conjectures on these kinds of learning follow.

1. Survival Learning

The first kind of learning in the lifespan is *survival learning*. The infant has one purpose — survival. The infant's learning is the most astonishing accomplishment of all learning. Essentially helpless, lacking speech communication, without formal instruction, incapable of doing anything for himself except learning, he learns the most complex and difficult things in a relatively short time. He survives in what must be an alien and sometimes hostile world of dangers and deprivations. The powerful motivation of sheer survival overcomes all, and the reinforcement of success propels him to new learnings.

It has been customary to classify the "maturation" accomplishments of infants and children outside the sphere of learning. Klausmeier and Ripple state that

> *learning* is a process or operation inferred from relatively permanent changes in behavior that result from practice. On the other hand, relatively permanent changes that result from maturation and temporary changes that result from drugs, fatigue, and the like are not considered to be learning. . . . When a child first walks upright, runs rather than walks, or does any of the similar things that all children do without practice or instruction, it is maturation rather than · learning.[38]

However, at the other end of life, it is clearly recognized that maturation is a quite uneven development or accomplishment. Not all adults mature to the same extent, in the same areas, or at the same time. The writings of poets, dramatists, novelists, and philosophers consistently suggest that what a person has learned in his lifespan (not the same as his educational qualifications) has an important relationship to maturation.

It is curious that with regard to infants and young children, psychologists have tended to be emphatic in separating learning from certain nontaught maturational achievements. But with regard to adults, the writers, philosophers, and artists have tended to be emphatic in including learning as significant in maturation. Maturation is usually defined as the process of becoming mature, of coming to full development; the emergence of personal characteristics and behavioral phenomena through endogenous growth (as in learning); the achievement of intellectual or emotional maturity.[39]

The difficulties of attempting to define learning in the lifespan context are many, in the face of the formidable literature at each stage of development and the breadth or narrowness of definition. As Tyler asks, "What are the relative contributions of intrinsic and extrinsic factors [maturation and learning] in development?"[40] But this question skews any answer that may be forthcoming by characterizing intrinsic (endogenous) factors as maturation. Yet Eccles, Tyler, Lipsitt, and others are emphatic in asserting the presence, at birth, of all the structures necessary for learning. In fact, Tyler states that

the individual at birth can . . . be said to be *overendowed*. He or she will develop far more brain cells than will be needed for the thinking that will actually be done in a lifetime. He or she has the equipment that would make it possible to learn millions of facts or skills. He or she can make all sorts of movements, can utter a tremendous variety of sounds. The selection of possibilities to be actualized, begun during pre-natal life, continues after birth.[41]

The absence of a teacher, of direct, purposeful intervention and instruction, may be the reason that psychologists and learning theorists find it difficult to perceive that learning can take place in infants. (Most infants who achieve normal measures of maturation have a parent or parent figure to encourage development. This is not the same as a professional teacher, however. The motivations, communications, and interventions are different.) Anyone who has closely observed infants must be impressed by the persistence of practice in learning such things as grasping, standing, walking, speaking. The surprise, delight, and joy evident in successfully performing these untaught accomplishments, or the frustration, anger, and impatience evident in failure, are unmistakable. These, it is suggested, are survival learnings, motivated by intrinsic as well as extrinsic factors and situations toward survival.

In survival learning, the learner is autonomous, reacting, adapting, trying over and over again with seemingly random but purposeful effort to do something essential to survival. Learning is natural because the organism (the person) perceives the need and acts directly to satisfy it, gaining satisfaction as well as survival thereby. This learning is driven intrinsically, but is also affected by extrinsic factors.

2. Surrogate Learning

The second kind of learning occurs when the learner goes to school. This may be called *surrogate learning*. In school a shift away from directly perceived needs and the satisfactions of achieving them takes place. The school and the teachers deal more and more with other-determined needs, that is, needs not perceived as part of the life reality of the learner. These are surrogate needs. An immediate problem arises. Children quickly lose enthusiasm or motivation for this kind of learning because they no longer feel the genuine satisfactions resulting from accomplishment. So a surrogate reward-punishment system is invented (grades, promotions, rankings, etc.). As the learner moves through school the purposes, motivations, rewards, and punishments tend to become more and more "academic," removed from real-life problems and satisfactions. Instruction becomes more and more abstracted. The learner copes with this pseudo-reality by gradually yielding up to authority the independence that formerly characterized his learning; he becomes to a greater degree dependent. His school learning becomes other-directed; his goals are determined by others; the processes of learning are in the control of others; the determination of success-failure is in the hands of others. Whereas in school his learning is dependent and surrogate, outside he may still be learning in an independent manner. (It has often been observed that many underachievers in school are active, successful learners outside of school.)

3. Independent Learning

The third kind of learning occurs when the learner is returned by the school to society, presumably ready to take charge of his affairs, cope with problems, perform occupational-vocational-professional skills with some degree of predictable as well as actual competence, continue learning in a changing society, assume responsibilities, and grow in maturity, wisdom, and self-identity. If all of this is actually to happen, with the individual on his own, self-directed, there must obviously be an assumption, however unstated, that the person can be an independent learner. So this third kind of learning may be called *independent learning*, very similar to the *survival learning* of infancy and early childhood, but broader, in that sheer survival is not the same imperative it was for the infant. Many other needs and motivations actualize the adult, who must now seek to achieve his needs through autonomous or independent learning.

The problem encountered at this point is that through long exposure and adaptation to schooling (in which, it will be recalled, independence is yielded up to authority for a more dependent role) the person may have great difficulty in reasserting that independence which once characterized his learning. Submission to authority tends to alter not only learning behaviors, but also self-identity, perhaps of crucial importance in continuing learning. Nevertheless, any study of the learning that adults do without the formal interventions of schools and teachers is impressive; so there is evidence that many learners do satisfactorily achieve this third kind of learning, although others do not.

The Jumbled Sequence

Earlier it was stated that the three kinds of learning that characterize the lifespan are not strictly sequential and hierarchical, but that they coexist in different sequences and mixes throughout the lifespan. However, in presenting the three kinds of learning, a sequence was employed to contrast the three kinds of learning. While for many learners the sequence suggested may be relevant, for others (because of differences both intrinsic and extrinsic) the sequence will be different. As Tyler notes, "At any point in time, the organism *is* its total history from conception to the present instant. . . . *What will be* arises from *what is,* and *what is* is a resultant of the whole history of what has happened when the processes coded in the chromosomes occurred under particular circumstances."[42]

The different kinds of lifespan learnings are not, then, a neat and tidy sequence of one-at-a-time learnings, succeeding each other according to some cosmic cycle. The learnings are jumbled together because the needs of learners, the purposes of learning, the immediate circumstances in which the learning occurs, the effects of earlier learning, and the human relationships involved are a complex mix never twice the same. Even if one were able to hold the first three variables constant, the last two by their very nature alter the individual so that he is thereafter different.

In all probability all three kinds of learning are engaged in by learners throughout the lifespan, but at different levels of intensity. An exception may be the newborn infant, whose learning may be assumed to be of the survival type. However, recent studies have discouraged the idea that the newborn is without "experience"; at birth the newborn has already had sensory and other kinds of experience that not only make him unique but which may predispose him in certain ways to developments upon and immediately following birth.

Babies, for example, would seem to do more than survival learning. They learn things like object permanence, which is independent learning.

They also acquire skills in and around the bathroom which are, fundamentally, surrogate learnings. But mostly they learn for survival: (a) the motor and coordinative skills that for so long have been called maturation because no external agent, teacher, or purpose directs and controls the process; and (b) they learn how to manipulate others in the social context in which they must survive.

But survival learning is not sloughed off when the person goes to school and surrogate learning becomes a necessity. Survival learning is important throughout life, though at different levels of intensity. Among the aged, for example, the "future shock" phenomenon may be an example of conditions that revive the need for survival learning. On the other hand, among youths and adults reared in ghettos, survival learning may persist long after it is appropriate because the survival learning pattern or set has inhibited the possibility of acquiring or employing surrogate or independent learning.

The surrogate learning that is characteristic of schooling (other-determined, directed, controlled, and evaluated learning) may help explain the low impact of such learning on society despite its cost, and the prevailing and largely false notion that schooling occupies most of the time of children and youth. Television, sports, and entertainment now occupy children and youth far more than schooling does. Clasen points out that schooling generally occupies 49 percent of the time available in a school year.[43] In view of the low profile of schooling, and the situation in which schooling occupies less time in the education of youth than some other activities, it would seem desirable that schooling concentrate less on surrogate learning than it does.

Given the human internal dynamic towards self-actualization (independence in learning as in other activities), and the virtual inability of the human being to "turn off" brain activity, even in sleep, it is understandable that children and youth in school tend to be selective and discriminating in what they learn or don't learn in school. Learning is hampered, furthermore, by faulty perceiving mechanisms, emotional focusing mechanisms, first (survival) priority mechanisms, and the cumulative maladaptive habits acquired by learners when surrogate learning is not personally fulfilling.

Independent learning has the potential to become the most advanced kind of learning. But since survival learning is not a pre-condition for surrogate learning, nor surrogate for independent learning, it is unlikely that these three kinds of learnings are developmental or hierarchical. The three kinds of learnings suggested reflect observations on the ongoing phenomenon of learning throughout the lifespan. Perhaps the three types of learning are primarily a perception of learning as it continues through life from a relationship-to-others viewpoint. Cognitive-field theorists and associationists have not said that human beings learn differently at school than elsewhere, yet it appears that the learner's relationships to other-direction and to the processes of goal-setting and evaluation do significantly alter the learning mode or type engaged in. Perhaps a change of learning type is an adaptive behavior; if so, it would seem to be an affective response.

The relative intensity or emphasis of each kind of learning changes throughout the lifespan, as suggested by Clasen in figure 13.[44]

Constructing a lifespan view of learning, with the learner central to the phenomenon, is difficult because the conventional language of education is institutional and teacher centered. Describing, from a fresh perspective, the kinds of learning that seem to be involved in the lifespan is equally difficult, but the effort must be made if the concept of lifespan learning is to have a significant impact on the understanding and revitalization of learning in our society. If the three kinds of lifespan learning suggested here have validity, it will then be possible to think anew about lifespan learning, instructional design, the alteration of curricula, the deployment

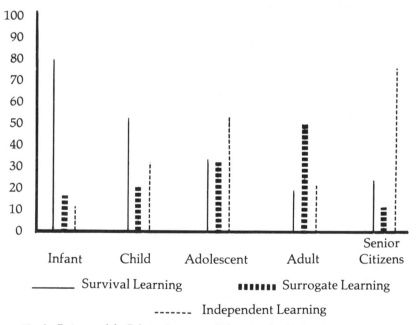

Figure 13. An Estimate of the Relative Intensity of Three Kinds of Lifespan Learning at Different Times in Life (after Clasen)

of resources, and the development of materials and methods that make the learner and learning central to the lifespan learning society.

Non-traditional learning in the lifespan is not only important to those who engage in it, and to the society that is its secondary beneficiary; it is also important because the non-traditional learning phenomenon is compelling the attention of educators at all levels towards a more holistic understanding of all the learning that occurs in the lifespan.

XI
Education for What?

The growth of non-traditional learning in the United States adds a new dimension to the continuing debate on the purposes of education. Once almost entirely the province of philosophers, educators, professionals, and statesmen, questions about the ends of learning are being decided by the thousands of learners who, as part of their independence and autonomy, match their needs, concerns, and aspirations against the educational opportunity and access available to them. This process is no high-flown literary or philosophical dialectic; it is homely, grass roots, idealistic, and practical. However, a learner's determination of purpose is rarely simple, in the sense of a knee-jerk reaction or a careless or thoughtless decision. Intrinsic motivation to learn plumbs the self in the small or large society that, at the moment, is part of the situation that activates the learner. Klemp has pointed out that "motivation is, after all, a need state – a prerequisite for behavior . . . [and] an important variable. This variable describes a person who habitually thinks in terms of causes and outcomes as opposed to one who sees the self as an ineffective victim of events that have an unknown cause."[1]

The non-traditional learner makes choices to learn out of a hope, verging on conviction, that he can maintain some measure of control over himself and his life. He undertakes learning to obtain consequences that will be favorable to himself, his job, his family, and the things and persons he believes are important. Such learners, male or female, think in terms of causes and outcomes, as Klemp has suggested above. The majority of learners probably do not seek learning as an end in itself, but as a means to other desirable ends.[2]

Instrumental Learning

Education for most learners is instrumental, as Billie Wendlandt implies in her letter of application to a non-traditional university program:

> I just turned thirty-four. That may be a little late to be looking for more education but I think you will find that we adult freshmen will appreciate our education ten times more than eighteen-years olds. . . . I have been looking and hoping for an opportunity like this for a long time. . . . I have always regretted not going on to college right after high school, but it seemed impossible at the time for financial and other reasons. My husband is willing to cooperate in whatever way he can to help my education. If I am able to complete it and become a teacher, one attractive by-product will be helping my sons to go to college when the time comes. So, I stand ready and willing to devote all the effort and time I can spare (and maybe some I can't) to this long awaited education. It is a second chance at something I have regretted missing.[3]

In the letter above, education is perceived as an instrumentality undertaken to bring about results in the person, leading to possible employment, affecting a wide range of responsibilities and relationships. The letter also illustrates the differences and complexities that mark the non-traditional learner's role and role behaviors, as compared with those of the traditional learner.[4]

Immanent Learning

On the other hand, there are also non-traditional learners who pursue learning as an end in itself, in leisure (nonwork) activities, undertaken on the learner's own terms, for an immanent result only. The result sought, as noted by Adler, is "the beneficial effect on the person . . . the improvement of his mind or his character."[5] Less is known about such non-traditional learners, and it is widely assumed, as indicated by Tough,[6] that immanent learning is less common than instrumental learning.

Socioeconomic class undoubtedly has an important bearing on how learners perceive education. Whether class and culture influences are as distinct as suggested by Linskie[7] is uncertain respecting non-traditional learners. Certainly non-traditional learners, especially those toward the extreme end of the independence/autonomy scale, are not usually identified in the statistical reports, even of continuing education institutions, whose courses probably would not attract, and might impede, their progress. Such well known non-traditional learners as Eric Hoffer, Irwin Edman, and Albert Einstein may, however, be only the visible tip of an iceberg of invisible immanent learners known only to friends, family, and the librarians who cater to their needs.

Such learners do enroll and participate in formal education, but in non-instrumental ways. Modern universities and colleges, for example, may open regular courses to the elderly without requiring formal admission, tests, or grades. Elderly persons may attend and participate at reduced or no fees at all, if there is room for them. That is, regular students at regular fees, pursuing largely instrumental learning, have first priority. The non-traditional and possibly non-instrumental learners are welcome when there is room. In such ways, institutional policy reflects the instrumental view of learning common throughout society.

Whether viewing education as instrumental or immanent, non-traditional learners at the back doors of institutions are an invaluable asset to our society as it develops. Bowen pointed out that "it is only as we improve our people that we can hope to improve our society."[8] For hundreds of years non-traditional learners have been going about the task of self-improvement at little or no cost to society, and largely beyond the usually well intentioned but frequently unsympathetic efforts of educators in traditional institutions. Adler pointed out that "the old aristocratic ideal [of education, especially of higher education] was stated in terms of intellectual content [and] we must replace that ideal with one more appropriate to our kind of society and our commitment to the education of all or at least helping all to become educated."[9]

The needs and maturities of learners that motivate learning cover a broad spectrum. In consequence, education must similarly provide an adequate range of support, opportunity, and access to serve learners through the lifespan. Edgerton asked, "How can we combine the advantages of a liberal and general education with the necessities of equipping people with the means to secure jobs?"[10] This is the basic question, for whether learning is instrumental (a means to some other end), or based on its immanent value (inherently valuable, an end in itself), neither can be ignored.

Whatever the class, needs, culture, and maturities of traditional or non-traditional learners, the range of institutions that serve learners must be responsive. The learners themselves, in a feisty, bored, dependent, or independent response to institutional programming, give the final answer to the question, "Education for What?" In the past, more often than not no one was listening, and the non-traditional learners at the back door went their own way, a yeasty element in our society that contributed much to its diversity, adaptability, and survivability.

Non-traditional learning became a necessity for an increasing number of learners for many reasons. Some were personal-situational (the learner was poor, lived in a place remote from opportunity and access, could not meet traditional qualifications for admission, had to work from an early age and could not match his free time with the hours set for schooling, could not commute to school, etc.) and some were institutional. Among the institutional reasons forcing learners into non-traditional learning were early learning trauma suffered in unresponsive schools,[11] and curricula that did not seem appropriate to the learner. Any curriculum gives an answer, in a very specific way, to the question Education for What?

Age-Based Curricula

The lifespan education that is increasingly the need of people and the concern of educators is more and more a blend of schooling and non-traditional learning. Because of the age-fragmented way in which we view education, it has been customary to separate successive stages of education and — even though we know learning is incomplete at each stage and that learning must follow each stage — to regard each stage as essentially complete and self-contained for its level.

The learner uses the block of learnings achieved in each stage to advance to the next stage. At each junction of blocks there are usually opportunities to remove deficiencies so that learners are able to proceed. Or, learners who are demonstrably ahead may be permitted to go directly to more advanced courses. The building block process can, to some extent, provide continuity of learnings that are intended to match the changing needs and objectives of developing learners.

Perceived needs, learning objectives, and the instruction provided to meet them, are derived from the age-based curriculum concept. The curriculum is determined, for most students, from the top down. For a student who will enter college, for example, the college curriculum determines the secondary school curriculum, which determines the elementary curriculum. This is a rational plan intended to make possible the progress of children and youth through successive, age-based learning experiences to reach the long-range objective of a college education.

Students who do not plan to enter college may follow secondary school curricula that prepare them for other objectives, largely vocational. But vocational curricula are also rationally derived from the top down: the requirements for employment in various occupations. For example, as Wirth points out, "The school in both its vocational and liberal aspects is modeled on the job archetype."[12]

When the student enters college, the curriculum he chooses is also determined from the top down: the requirements of professions, or of subject matters. The intent is for all students to get some general education and some technical education at successive levels. But the farther up they go, the more they are expected — and often required — to follow one or the other route, and their learnings become narrower and more specialized. Consequently, there is concern that secondary, post-secondary, and higher education graduates may not be able to integrate the liberal and technical-vocational aspects of education in ways that society is now beginning to demand. According to O'Toole, "Traditional vocational and liberal approaches to higher education are inappropriate to this challenge, because they are based on outmoded assumptions about the nature of the tasks that need to be done in the world."[13]

Granted, there is a certain utility in the deterministic curriculum development process. But there is also a difficulty: what if learners, and the society of which they are a part, do not need one *or* the other kind of education? This is not an imaginary issue, for at the top of the pyramid that determines the curricula requirements that filter down through the learning building blocks, the experts and guardians of educational content and quality are deeply divided, and the division is historic. The debate — sometimes bitter, always energetic, frequently erudite, and occasionally vain and frustrating — splits the academic ranks. Who should learn? What should be learned? How should learning be related to life itself? Disagreement over liberal education on the one hand, and/or technical-vocational education on the other, is as contemporary today as it was 2,500 years ago.

Non-traditional learners — because of the autonomy they exercise over their choice of curricula and their distance from counseling — are less exposed to the advocates of these two schools of thought. One result is that some learners follow narrower and even more specialized curricula than their more dependent counterparts in regular schools. But it is also true that other non-traditional learners select curricula that are broader than those in regular schools. And truly independent learners build for themselves learning programs of exceptional range and scope beyond anything available in institutions.

Learner age as a basis for curriculum building is not wholly a bad idea, even though it seems to lump disparate learners together in disregard of widely varying individual differences. The age of the learner is frequently related to the activities, responsibilities, situational characteristics, and concerns of others of similar age. Cultural sanctions as well as normal developmental patterns seem to produce at least a superficial age-level congruency among peers.

Other Ways of Determining Curricula

Are there other, perhaps better, ways of determining curricula for learners? Should required or recommended curricula reflect the physical, psychological, and chronological activities, self, social needs, and aspirations of learners? All of these, no doubt. And what about the needs of society? Numerous curriculum and developmental theories suggest various stratagems for discovering and providing curricula at different learner stages, if not ages.

Erikson's epigenetic stages of man,[14] and his concept of human generativity (all that is created and enduring from one generation to the next, such as children, products, ideas, works of art),[15] are useful in understanding the stages of human development and intrinsic motivations for learning. Vaillant's study of the "best-worse" outcomes[16] of the coping mechanisms employed by promising undergraduates (followed into middle age) seems to imply that Erikson's concept may indeed be helpful in groping towards answers to that most meaningful question, "Education for what kind of life?"

Havighurst's developmental tasks[17] and his idea of dominant concerns appearing at different decades of life have direct implications for the development of curricula.[18]

If educators know such theories, does this knowledge help them to develop curricula and engage intrinsic motivations for learning? Roberts[19] found a gap between the knowledge of a group of adult educators concerning life developmental theories, and the educators' application of such knowledge in their analyses of learning needs. Discontinuity between knowledge and its application is not, of course, confined only to educators of adults. It is a common problem of all learners, and suggests again that learnings are not complete until evaluation-application has occurred.[20]

What happens when learners try to evaluate and apply information? Suppose an educator wants to apply information about life development needs in shaping curricula for learners. He might take Havighurst's concept of concerns, for example, and ask himself what, in his previously acquired knowledge and experience, confirms, modifies or denies the possibility of concerns as a basis for developing curricula of intrinsic interest to learners. He has to "think" about concerns, not merely store information. He asks further questions, tests tentative answers, searches for more information and understanding, begins to hypothesize things he could do to employ the information and understandings that are stirring in his mind. No person's search for learning — all the way to evaluation and application

—is like that of any other's. But perhaps an educator might pursue a line of thought as follows—

Concerns and Curricula

Could the concerns of learners be used by schools, teachers, parents, or learners themselves to devise curricula for learning? What is a concern? A concern is something the learner feels is important. A concern has three levels of strength or intensity: (1) A concern relates one thing to another as a matter for consideration. (The car won't start, and concern extends to the battery, ignition, or carburetor.) (2) A concern may express a strong interest or regard arising from a personal, experiential, or responsible relationship in the matter under consideration. (The car is the prized possession of a brother who is soon leaving town.) (3) A concern may be an uneasy blend of interest, regard, uncertainty, and apprehension about a present condition or future development.[21] (The brother must have his car in two hours for a critical business trip that will affect his job and family situation.)

Any intensity level of concern may motivate a person to learn, depending upon a number of conditions—time, availability of learning and instructional resources, formulation of a goal, finances, and personal, familial, and job relationships.[22]

Now suppose the educator tries to think of concerns that are persistent and developmental; that is, concerns that develop and continue through the lifespan but are at different levels of intensity at different periods. "Persistent life situations," however, are believed to last throughout life.[23] Concerns are related to developmental tasks and persistent life situations, both of which have been used to develop school curricula. Concerns, the product of tasks and life situations, might be useful in curriculum building (from the institutional viewpoint) and selection (from the learner's viewpoint).

Non-traditional learners who choose their courses are likely to select on the basis of their concerns. Institutional curriculum makers are likely to build curricula on the basis of subject matter, tasks to be accomplished, or situations to be faced. The learner, however, tends to be responsive to his concerns, which are the product of tasks, situations, and aspirations, signals from within and without that intrinsically motivate him to do something—learn, for example—in progressively coping with present or future situations.

Dependent learners in school will be told and counseled about tasks to be learned in preparing for life situations to come. They will be extrinsically motivated by the prospects of institutional rewards (grades, certificates, privileges) and punishments.

What sorts of concerns do human beings have? What can the teacher, parent, or learner think of according to what each knows about himself and others as learners? Would these be "universal" concerns?

1. concern with self
2. concern with social adequacy
3. concern with being important to another or others
4. concern with understanding the physical world
5. concern with understanding the mental, emotional, spiritual world
6. concern with earning a living, with survival
7. concern with reaching one's potential
8. concern with being secure
9. concern for others — in the family, the immediate circle of friends, among peers and colleagues, in the community, and as a part of society
10. concern for values to guide one's life towards the greatest possible fulfillment, happiness, and contribution to life.

There are other concerns, of course. Concerns are not of the same strength or consistency (do not have continually the same power to motivate) at different periods in life. Take the first, concern with self. Children and youth have a high concern for self, which recedes in importance through young, middle, and mature adulthood, but rises again in older adulthood as the person may begin to disengage from concerns outside the self. Concern with being secure follows a somewhat similar course.

Concerns are interrelated, and supporting or reinforcing. For example, concern with self may be paramount at some periods, but also linked to concern with social adequacy (the self in the wider world), with being most important in the eyes of some other or others, with survival, and with being secure. At other periods, the relationship remains, though the priority or order of power for self-actualization and motivation for learning, is different.

The Venables *Report of the Committee on Continuing Education* for the British Open University recommends "adult concern" courses which "should start with a particular well-defined and well-known problem, which should trigger off, if the student so desires, a whole series of connected topics and problems which have as much or as little academic depth as appropriate." The report suggests six categories of adult concern, and related topics and problems:

a) Day-to-day problems of dealing with different authorities — housing, taxation, education, social security, employment, etc.

  — individual rights and responsibilities
  — financial management and taxation
  — the choice of your child's school
  — improving your home
b) Understanding the rules, procedures and policies of particular authorities
  and the methods by which they are made accountable.
    — learning to live with local government
    — how central government affects the individual
    — local transport problems
c) Participating in change, where a "major issue" arises or where a group is
  conscious of conflicting priorities within an authority.
    — how tenants associations work
    — running a local pressure group
    — planning your own neighborhood
    — parents, managers, governors and schools
d) Understanding how society affects the individual.
    — young people and unemployment
    — industrial relations, work and its rewards
    — problems of a multi-racial society
    — social implications of science and technology (or how technological
    change affects decision-making)
    — resources and the environment
e) Understanding the individual in society.
    — family relationships in middle life
    — child development in single parent families
    — health: your rights and responsibilities
    — the handicapped person in the community
f) Basic educational skills.
    — numeracy: as a supplement to a course for teachers
    — literacy supporting . . . and extending . . . communication skills in
    general
    — how to study[24]

Each institutional planner, curriculum developer, teacher, learner, or
parent will conceive a somewhat different list of concerns around which
to build or select a curriculum of courses. Yet all lists will have some similarities in spite of differences of language, culture, and situation, for concerns do reflect basic human responses to living.

Concerns as an avenue leading to the planning or selection of courses
and curricula have the advantage of placing the learner near the center of
the teaching-learning process. As Renshaw indicates, "It is important to
help students take and feel more influence over their own lives and events
in their lives. It is important to raise the possibility of making more conscious choices of lifestyles in work, education, relationships and families
and begin to create support within the educational system for helping stu-

dents make and implement these choices."[25] Concerns, properly identified and used, can relate the learner more closely with the educational institution and program, and/or to teaching-learning resources.

The rational, deterministic age-grade curriculum development discussed earlier is particularly unsuited to the needs and motivations of non-traditional learners. Such learners are wary, from earlier school experiences, of being helplessly caught in the schizoid conflict of values that has weakened American education and continued the old debate over content. Wirtz comes out flatly against the values dichotomy that has consistently separated practical, vocational, and technical learning from liberating learning: "A two-dimensional education-work policy — bowing to education's manpower training obligations on the one hand and then, on the other, pleading its broader values to those who cannot find jobs — is not going to work."[26]

Our exploration of the ways in which curricula are developed for traditional or non-traditional learning has brought us again to the question, "Education for What?," and the debate over liberal versus vocational or technical education. It is necessary, now, to look at the arguments for each, and the possibilities for, if not a truce, at least a blend.

The Great Debate — the Liberal Arts

The Liberal Arts are those studies which originally comprised the trivium and quadrivium in the middle ages — language, philosophy, history, literature, and abstract science. Sometimes called the "humanities," these studies (including mathematics) are regarded as having primarily a cultural and liberating character.[27]

The idea of liberal studies derives from Aristotle and Plato, as the education appropriate for freemen as opposed to slaves. It had four essential features:

a) It is education that is not "mechanical"; that is, it demands more than routine; it demands higher abilities as part of the good life.
b) It is not utilitarian, but is worthwhile in itself; it has intrinsic, not extrinsic, value.
c) It is not narrow but broad; it views specialization as restricting to the mind, which should be free to attend to all matters of value and importance for the good life.
d) It must be pursued for its own value, not to impress others or to earn a living.[28]

Aristotle equated the pursuit of reason, of excellence in intellectual and moral activities that lead to truth, as the good life. Useful skills and physical training were not denied, but were perceived as means to ends, whereas liberal studies were ends in themselves. "This is what the Athenians did. . . . They made their society one designed to bring all its members to the fullest development of their highest powers. . . . Education was not a segregated activity, conducted for certain hours, in certain places, at a certain time of life. It was the aim of society."[29]

Over the centuries since Aristotle and Plato, immense and significant changes have occurred. The power and nobility of the Aristotelian-Platonic concept of liberal education spread throughout the world, waning and waxing as societal contexts and values shifted, but always important, even fundamental, wherever knowledge, human values, and learning were discussed. As a consequence, "The academic community has an ancient tradition of liberal learning. The specific purpose of this kind of learning was to free the mind, to encourage inquiry, to consider the great moral and social issues, to promote a philosophical cast of mind, to cultivate the arts, literature and other sources of humane values, and to foster understanding of the world of science and politics."[30] Liberal arts or general education today can be pursued at the secondary, collegiate, and adult levels, can be degree programs, woven into a variety of majors or pursued for its own liberating values.

Technical and Vocational Education

The rise of science, the scientific method, technology, the altered contexts of societies moving towards industrialization, the democratic and egalitarian processes, brought opposition to the liberal arts concept, and provoked the crisis-laden turbulence that has been the history of liberal arts in modern times.[31] The rise of professionalism (a higher name for vocationalism), the social trends away from elitism and towards progressivism and eclecticism, either diluted or enriched—depending upon one's viewpoint—liberal arts into general education.

More recently, the effects of scientific and technological change, the development of new knowledge, changes in old assumptions, and the reordering of principles and priorities according to new societal contexts, brought technical and vocational education into prominence. Science and technology affects the way work is done, changes the economy, and puts heavy demands on education. Hence education was forced "to fit groups of people who were once self-sustaining with very little schooling for a society which demands more and more skills and knowledge of the individual if he is to have economic and social competence."[32] What resulted was the schizoid conflict of values in education noted earlier and an unyielding "hold the fort at all costs" attitude on both sides of the Education for What? question.

Technical education met genuine need; it filled a gap left dangerously open in the contexts of a simpler society. Technical education rose as a terminal occupation education that prepares for employment in industry, engineering, business, health, public service, and agribusiness technologies. It can be both professional and vocational in aim and level, is pursued at secondary, collegiate, and adult levels, can lead to degrees as well as technical certification, and it, too, may be pursued as an end itself.

Who Decides What Content to Follow?

Who *should* determine the education that people obtain? Traditionally, the schools, the professionals in institutions, determined what should be learned. Dodes, for example, believes that the liberal arts should be based on the work and place of professionals in society — the materials, instruments, basic principles and insights of content "decided by professionals, taught with dignity, and learned with respect."[33] On the other hand, the consumers of education have also expressed their choices. Howe points out that "the parents want teachers who respect their children, education which leads to a good job, and schools which take seriously the obligation to create success as opposed to schools which insist that students who do not meet their standards are failures."[34] Furthermore, industry, business, and government are now in on the act. Professional and technical workers nearly doubled in the period 1950-1965, and constitute the fastest growing category within the white-collar group, increasing almost four-fold between 1950 and the present, and will account for 55 percent of the labor force by 1980.[35]

It is not surprising that student/parent goals for education are different from professional and institutional goals. Each set of goals is differently derived.

Nor is this the full extent of the dilemma and the argument. The Aristotelian-Platonic disparagement of learning related to work and technology persisted through generations, advocated by such spokesmen as William Blake, John Ruskin, Aldous Huxley, Charlie Chaplin, George Orwell, and Louis Mumford. Our education system has been shaped, in large part, by generations of professionals whose self-concepts depended upon a hierarchical ordering of knowledge in which the liberal arts and humanities are at the apex, superior to other kinds of knowledge because of nobility or purpose as well as content. In 1959, the English novelist and scientist C. P. Snow introduced the expression "the two cultures" into our society.[36] Snow was following the old, pessimistic-protective view that science and technology are incompatible with humanism. Snow's famous phrase continued the polarization: the scientists, engineers, and technologists at one pole; the humanists at the other.[37]

Educational institutions, staffed by professionals, reflect this polarity, which reinforces the ancient and continuing struggle over what constitutes an appropriate curriculum for learners: the liberal arts, or technical education? Non-traditional learners are as much affected by the split personality of education as are traditional learners. What is handed out at the back door is not much different from what is obtained at the front door, except as modified by self-selection and self-direction.

Technology: Hero and Villain

What is it about technology that so often and so long has caused it to appear as hero to some, and as villain to others? However viewed, science and technology have had a potent influence in shaping cultures, affecting work and economics, and attracting or repelling scholars and learners. Pirsig, in his book about self-discovery on a motorcycle odyssey, writes about the love-hate emotions people feel toward technology. He is confronted by the anger, resentment, and frustration of others over the maintenance of the motorcycle and other things, and analyzes these emotions:

It's not the motorcycle maintenance, not the faucet. It's all of technology they can't take . . . a kind of force that gives rise to technology, something undefined, but inhuman, mechanical, lifeless, a blind monster, a death force. . . . All this technology has somehow made you a stranger in your own land. . . . So the final feeling is hostile. . . . Anything to do with valves and shafts and wrenches is a part of that dehumanized world. . . . I disagree with them about cycle maintenance, but not because I'm out of sympathy with their feelings about technology. I just think that their flight from and hatred of technology is self defeating. The Buddha, the Godhead, resides quite as comfortably in the circuits of a digital computer or the gears of a cycle transmission as he does at the top of a mountain or in the petals of a flower. To think otherwise is to demean the Buddha — which is to demean oneself.[38]

Fear and distrust of science and technology is not new. In the late Renaissance period, Roger Bacon led a revolt against the calcified higher education that was stifling scholarship in England and on the Continent. He invented a new way of discovering knowledge (what we now call the *scientific method*) and helped turn the universities of his day away from an exclusive focus on the beliefs of the Ancients, to a more direct study of nature that would serve some social purpose and improve man's existence. Bacon's purpose (shared by Francis Bacon in the seventeenth century) was truth and a humane concern for mankind. He was nevertheless reviled by traditionalists who followed ancient authority; he was called a witch and sorcerer, and lampooned in a dramatic comedy.[39]

Yet abstract science was part of the liberal arts and humanism of Aristotle; it evolved out of philosophy, was respectable. It would appear that when science split away from philosophy in pursuit of new knowledge derived from a process of observation, hypothesis, verification by proof, and the practical applications now called technology, the scientist was cast in the role of heretic, and his technology disparaged as something akin to black magic.

The noble purposes, methods, and materials of the humanists, drawn from mankind's best thoughts, feelings, and accomplishments, inevitably and properly look back in time; science and technology look forward, toppling older authority with new knowledge and applications.

Applications of knowledge cause change, affect the way people live and work, and challenge old assumptions, values, and priorities. Applications directly bring the world of work, practical considerations, and unanticipated consequences, into the world of humanistic knowledge. It creates technology, the work-related professions and subprofessions that occupy roles between those of scientists, philosophers, and workers. Workers must know more and more about technology to perform their tasks, and work-related knowledge has to be disseminated across nearly the entire spectrum of human beings. As consumers, all of us, no matter how liberated or confined by the education we have obtained for ourselves, live in a new world of technical dependency. We are more and more dependent not only upon things, which we think we can manage, but upon technical services, which we know we do not.

So long as science remained abstract — an extension of philosophy — it was thought to be humane. But when science was applied, generating the technologies that provide us with useful or useless things, requiring technical services for their maintenance, we then began to feel trapped, captives in the world we had made to liberate ourselves. The search for freedom in being and highest self-development — that was the noble purpose of liberal arts and general education — seemed instead to cast us into a serfdom of gritty technological dangers and dependencies.

While the humanist/liberal arts curricula have been put on the defensive, so also has technical-vocational education been put on the defensive. Science and technology, "running wild" (as their detractors put it), succeeded in pushing certain kinds of knowledge to ever-new boundaries, and made possible applications that have created a dangerous world lacking the balance of stabilizing humane values. Aristotle's aim of knowledge to produce the good person, the good and moral life, has seemed ever more desirable and necessary, yet ever more remote and unattainable.

Value Rigidity

Perhaps the problem does not lie in either the liberal arts or technical-vocational education, but in the unfortunate dichotomizing of education into two separate streams. The question "Education for What?" has been answered by presenting learners with two different kinds of curricula and two different value systems, rigidly kept apart by the competing advocates of each side. Pirsig tells a story about a monkey trap to illustrate the effect of value rigidity:

> The trap consists of a hollowed-out coconut chained to a stake. The coconut has some rice inside which can be grabbed through a small hole. The hole is big enough so that the monkey's hand can go in, but too small for his fist with rice in it to come out. The monkey reaches in and is suddenly trapped — by nothing more than his own value rigidity. He can't revalue the rice. He cannot see that freedom without rice is more valuable than capture with it.[40]

Is the education provided by our institutions a kind of trap because of the way it dichotomizes and rigidifies liberal versus technical-vocational values? Chickering comments,

> We should not underestimate the importance of integrating professional and vocational preparation and liberal studies. . . . The liberal arts can expand the capacity to love life, to experience it more richly, to continually increase one's range of satisfying activities. Effective professional and vocational studies prepare us for productive work but also help us grow in scope and capacity. . . . But one in the absence of the other leaves us crippled, hopping along with one leg, negotiating rough terrain with difficulty, feeling less than we ought to be, and getting less from our living than we know we should.[41]

Must historical-cultural biases of the past forever influence a choice of either the liberal arts or technical-vocational education?

Extremes and Self-Perceptions

John Dewey remarked in 1938 that "mankind likes to think in terms of extreme opposites. It is given to formulating its beliefs in terms of either-or, between which it recognizes no intermediate possibilities."[42] Yes, and if someone wishes to protect his vision of mankind, the world, knowledge, and learning, he can best do so by keeping it separate and distinct from the views of others. A kind of intellectual territorialism? Perhaps, but it is even more than that. Our values, structures, and beliefs are *learned* from others who are models, and with whom we closely identify. Thus the things we eventually profess are part of our self-concept, and when these things are threatened, our very concept of self is threatened. This is a devastating event, and it generates not sweet, pure efforts to seek the truth in compromise and collaboration for the good life for all, but adrenalin-charged flight or fight for the protection of self. Gulfs widen instead of narrowing.

Snow was right in calling the dispute "the two cultures." Cultures are givens that are learned, internalized, applied, become significant elements in our self-identity. They stubbornly resist change because it is almost unthinkable to "be born again," for that — almost literally in terms of self-perception — is what is required if we are ever compelled to abandon our beliefs, turn out backs on revered models, and dismantle the mental and emotional structures that cradle the concept of self. To profess something that violates self-concept may be worse than admitting error; it is the destruction of the old self in whom that which is now called error was truth. This is not a rational process; it is a deeply disturbing self-induced aggression against the old self and what it stood for. Yet some people undergo this process and are not destroyed, and in religious and philosophical literature there are mystical and exquisite paradoxes that describe the process.

So "either-or," as Dewey noted, is firmly established, and many think it unlikely that professing humanists or scientist/technologists will learn enough of each other's culture to understand and collaborate in curricula that effectively combine the essentials of both liberal arts and scientific/technical education. Nevertheless, the ever more frequent efforts to create this kind of curriculum, often maligned and denigrated, and frequently resulting in products badly patched together without great intrinsic merit, point in the right direction.

Small Bridgeheads

Soderberg, writing about engineering education, pointed out that educators now "advocate humanistic and social studies for engineers so that they as prime agents for change will be able to appreciate more fully the interaction between human values and attitudes and the progress of technology."[43]

The difference between humane values and cultural-technical progress was accidentally suggested to an American professor who was invited to give a paper in Moscow. As he prepared his paper, he had a brilliant idea: if he could deliver the paper in Russian, he could humanize the presentation more effectively than speaking through an interpreter. The Slavic Department translated his paper, and taught him to read it in Russian.

The big occasion arrived, and in the great Moscow banquet room the professor noticed how formal and correct every toast was. Suddenly he was struck by a terrifying thought. He did not have a salutation for his paper. In a panic, he remembered that many people, after the numerous toasts, had left the banquet hall before the next course. Aha, he thought — all I have to do is go out in the hall, observe where the men and women go, copy down the words on the doors they enter, and use them to open my paper.

When he began his paper with the hastily-contrived salutation, he noticed a few furtive glances, suppressed smiles, and stifled giggles. But the paper went well, and he was roundly applauded.

Afterward, he asked his host about the smiles and glances.

"Oh," said his host, "your pronunciation was all right. But you must realize that we have never before been addressed as 'My dear urinals and water closets'!"

The humane thought; the unintended cultural-technical consequence.

Weinberg, in discussing technological change, asserted the need in the future "for an emphasis in education on cultivated general intelligence, abstractions, and basic academic skills."[44] In a paper on the humanities and education, Olafson points out that the humanities/liberal arts have been criticized because the graduates of such courses have not been informed by the substantial knowledge, scientific and technical, that only other forms of education can give. "The future of humanism," he adds, "is likely to depend upon the successful resolution of this conflict between the demands of specialized knowledge and the humanistic aspiration to keep humane and moral concerns at the center of personal culture."[45] King and Brownell urge that "every student is worthy of an encounter with the disciplines of knowledge,"[46] and Hirst suggests that liberal education should include the full range of the distinctive forms of knowledge and understanding to develop in learners rational abilities, qualities of mind, and the all-around development of reason, important for all.[47]

Small bridgeheads are emerging between the two cultures which may lead to an effective communication and collaboration that could help revitalize all of education. O'Toole observes:

A prime concern for education must be to prepare young people for a changing and uncertain future. . . . the new vocationalism is inappropriate to this task. . . . [and] unfortunately traditional liberal arts programs are also inappropriate to the needs of many students. . . . Consequently, forms of eduation that seek to fuse the best of liberal and technical education seem most appropriate. . . . .[48]

Common Concerns and Common Learnings

But the best hope for the resolution of the problem may not lie within conventional educational institutions at all. Plagued by uncertainty over their intellectual role, institutions are confused within and misunderstood without. As Gould points out, "The needs of society are contrary to what the traditionalists in universities would like its concerns to be."[49]

The rapid growth of continuing education for adults, via various non-traditional methodologies, may be the most promising area for employing those bridgeheads for blending the opposing cultures. Adults insist upon having a voice in shaping the education they obtain for themselves. The enormous costs of our various systems of education are paid by them, and they now begin to see education as lifespan, not confined to children and youth. Hence another category of protagonists enters the field. This new force will undoubtedly have a marked influence on the re-structuring of curricula for a lifespan learning society. It would take the design of education out of the sole jurisdiction of the institutions that primarily serve children and youth. While Wendt points out that "it is the level of technology and organizational complexity that is the primary determinant of continuing education needs,"[50] there is also ample evidence of the interest of adult learners in bringing values to business and technology, to learning itself, and to the enrichment of individual and community/national development.

It is the new place of, and interest in, learning in the larger society, that signal fundamental changes to come. The debate between the two cultures will be affected by the rise of lifespan, non-traditional education.

We are living, teaching, and learning in a different society from that in which our long line of ancestors in the ancient either-or dispute lived their lives, thought their thoughts, and defended their intellectual territories. Today's problems in energy, pollution, health, and peaceful coexistence (to mention only four) are to a large extent dependent for solution on changing our behaviors. That means learning, for we human beings and our present behaviors are the problem. As Bowen points out, "It is only as we improve our people that we can hope to improve our society."[51] The most profound changes in our society by the year 2000 may very well occur in education — no longer strictly technical or strictly moral and humanistic. Learners within schools and outside will follow or select curricula that blend value-laden and behavior-affecting learnings with scientific-technical learnings, complementary and side by side. All educational institutions will undergo change, but Gould thinks it possible that a realignment of purposes and energies in the universities might bring about a new concept of the intellectual role of universities, and new curricula for learners across a broad spectrum of ages, learning styles, and content. If this should happen, Gould describes the result:

> When the University performs its task properly and effectively, a person emerges who can find for himself a stable economic life technically or professionally; who can weave richer and deeper patterns of living through his cultural awareness and appreciation; who can assume a position of activity and even leadership in the expansion of knowledge and the pursuit of truth; who is constantly aware of the swiftness of change . . . and is receptive; who can be moved to understand and desire world peace; who understands the responsibilities of freedom together with its rights and insists upon these responsibilities and rights for others as well as for himself; and who is motivated to help solve the major social problems of his age. In its intellectual role the university couples intellect with character, it joins thinking with doing, and it places the educated man squarely in the center of his society and keeps him there.[52]

If Aristotle and Roger Bacon were alive now, and resident in *this* society, they could probably agree that the foregoing is an appropriate statement of educational purpose to which each could subscribe, useful whether animating the learning of traditional or non-traditional learners. The two cultures—so long separated—could become, not one or the other, but a new culture with a new wisdom and ethic.

And Jonathan Swift, if he were here, would exult in the role played by legions of back door learners, and the elimination of arbitrary and harmful restrictions to learning on the basis of elitism, intellectual territorialism, and the absurdity of propagating different cultures for different groups of learners so that they are kept in opposition instead of cooperation throughout their lives.

The common concerns of all human beings may yet — if we have choice — bring us to common learnings. "Education for What?" must certainly mean an education for all, that will improve the lifespan quality and meaning of living for all.

If motivation is a need-state, a prerequisite for behavior, then the fundamental need-state that underlies all the concerns that activate learning is the awareness of and capacity for learning throughout life. Lifelong or lifespan education would thus imply a major goal intrinsic in non-traditional learning — the continual strengthening of the capacity and desire to learn.[53] The ancient academic, philosophical, and territorial disputes over which of the two cultures to learn overlooked the basic culture — the learning culture — which fortunately has been kept alive and vigorous in non-traditional learning.

XII

Back Door Learning in the Learning Society

Carl Sandburg's advice to a youth coming of age is relevant to non-traditional, back door learners of any age.

> Tell him to be alone often and get at himself
> and above all tell himself no lies about
> himself whatever the white lies and protective
> fronts he may use amongst other people. Tell
> him solitude is creative if he is strong and
> the final decisions are made in silent rooms.
> Tell him to be different from other people if
> it comes natural and easy being different.
> Let him have lazy days seeking his deeper
> motives. Let him seek deep for where he is a
> born natural. Then he may understand Shakespeare
> and the Wright Brothers, Pasteur, Pavlov,
> Michael Faraday and free imaginations bringing
> changes into a world resenting change. He
> will be lonely enough to have time for the
> work he knows as his own.[1]

In a society in which education is dominated by traditional institutions, methods, and practices, the non-traditional learner knows loneliness, not so much in a social sense, as in the sense of identity as a learner.

Back door learning has been something of an embarrassment to traditional institutions. To learners, non-traditional learning is sometimes a frustrating kind of satisfaction, fulfilling to the self, but eliciting from a schooling and credential-oriented society an incomplete and distorted image of actual accomplishments. In ways characteristic of any bureaucracy, the viewpoints, policies, and procedures of traditional education have denigrated, dismissed, or downplayed the self-initiated and self-directed efforts of learners. It is almost as though such learners don't really exist; as though their achievements in learning can't be identified, measured, and compared with the achievements of traditional learners. Similarly, studies of non-traditional learning have, by and large, been ignored.

Yet by any standard, non-traditional learners and their achievements constitute the equivalent of a great natural resource in America. As the kind and quality of education a person obtains for himself becomes more urgent, non-traditional learning more and more replaces, supplements, extends, or builds upon learnings acquired in traditional ways. This great but largely invisible national resource spreads and renews itself at little cost and great benefit to the nation. Even back doors to education, it appears, "once opened, cannot be shut."[2]

It is said that "forty years ago, Robert Binkely at Western Reserve University stumbled onto what he came to call the 'amateur scholar', and recognized an intelligentsia in America invisible in every way save locally."[3] Currently, Gross is studying the

serious, advanced intellectual work conducted independently. . . . to call attention to the passionate pursuit of truth beyond academe, by all kinds of people in all kinds of realms: the hard sciences from microbiology to astronomy, the humanities from history to metaphysics, the social sciences from demographics to environmental activism; other realms of knowledge denigrated or undreamt of by the academy . . . utterly voluntary, pro-active, self-directed, autonomous, idiosyncratic, non-institutionalized, productive, innovative, and joyous.[4]

Non-traditional learning at the back door encompasses a broad and diverse range of activities. At one end is learning undertaken, as Gross notes, with complete autonomy and independence. At the other is learning undertaken in a transactional relationship with educational programs and institutions, but entered into by the choice of the learner on the basis of his own needs, concerns, and aspirations. Such learning employs non-traditional methods that afford opportunity and access irrespective of learner location and situation, and that in varying degrees place the learner at or near the center of the teaching-learning relationships. Distance, independent, and open learning are terms in wide use today for certain kinds of non-traditional learning, but such terms are imprecise, ambiguous, and overlapping. Even the catch-all "non-traditional learning" is almost undefinable, and preserves myths and misunderstandings about learning.

Non-traditional learning is not new, but rests upon a long history of learning before education was institutionalized, and the vigorous effort in earlier America to bring some semblance of civilization to the settling of diverse peoples in a vast wilderness. Lyceum, Chautauqua, debating societies, subscription libraries, self-improvement societies, churches and informal study groups began the democratization of education even while schools, academies, colleges, and universities tended to preserve the elitism in education that was part of the European heritage of the America-seekers. The self-made (meaning self-educated) person was — and to some extent still is — a persistent and enduring folk model.

The societal contexts that in earlier times had produced school, college, university, and adult institutions and programs changed during the growth, industrialization, and democratization of America. Yet the educational institutions created out of those contexts did not altogether keep up with the new contexts that were evolving. Eurich, commenting on a statement by Drucker, pointed out that knowledge in earlier times was regarded as an ornament of man and society, but that in the modern world has become a meal ticket for the one and a charm against disaster for the other.[5] Before the twentieth century, to be educated meant being unproductive, a condition that society couldn't afford in too many people. But by the latter part of the twentieth century the exact opposite has become true: being educated is equated with being productive.

Of course, the pre-twentieth century education referred to as ornamental and unproductive was formal, traditional education obtained at schools, academies, colleges, and universities, which had not kept up with the changing needs, circumstances, and aspirations of American society. In histories of education, little attention is given to the other kind of education obtained by Americans on their own initiative. This non-traditional education has been a significant factor in America's innovation, self-reliance, and unparalleled productivity in agriculture, science and technology, music and the arts, business and manufacturing, and social-civic adaptation. If formal, traditional education was regarded as ornamental and unproductive in early America, there was alongside it an educational process that was eagerly sought for productive self and community improvement.

Long notes that in the Colonial period,

Young men, and to a lesser degree, young women of "low" birth or social station could aspire to great achievement. Perhaps more than at any earlier era, learning could produce immediate tangible results. . . . Prior to the Revolution there was a kind of spirit that nurtured the idea of a learning society. . . . all of society was instructive; each individual was both learner and teacher. Within three generations of the Revolution, however, a changed attitude could be noted; "learning" became the responsibility of teachers and schools, and an activity reserved for juveniles.[6]

Long comments, "It could be argued that some of what would be considered non-traditional forms of education today were more likely to have been 'traditional' two-hundred years ago."[7] For example, in the colonial period "independent learning among adults was more a tradition than was dependence on 'schooling'. That condition can be contrasted with the contemporary situation where independent study is labeled 'non-traditional'."[8]

Foreign visitors to early America found things they liked and disliked, and some things that surprised them. De Tocqueville, in the 1830s, was struck by the fact that he did not find Americans culturally deprived. The American pioneer, he said, "is a highly civilized being who consents for a time to inhabit the back woods. . . . It is difficult to imagine the incredible rapidity with which thought circulates in the midst of these deserts. I do not think that so much intellectual activity exists in the most enlightened districts of France."[9] These comments may be taken as an oblique reference to the vigor and effectiveness of early nineteenth-century education, especially that now called non-traditional. But de Tocqueville, it will be said, was something of a romantic, and he did not see all of America.

Charles Dickens, English novelist and social critic, visited America in 1842. Defrauded in a land scheme and appalled by the brutish toil, ill manners, violence, chicanery, and libertarian boasting of some Americans, he criticized the country in ways then thought to be severe. Yet Dickens was startled by the extent of self-education in America by persons who, in England, would have remained uneducated. In *American Notes* (1842) he describes the fervor of young American women (mill workers from the countryside, working twelve hours a day and living in town boarding houses) to rise above their present condition by self-initiated study, reading, music, and (this really astonished Dickens) by writing and publishing a magazine.

I am now going to state three facts which will startle a large class of readers [in Britain]. Firstly, there is a joint-stock piano in a great many boarding houses. Secondly, nearly all these young ladies subscribe to circulating libraries. Thirdly, they have got up among themselves a periodical [in which] it is pleasant to find that many of its Tales are of the Mills and of those who work in them; that they inculcate habits of self-denial and contentment, and teach good doctrines of enlarged benevolence . . . feeling for the beauties of nature . . . A circulating library is a favourable school for the study of such topics. . . ."[10]

Dickens, the social critic, anticipates that the response of his English readers to such learning efforts will be "preposterous . . . These things are above their station." He continues, "I know no station which is rendered more endurable to the person in it, or more safe to the person out of it, by having ignorance for its associate. I know no station which has a right to monopolise the means of mutual instruction, improvement, and rational entertainment. . . ." Despite his ambivalent feelings toward America, Dickens put a discerning finger on a major educational difference between the Old World and the New: the power and popularity of self-initiated learning as a means of removing class distinctions in America.

Learning had, of course, other uses. Turner, writing about the American pioneer, said that in the New World "he was forced to make old tools serve new uses; to shape former habits, institutions and ideas to changed conditions; and to favor new means when the old proved inapplicable."[11] Making old tools serve new uses, shaping habits, institutions, and ideas, and favoring new means all signify skill, cognitive and affective learnings however and wherever initiated, sustained, evaluated, and applied. Some may call it improvising, but it should be remembered that improvisation has much in common with the trial-and-error problem solving associated with idiosyncratic learning, and that when disciplined and formalized it is part of the intellectual development of hypotheses to be tested.

As the pioneer period faded, many new problems confronted Americans, and old settlers and new immigrants responded with the same spirit that had been shown earlier. Speaking of the latter part of the nineteenth century, Gould comments:

Americans looked to themselves for solutions to the host of problems that beset them in the seventies and eighties. The Chautauqua movement [begun in 1874] lay ready to hand, and they used it. They subscribed to Chautauqua courses, copied Chautauqua forums, hired Chautauqua speakers, emulated Chautauqua ideals. . . . Chautauqua paved the way for extension courses, community colleges, adult education centers, and dozens of other educational ventures. . . .[12]

But Chautauqua "lay ready to hand" because of what had gone before.

It was, fundamentally, a response to an unspoken demand, a sensitive alertness to the cravings of millions of people for "something better." It was part of that tradition of revolution without dogma that has been typical of America since the first settlers landed on our shores. One of several waves of mass enthusiasm for self-improvement, social betterment, and reform. . . . it filled a vast need . . . provided a free platform for the discussion of vital issues . . . introduced . . . new educational concepts, ideas and opportunities. . . .[13]

Chautauqua became a university, chartered by the New York State Legislature in 1883, signifying in a unique and unprecedented way the willingness of Americans to improvise with higher education. As Gould points out, "Certainly no one would have been hardy enough to predict that this freak among universities would put the stamp of its own uniqueness on all of American higher education. But that is what happened. . . ."[14] For millions of back door learners, Chautauqua was the nearest thing they had to front door opportunity in higher education, for a while at least, until the varied programs that Chautauqua developed were replicated and institutionalized in the land grant universities and other institutions that eventually took over Chautauqua's programs.

Now, approximately a century after the "great change" wrought by Chautauqua, Gould perceives another change. "The individualism which spurred so many to learn . . . to enroll in a demanding course of study, or to swelter in a brown canvas tent for the sake of 'culture' is no longer a vital force in our lives." Gould may have been contrasting the great self-taught heroes of earlier days (Thomas A. Edison, Henry Ford, Abraham Lincoln, and many others) with the devotees of the new barbarianism, the counter-culture movements of the early sixties. He continues, "We tend to think of ourselves in terms of our membership in a social class, a union, a profession, a minority, or simply an interest group; we passively accept the group values, and thereby surrender our identity. . . . we are passive observers."[15] Are we?

Perhaps. But Gould wrote his commentary on Chautauqua, an incident in the continuing American revolution, in 1961. Yet the remainder of that decade witnessed an astonishing surge of innovation at all levels of education, but most particularly in non-traditional learning for adults. In 1964, with partial funding from the Carnegie Corporation, a unique four-year experiment in the opening of higher education to persons excluded from it was inaugurated by the University of Wisconsin. This experiment, called AIM (for Articulated Instructional Media) laid the theoretical, academic, technological, and operational bases for the creation of new institutions of open, distance, and independent learning.[16] The experiment ended in 1968, and the principles it had established were almost immediately applied in the new (1969) Open University of the United Kingdom. Thereafter followed an explosion of new institutions.

In 1970, the Commission on Non-Traditional Study was set up by the College Entrance Examination Board and the Educational Testing Service to study the pros and cons of non-traditional study.[17] By 1974/5, there were, in the United States alone, nearly one hundred new institutions or programs employing in a variety of ways the open, distance, and independent learning approaches.[18] Studies were under way in numerous states and foreign countries to assess the feasibility and desirability of creating new institutions of these kinds.[19] In 1975, UNESCO published a world survey of selected open learning case studies.[20] In the seven years between the end of the AIM experiment and the UNESCO report there was an upswelling of new institutions, experiments, programs, studies, reports, conferences, articles, and books on non-traditional learning, such as few issues in education have ever generated. Self-initiated learning at the back door, far from declining as Gould had suggested in 1961, was proliferating at an unprecedented rate.

During these years great progress was made in several fields related to non-traditional learning: the how-to aspects of building and evaluating non-traditional programs; the design and development of instructional materials; the development of cooperative, apprentice, and work-study programs; linking learning with community resources beyond the schools; different ways of organizing knowledge and relating disciplines in curriculum building, materials development, and instruction; studies of adult learning projects, which have yielded new information on the learning of adults; the place of technology in providing opportunity and access to learners; the testing and employment of new technologies and media in teaching and learning (television, the telephone, blackboard by wire, the satellite, cable, the newspaper, cassettes); demographic and marketing studies to determine learner needs; coalitions and consortia of institutions combining resources to create non-traditional programs on national or regional bases.

A whole new vocabulary relating to non-traditional learning came into being: *learning exchanges, Elderhostels, educational brokering, free universities, learners' cooperatives, self-chosen learning, learning networks,* and other terms. New periodicals on different aspects of non-traditional learning appear regularly, sponsored by a wide variety of interested groups. Their names suggest the vigor of the movement: *Second Thoughts, Basic Choices, Setting the Pace, Community Memory.* There is even a new organization, The National Alliance for Voluntary Learning, which will work against MCE (mandated continuing education), to preserve continuing education free from compulsion and to save it from the groupy blandness and other-direction of schooling.

Gould ended his 1961 book on Chautauqua with these words: "Changed times must bring new improvisations."[21] The new improvisations called non-traditional learning continue to reflect active, not passive, roles for non-traditional learners, and a healthy state of innovation in education. The purpose of this book has been to reflect the new urgency of learning that has brought about so rapid a development of non-traditional learning, to link this development with past as well as present, to suggest the significance of non-traditional learning respecting education in general, to relate non-traditional learning to general learning theory, and to the need for a lifespan view of learning.

What now needs to be done to secure and consolidate the advances that have been made in non-traditional learning and to continue the improvisations and innovations that are needed? The major themes of this book are briefly restated in the following commentary, along with their implications.

Themes and Implications

1. *The new urgency respecting learning, to cope with societal behavioral problems (health, energy, crime, human rights, resources, peaceful coexistence, population, pollution, etc.), signals the need for educational approaches that recognize and acknowledge the significance of non-traditional learning throughout life.*

Man is essentially a learning animal. Learning implies freedom to choose among alternatives. It implies that Man makes himself and his world. Learning is a renewable human resource that is not confined to schools or to any age group. Non-traditional learning carried America through great and small crises of development when schools and universities were too few in number, too poor, too slow in responding to needs, or too inefficient to meet the needs of all. More learning goes on outside of schools and classrooms throughout life because learning occurs where learners survive, meet, and act upon their needs, problems, concerns, and aspirations. Intrinsically driven learning is the most powerful of all learning. Presently learners find opportunity and access for such learning mainly in non-traditional programs or institutions, or in completely independent learning pursuits.

It is time that any significant learning, whether accomplished in formal schools or in non-traditional ways, be recognized. Some "cross-over" system should be available to non-traditional learners — if they want and need it — that would recognize and accredit their learnings.

We should not respond to the new urgency for learning by building more conventional schools and institutions, but by encouraging, recognizing, and accrediting — when wanted and needed — the non-traditional learning that already exists in our society, and that could be enhanced by the selective creation of new open, distance, and independent learning institutions.

2. *Non-traditional learning is an important and desirable kind of learning. It is not simply an alternative to, but in some ways is the opposite of, traditional schooling. It could be a model for revitalizing all learning in America.*

The vigor, success, persistence, economy, and social-individual adaptability of non-traditional learning, although well demonstrated from the Colonial Period on, is almost unknown to professional educators and much of the public at large. Schooling is the cultural artifact that symbolizes education. Yet even leaders in education, and a growing segment of the public, are worried if not convinced, as Richmond put it, that "something is seriously wrong with institutional schooling in its present form. . . ."[22]

Schooling is not learning. Schooling is the chief medium, process, or method provided by formal educational systems for the teaching of learners. As Cropley, commenting on Delker,[23] notes, ". . . learning is a normal and natural process which does not need teachers or even awareness that the process is occurring . . . [but] Education . . . focuses on experiences which influence learning . . . those activities which have a conscious educative purpose."[24] Education has tended to focus on institution-directed processes, teaching, systems of reward and punishment, attendance, evaluation, and conformance. The teacher and the learning activities of the class are central, and the learner, despite all the effort ostensibly put forth in his behalf, is placed in a reactive mode.

America is fortunate that from its beginnings it has had a vigorous non-traditional learning subculture which has, first, provided opportunity and access to those who, at any age, could not get the education they needed from the regular schools, and second, has preserved a range of learner autonomy and independence — key ingredients in successful learning and development to maturity. Holtzclaw, confirming Rogers,[25] pointed out that "the free learner, a self-directed individual operating on the belief that he can make his own decisions and take responsibility for them, has been and continues to be the cornerstone of our democratic society."[26]

Non-traditional learning counteracts the effect of traditional learning, which tends to make learners passive.[27] It is harder, more rigorous, more natural, intrinsically more joyous and more productive. Traditional schools should not be abolished or replaced, but improved. "What is needed is schools which have the effect of producing people who are capable of learning after [leaving] school."[28]

All learners, it seems, could benefit from some non-traditional learning as a part of schooling, discovering how to learn proactively according to the ebb and flow of needs, self-motivation, self-direction, and self-evaluation, to achieve the goal of all education — learner self-sufficiency. This could revitalize all learning.

3. *Learning, whether traditional or non-traditional, should lead to humanistic ends.*

People should not study either liberal arts or technical-vocational subjects, but a blend which will ". . . change things for the better and help people . . . in harmony with their day-to-day lives."[29] Schools and universities are not able to do this, alone, for their learners. The young non-traditional learner, for example, studying at home to supplement regular schooling, may have advantages not perceived by others. "The place where the individual learns most, and most quickly, both about himself and his environment and the way that he can live with other people, is the family."[30] These learnings are the foundation needed for a lifetime of humanistic learning. If, as Windham, Kurland, and Levinsohn assert, traditional learners are captives of educational institutions which do not adequately meet their needs,[31] they ought, through exercising choice, to take a hand in selecting, directing, and evaluating the education they obtain for themselves. In the quest for a better life and a broader humanity, ". . . autonomy is better than conformity, open-mindedness better than dogmatism, democracy better than elitism, sharing better than authoritarianism. . . ."[32] Such humanistic ends of learning provide a better chance, throughout life, that learners will enjoy an education that improves the quality of living as they themselves become ". . . emotionally robust, autonomous and 'inwardly youthful.' . . . The goal of lifelong education can be seen as that of developing a 'new man', eager to learn throughout life, capable of doing so, able to set priorities and judge results, democratic, concerned about fostering the quality of life. . . ."[33]

Learners will not only benefit from a blend of heretofore academically separate subject matter areas, but also from a blend of traditional and non-traditional learning activities. The line between formal and informal education and institutions will probably be blurred as more learners seek a practical, humane, and personally meaningful education through autonomy, choice, and independence.

4. *It is necessary that new and better understandings of learning as a natural survival behavior throughout life take the place of the older concepts of learning that underlie formal education.*

Learning is widely misunderstood because of narrow and incomplete learning theory and the dominance of the traditional classroom. Learning theory for children, youth, and adults does not articulate well; it leaves gaps and inconsistencies. Derived chiefly from the study of learning in school or laboratories, and of animals in cages, learning theory fails to account for the vast amount of learning that goes on in society without the formal intervention of schools. Most of our assumptions about learning seem inappropriate in today's world because of changed societal contexts and the existence and gradual recognition of the non-traditional learning that goes on throughout life. A more creative approach to theoretical research in learning is needed, not only to broaden our understanding of lifespan learning, but also to counteract the tendency of scientific specialists, in any field, to attach more credibility to conventional theory than may be warranted.[34]

The emphasis on teacher, classroom, and subject matter that has been characteristic of schooling rests on rather tenuous grounds: that knowledge is finite; that learners are mainly passive or hostile to learning; that to learn one must be taught; that learning is the receiving, storing, and repeating of information; that learning is an act of social interaction; that the classroom is the only means for teaching-learning; that speech communication between teacher and learner is so important that physical distance between teacher and learner (requiring other communications media) is a deterrent to learning; that the environment for learning is a special, designated place where teacher and resources are supplied; that learning can and should be separated from normal living and working in the total community; that learning is defined chiefly as the product or consequence of teacher effort and intervention.

The items above are more in doubt each day as "Eminent forward-thinkers . . . are losing interest in the narrow sector occupied by the learner's school days and focusing their attention on the problems and prospects arising in the field of lifelong learning."[35] While a declining number of educators would support the items listed, these beliefs still persist in the traditional classroom. Non-traditional learning throughout life is providing opportunity for broader study of such matters, and new theory revises our understanding of learning as the earlier gaps, inconsistencies, and cultural stereotypes of learning theory are removed.

   5. *The preparation of teachers and other school professionals should include an understanding of, experience with, and a commitment to non-traditional learning through the lifespan.*

The aim of all education has been the preparation of learners who could "go on their own" when they left school; but the preparation of teachers has left them without an understanding of learning that is independent of schools and teachers, is self-initiated, self-directed, and self-evaluated, and employs other means than the classroom. Teacher self-concept has been dependent upon fulfilling roles derived from models in traditional education. Hence teachers, while professing a commitment to developing learners who will learn independently after leaving the classroom, have instead sanctioned and reinforced a dependency in learning that is incompatible with society's and education's goals and needs.

As Richmond points out, "Modern man is in the unprecedented situation of having at his disposal a whole range of resources for learning . . . [but] an information-rich society is not necessarily an educative or a learning society unless its members can make systematic, selective and critical use of the resources. . . ."[36] Henderson suggests, therefore, that "educators need to recognize that they must change too and that their institutions have in some cases become obsolete. In media-rich cultures such as our own, it makes sense to move toward more non-institutional learning, more apprenticeships and internships, and more learning in the context of communal production modes and self-managed [learning] enterprises."[37]

Lynch believes that

. . . we are at the moment in a transitional stage in our conceptualization of the role of the teacher. . . . A general trend can now be observed away from schooling to learning . . . more open teaching and learning imply new tasks for teachers and other educators. . . . Instead of the learner being totally accountable to the teacher as was formerly the case, the pendulum will swing and the teacher will increasingly be accountable to the learner.[38]

The new roles for teachers may include participation in team teaching and interdisciplinary efforts, the preparation of materials for learners outside of school, the use of communications media, and the employment of special program development processes such as instructional design and formative evaluation. Teaching and learning will be studied and understood from different perspectives and disciplines, such as the Ghatalas' use of sociology and psychology to prepare teachers of non-traditional learners.[39] Whether traditional or non-traditional, formal or informal, all learning will be the concern of the teacher-facilitators whose preparation and experience will have to include non-traditional learning.

  6. *The historic growth and development of non-traditional learning, and the knowledge explosion of the mid-twentieth century, are changing the way in which knowledge is perceived.*

The Platonic structure and organization of knowledge, an ancient given in education and the learned professions, is undergoing change. Knowledge is less and less perceived as something separate and apart from the human being, and more and more perceived as the totality of understandings from the world of experience with which humans are connected. Paul Lengrand puts it this way:

The traditional concept of knowledge is itself increasingly in doubt. [The] accumulation of facts and data constitute knowledge only in a relative sense. . . . knowledge means the particular, original, living relationship of an individual with the field of his experiences. . . . The notion of a knowledge external to the perceiving individual is one of the illusions which must be abandoned. . . . There is no other knowledge than the relationship the individual establishes with the object he wants to know. . . . Knowledge itself is an internal operation carried out by a mind which resolves a problem, finds an answer to a question, discards an illusion or adds something to its stock of knowledge.[40]

Non-traditional learners, outside or at the back door of education, made contributions to this perception of knowledge, contributions which were not known or were ignored by traditional knowledge storing, retrieving, disseminating, and creating institutions. The knowledge explosion after World War II burst the remnants of the traditional structure and organization of knowledge. Modern knowledge-generating institutions are in many respects non-traditional learning organizations.

Is knowledge an end in itself, or a means to other desirable ends? Both, it would seem, as new non-traditional institutions emphasize knowledge as means, alongside older institutions which stress knowledge as an end. Duality of mission in other institutions, while more difficult to maintain because of narrow concept space between missions, is likely to continue. The way knowledge is perceived, and the knowledge missions of educational institutions, affect curriculum and the goals of instruction. Non-traditional learners, exercising choice and independence, and learning at a distance if necessary to gain access to opportunity, select to a greater degree their own curricula and set their own goals respecting knowledge.

   7. *Non-traditional learning occurs throughout the lifespan. The term* lifespan learning *refers to all the learning, traditional and non-traditional, that a person engages in from birth to death.*

From a lifespan view of learning, a new perspective on the jumbled sequence of learnings, throughout life, is possible. The term *lifespan learning* is used in place of such other terms as *lifelong learning* and *continuing* or *continuous education*, because these terms to many in America seem to imply post-secondary or adult education. The concept of lifelong education as defined by Lengrand[41] is more widely accepted in other countries. Lengrand has cautioned against adding any new term to education unless it is a term that "does not refer to any particular structure, and which, furthermore, is only justified when it designates the comprehensiveness and universality of the educational process seen under various aspects and the diversity of its applications."[42] The *lifespan* term and concept are needed to clarify and give new perspective to the idea of learning throughout all of life. Lifespan learning also has some similarity to *permanent education* as defined by Huberman: "'Permanent education' means very simply solving the problems one faces in one's life . . . For some of these problems I need to use resources other than myself. I may need other people or books, or I may need instruments. I may even need an institution (e.g. to follow a course of study). . . ."[43]

Under the lifespan learning concept, the learning that people do during their lives can be described as survival, surrogate, and independent. These non-hierarchical kinds of learnings are the product of different mixes of learner needs, purposes, circumstances, the effects of earlier learning, and the human relationships involved at different times. In the lifespan learning concept the learner is central, as in non-traditional learning. The non-traditional learning phenomenon is thus an important

element in the perception of a holistic understanding of learning throughout life.

   8. *The "environment" for learning is the learner and his surround.*

   If learning occurs throughout the lifespan in different places, under different circumstances, and in different relationships with others, the only
"constant" in this jumbled and changing sequence is the learner. The learner
is central. What, then, and where, is the environment for learning?

   Educators find it appealing to think of themselves as the center of the
teaching-learning process, in an environment (the schools) set up to maxi-
mize learning. This is a benign delusion based on the assumption that
learning is the result of teacher-school-environment, acting on the learner
as object. The learner, in this view, is dependent — unable or unwilling to
learn by his own volition.

   The history of persistent learning outside of schools (non-traditional
learning) suggests that the learner himself, and his surround at any moment whether selected or fortuitous, are the significant environmental
elements always present in a lifespan of learning. This does not imply that
improving the school environment is foolish. But it does suggest that it is
more important to free the learner from the dependency created by teachers, schools, and special learning environments, and encourage him to
perceive himself, wherever and whenever, as the crucial environment for
learning. This simple truth means that more encouragement should be
given to learners to maintain, throughout life, attitudes and surrounds
conducive to learning.

   If, as Schaefer pointed out, "Research [indicates] that intellectual functioning is influenced by environmental stimulation. . . ."[44] then learners
should be helped to contrive the surrounds they need to enhance their
learning wherever they may be in a lifetime of learning. The enhancement
of individual surrounds in America is common, even among low-income
persons, for the purposes of play, music, recreation, and sports. Common
media (print, radio, television, telephone, cassettes, tapes, and other devices) link learners to happenings and resources anywhere, which, for the
moment, become part of the surround that can enhance learning just as
well as entertainment.

   Perhaps most important is that learners realize that they are the center
of learning and need not depend upon others, except as resources, to enhance lifespan learning. An enhanced home surround can be shared by all
in the family, setting patterns of learning and relationships that, irrespective of change in the immediate surround, continue to encourage learning
as a natural and proactive way of meeting the needs and problems of life.

   9. *Technology is hero to some, villain to others. It is of growing signifi-
      cance in non-traditional learning, and could aid in the revitalization
      of all learning.*

Technological media provide access to opportunity, to resources, to teachers, to experience and reality beyond one's own self, to dreams and aspirations, to the wider learning that can mean better living. Non-traditional learners have always had to use whatever technology and media were available to them to advance their learning. They learned to accept, use, and depend upon writing, reading, books and other printed matter, correspondence and newspaper courses, subscription and public libraries, museums, church, neighborhood, and community study centers, Chautauqua and Lyceum programs, and university extension and community college courses. More recently the electronic media of radio, television, telephone, cable, satellite, and computer have been employed in learning, multiplying the senses that give power and immediacy to communication in learning. This acceptance and use of technology was practical; some way had to be found to compensate for the schooling that went to others. Learners at the back door grasped whatever means they could find for improvement.

Teachers in traditional institutions, however, have been reluctant to accept and use technology for many reasons, some good, some self-serving. The difference of technology acceptance between teachers in traditional schools and non-traditional teachers and learners, sheds light on the academic disparagement of non-traditional learning. Academically oriented professionals have not been able to identify with learners at a distance, active, independent, involved, making choices, assessing learning from practical and personal short- and long-term goals, and communicating via low or high technology media. Such learners have seemed unreal to academics with a narrow understanding of learning. Locked into a teaching-learning model (the classroom) that determines space/place for learning according to the required communications mode (oral speech), academics have consistently put down, even ridiculed, non-traditional learning. Any subculture is likely to be the butt of sarcastic jokes by those who represent the status quo, at least until the quo no longer has any status.

Correspondence schools and students, for example, since the beginning of this form of non-traditional learning in the nineteenth century, have been lampooned in jokes and cartoons. Behind the sarcasm lay the incredulity of academics and professionals that there could be any need for non-traditional learning on the one hand, and learners foolish enough, on the other hand, to try to learn by any technology other than that represented by the classroom. Although all essential elements in the teaching-learning arrangement are still present and working, because the communication mode has changed (a very personal factor for teachers), non-traditional teaching-learning is often rejected by teachers.

Technology has theoretically been an equalizer of opportunity for learners. Practically, technology has provided learners with access to learning opportunity, not equal to that provided to those who enter at the front door, but essential and effective for self-improvement and the democratization of society.

There is another kind of technology that alienates academia. This is the technology of use that must be learned whenever a person goes from one technology to another. In some ways this is the hardest technology to accept. It means unlearning old ways of performing tasks, and learning new ways compatible with the new technology. The nuisance of learning to do familiar things in an unfamiliar way not only seems unjust, it is also threatening to self-concept.

Nevertheless, technology continues, whether seen as hero or villain, to affect in significant ways both teaching and learning. Does technology dehumanize? From the evidence, it has not dehumanized learning, for it has been important in achieving humanitarian and democratic purposes in education. If technology is charged with dehumanizing teaching (especially by those who have refused to employ technology), then there is urgent need of those who profess humanitarian motives in their teaching, to bring their humanity and expertise into the world of non-traditional learning. Technology is not either good or bad; it is the motives of the people who use technology which make it one or the other. To remain uninvolved when needed is to choose isolation from significant changes going on in education.

    10. *Institutions that provide open, distance, independent, and other types of programs to non-traditional learners find it desirable to make use of special processes for the planning, development, implementation, and evaluation of such programs.*

New competencies are demanded of those who work in these special processes, and new professional specialties are emerging alongside regular academic positions. The complex developmental processes for instructional materials intended for large numbers of learners and high visibility on public media have introduced new requirements for quality. Instructional design principles and practices for mediated instruction have replaced the formal-informal lesson plans of a previous generation of teachers. Teachers work in a team format with specialists in such fields as instructional design, media, demographics, library materials, production, evaluation, and learning theory. Decision-making is shared, and the entire development process is linked, when appropriate, to faculty development initiatives, administration, counseling, registration, and field personnel.

Establishing an institution for non-traditional learners is best guided by a systems approach with continuing formative evaluation. Formative evaluation is useful in monitoring every step, from planning through piloting and actual use of courses and materials.

The special processes are part of the technology of use that follows the adoption of new technology and media in instruction. The special processes are intended to improve access and opportunity for learners, humanize learning, provide effective two-way communication between teachers and learners, help the teacher supply the highest-quality instruction and materials, evaluate program and learner achievement, identify and correct program and learner problems, and recognize and deal effectively with non-traditional learner role behaviors.

A Watershed in Education

American education has reached a watershed in its development. The full democratization of education requires that all learners be treated equally, and their learnings — if they so choose — be assessed and accredited on a common basis. Learning is a vital, renewable, efficient, and economic resource, whether traditional or non-traditional. As Bok's law puts it, "If you think education is expensive, try ignorance."[45]

Non-traditional learning has worked very well in America, although short of support and recognition, something many learners need and want. When traditional academics are asked to authorize non-traditional learning, they are prone to comment that non-traditional learning "may succeed all right in minor areas in some courses, but of course it couldn't in my area." The comment is only half right. The reason it doesn't work in the traditional academic's area is that recognition has been refused in advance on an a priori presumption of inferiority, perhaps wholly on the criterion of the communication technology employed. If communication is other than speech in the standard classroom format, the non-traditional program is frequently refused recognition. Traditional faculties, professional associations, and administrative and accrediting agencies have adopted rules that in many instances prohibit credit or any other recognition for courses taken by correspondence, radio, or television.

Such rulings do not rest on studies of comparative learning by different media. Instead, by fiat, learnings achieved by different methods are ruled beyond comparison. Such elitist and unscientific reasoning is unworthy of the high educational and professional standards to which academic groups generally adhere. One consequence of such blunt-axe proscriptions is that some of the very institutions which pioneered and sustained non-traditional learning have been unable properly to accredit learners who have, by standard academic assessments, achieved a quality of learning comparable to that of traditional learners. This is the original back door learning syndrome all over again — in the country that has led the world in a communications revolution.

Certainly there are non-traditional schools whose courses and programs may be below standard. And there are non-traditional learners who have not achieved a level of learning comparable to that required of traditional learners. But to refuse recognition to all non-traditional schools or learners because some do not meet standards is patently unjust. Traditional schools vary in quality also, with some falling below standards. The academic professions have dealt with such schools on an a priori presumption that they are inherently good and useful and should be helped to raise standards before they are put off-limits to learners. Furthermore, each school is considered on its own merits after careful and periodic review by a team of evaluators. There is, for traditional schools, no collective ruling against all schools in a given class of institutions because one or some of the schools have not maintained a particular standard of instruction. Learners in traditional schools are generally assumed to have some rights of choice, and most institutions have elaborate procedures for settling disagreements over instruction fairly, if not amicably.

The a priori presumption that teaching and learning are inferior by any means other than the classroom is a cognitive-affective blend perilously close to the mechanisms of racial bias. Instead of skin color, the communications mode of an instructional system is prejudged as a mark of inferiority — all evidence to the contrary notwithstanding. The failures of the few are made the burden of the many, and the successes are ignored or rationalized away as nonsubstantive.

It should be immaterial whether a person has learned at the front door or the back door of the Palace of Learning. What one has learned — not where, or how, in what sequence, at what institution, or in what period of time — is the only criterion of supreme importance. Fortunately, the individual and social injustices against those who have learned via non-traditional methods have not stopped non-traditional learning. The learners involved have generally experienced personal satisfaction and improvement in quality of life, despite the slings and arrows of disparagement.

Socially, however, sharp questions have been raised about the political morality of a system of different standards for front and back door learners. The new open, distance, and independent learning institutions were a response to the unwillingness of traditionalists to recognize and accredit non-traditional learning. But, admirable and needed as they are, they cannot meet the needs of non-traditional learners without access to a sympathetic government, education profession, and unbiased accreditation. Curiously, there is some opposition to the concept of independent learning by social egalitarians who seem to fear individual enterprise, even in learning. For example, Pflüger, commenting on adult education, states that ". . . individualistic attempts to promote participation in education have no prospects of success. . . . Emancipation is not an individual affair, but only definable and practicable as a solidarity struggle for freedom from dependence on society."[46]

The call for "solidarity" seems more a political than a learning slogan. Learning is personal, idiosyncratic. While there is need for a more just and equitable system of assessing learning on a base common to all learners, solidarity of one group over another is what we have now. Another kind of solidarity merely creates new "ins" and "outs," and justice still may not be served. Solidarity too implies other-direction, control, and derogation of the individual — not really desirable conditions if unfettered learning is what is being talked about.

Non-traditional learning would unquestionably benefit from an assessment and accreditation system that is fully independent of traditional education; in fact, so would traditional learning. The regional accreditation associations in the United States are gradually moving toward greater independence. That trend should be accelerated. There is new willingness to review and even accredit special (non-traditional) institutions, and some progress has been made.

The other effort that needs to be made is to improve the availability of better courses for non-traditional learners — locally, regionally, nationally, and even internationally. Satellite retransmission for learning is just as feasible (already adequately demonstrated by the University of the South Pacific) as satellite transmission for international news, sports, business, and entertainment.

In view of the reluctance of traditional faculties to be involved in programs for non-traditional learners, the difficulties of sustaining dual institutional missions on a level of equal priority, and the apparent retreat of university extension from conflict with residence faculties over credit instruction, the greatest hope would seem to lie in the creation of new institutions. Community colleges and vocational-technical institutes have shown initiative. Regional consortia of institutions are being tried. Most promising at the moment are the University of Mid America, and the Educational Satellite Program of the Appalachian Regional Commission, a consortium of universities in the Appalachian region.

The University of Mid America is vigorously exploring the feasibility of becoming The American Open University. If this should come about, the learning opportunities of thousands of learners (back door and front door alike) would be immensely improved. The Appalachian program may, through access to cable systems, be able to extend its programs nationwide. To succeed, however, these innovative institutions will have to have control of curriculum and rewards for non-traditional learners, and not be forced to depend upon traditional institutions for accreditation policy.

The argument is sometimes advanced that learning, like virtue, is its own reward, and that non-traditional learners should be satisfied with courses intended for traditional learners, but without the credit. That is specious sophistry. Non-traditional learning, to learners and to society, is too important to be dismissed in such callous fashion. There are, of course, many fully independent non-traditional learners who do not need or want any sort of credit or recognition. But there are others who do need and want credit and recognition simply because certification is forced upon them, made a requirement by the upward mobility processes of traditional institutions in education, business, government, and industry.

What non-traditional learning does not need is anything that would diminish the freedom of choice, autonomy, and independence that has kept this kind of learning vital, practical, resourceful, innovative, and humane from the beginning of this country. Non-traditional learning works for thousands of learners because they link it to their needs, concerns, problems, and aspirations. A bureaucracy could not do as well on the personal learning side, but might help in the assessment of learning, which is a social problem.

Non-traditional learning is many things, but mostly it is a natural survival behavior. Roger Reynolds was seriously injured in a skydive. He writes,

A year after my fall, all the casts were off except the one from my left knee to the ankle. The ankle was weak after a bone-graft operation and the bone wasn't healing. The doctor said, "Rog, we're going to give it one more month. If it doesn't start to heal we're going to have to operate again." I was totally bottomed out emotionally.

For some time, I had been sneaking up to the medical library to read about orthopedics. I learned that in order to heal, bones need circulation and exercise. I figured I had one month to see if that would work.[47]

What Reynolds had learned about exercise worked. The learning that Reynolds did is characteristic of the kind of non-traditional learning that has helped sustain Americans and America: natural learning, intrinsically motivated, applied, and evaluated. It didn't make Reynolds an orthopedic specialist, but it solved his problem. This is the most powerful learning known. It is not schooling.

The American Dream meant the opportunity to become what one could become. For millions of Americans, that meant self-initiated learning, self-development, preparation for that better time that lay ahead. It meant catch-as-catch-can learning for mother or father, but sending the children to school, and to college, for the things the parents had to discover for themselves, and things they never had the time to learn. Perhaps the earlier way had some advantages, for then the person's own needs, concerns, purposes, and circumstances could motivate and determine the education one got for oneself. Living and learning were coterminous, with the accent on living, which supplied the need and motivation for learning. For non-traditional learners at the back door, it is still very much that way.

Will America's long, successful, but largely unacknowledged experience with non-traditional learning revitalize education? We must all hope so, for we must all be learners throughout our lives. We must make ourselves competent generalists in the areas that affect our survival and quality of life and specialists in the areas on which we depend for our livelihoods. Formal, other-directed, and classroom-based education reflects its origins in earlier labor-intensive societies. The knowledge-intensive society we have now entered gives prominence to self-acquired learning throughout the lifespan.

Isaac Asimov foresees the time when computers, in a symbiotic relationship with learners, will greatly expand and extend learning. "When that happens . . . for the first time in history [we] will be achieving something approaching intellectual maturity. And we will look back on everything before that time as simply the childhood of the human race."[48]

If America is on the threshold of becoming a Learning Society, non-traditional learning may be its most genuine ingredient.

Notes
Bibliography
Index

Notes

Chapter I:
A New Urgency Regarding Learning

1 Sir Peter Venables (Chairman), *Report of the Committee on Continuing Education* (Milton Keynes, England: Open University Press, 1976).

2 The National Research Council, *Telecommunications for Metropolitan Areas: Opportunities for the 1980's* (Washington, D.C.: National Academy of Sciences, 1978), p. 15.

3 National Research Council, *Telecommunications*, pp. 15–16.

4 National University Extension Association, *Newsletter*, 14 April 1978, p. 6.

5 Ralph Schillace, "Theory: The Midwife of Invention," *IRTHE* (The University of Cincinnati Institute for Research and Training in Higher Education) 5, no. 3 (1978): 1.

6 Schillace, "Theory," p. 1.

7 Lord Walter Perry, *Open University. A Personal Account by the first Vice Chancellor.* (Milton Keynes, England: Open University Press, 1976), pp. xiii–xiv.

8 *Webster's Third New International Dictionary*, s.v. "theory."

9 Jindra Kulich, "An Historical Overview of the Adult Self-Learner," mimeographed (Vancouver: Department of Adult Education, University of British Columbia, 1970) p. 1. Also, *Journal of the International Congress of University Adult Education* 9, no. 3 (September 1970): 22.

10 Kulich, "An Historical Overview," p. 10.

11 René Dubos, *So Human an Animal* (New York: Charles Scribner's Sons, 1968), pp. 222–42.

12 Quoted in Arthur Koestler, *The Act of Creation* (New York: Macmillan Co., 1969), p. 233.

13 Donald T. Campbell, "Qualitative Knowing in Action Research," mimeographed (An address to the American Psychological Association, New Orleans, 1974. Evanston, Ill.: Northwestern University), p. 4.

14 Sir John C. Eccles, *The Understanding of the Brain* (New York: McGraw-Hill Book Co., 1973), p. 222. Used with permission of the publisher.

15 Roger Bingham, "Trivers in Jamaica." *Science 80* 1, no. 3 (March/April 1980): 63.

16 Reported by Constance Holden, "Twins Revisited." *Science 80* 1, no. 7 (November 1980): 55–59.

17 Reported by Paul Bohannan, "Being Human (The Gene Pool and the Meme Pool)." *Science 80* 1, no. 7 (November 1980): 25–28.

18 Eccles, *The Understanding of the Brain*, p. 191.

19 Eccles, *The Understanding of the Brain*, pp. 222–23.

20 Quoted in Campbell, "Qualitative Knowing," pp. 42–44.

21 Dubos, *So Human an Animal*, p. 131.

22 Nicholas A. Wheeler, "Toward Safe Routes to the Strange Future," in "Point of View," *The Chronicle of Higher Education* 16, no. 18, (10 July 1978): 32.

23 Fred Harvey Harrington, *The Future of Adult Education.* (San Francisco: Jossey-Bass Publishers, 1977), p. 2.

24 Harrington, *The Future of Adult Education*, pp. 2–3.

25 Harrington, *The Future of Adult Education*, p. 5.

26 Harrington, *The Future of Adult Education*, p. 5.

27 Harrington, *The Future of Adult Education*, p. 9.

28 U.S. Census Bureau. "More People Over 25 Are Going to College," *The Chronicle of Higher Education*, (10 April 1978).

Chapter II: Learning at the Back Door

1 Jonathan Swift, *The Tale of a Tub*, 1704.

2 Sir James Mackintosh, *Vindiciae Gallicae*, 1791.

3 Jacob Bronowski, *The Ascent of Man*, British Broadcasting Corporation, London, 1971. And book of same name (Boston: Little, Brown & Co., 1974). See especially the final television show and chapter, "The Long Childhood of Man."

4 René Dubos, *So Human an Animal* (New York: Charles Scribner's Sons, 1968), pp. *vii, xii*.

5 University of Wisconsin Center for Demography and Ecology, Madison, Wisconsin, (in a conversation with author), 23 January 1979.

6 Joseph Campbell, *The Hero with a Thousand Faces* (New York: Meridian Books, 1956), pp. 382–83.

7 Joseph Wood Krutch, *The Measure of Man* (New York: Bobbs-Merrill Co., 1953), pp. 256–57.

8 Dubos, *So Human an Animal*, p. 117.

9 Quoted in Dubos, *So Human an Animal*, p. 115.

10 Albert Schweitzer, *The Philosophy of Civilization* (New York: Macmillan Co., 1950), p. 113.

11 Edgar Weinberg, "Technical Change and Education," in *The Encyclopedia of Education*, vol. 9, ed. Lee C. Deighton. (New York: Free Press, 1971), p. 114.

12 Thorstein Bunde Veblen, *The Instinct of Workmanship and the State of the Industrial Arts* (New York: W. W. Norton & Co., 1914), p. 307.

13 Stephen P. Dresch, "An Historico-Economic View of the Evolving Role, Structure and Financing of Post Secondary Education," in *Report of a Conference on Lifelong Learning: Diagnosis and Prognosis*, (New York: Commissioner of Education, May 1974), p. 48.

14 Alfred North Whitehead, "The Aims of Education: A Plea for Reform," in *The Aims of Education and Other Essays* (New York: Macmillan Co., 1959), p. 1.

15 Whitehead, *The Aims of Education*, p. 3.

16 Whitehead, *The Aims of Education*, p. 51.

17 Whitehead, *The Aims of Education*, p. 10.

18 Alexander Meiklejohn, *The Experimental College* (New York: Harper & Row Publishers, 1932), p. *xi.*

19 Theodore J. Shannon and Clarence A. Schoenfeld, *University Extension.* (New York: Center for Research in Education, 1965), p. 1.

20 Merle Curti and Vernon Carstensen, *The University of Wisconsin 1848–1925,* vol. 2. (Madison: University of Wisconsin Press, 1949), p. 594.

21 Richard Moulton, National University Extension Association Conference, Madison, Wisconsin, 1915, *Proceedings* (Washington, D.C.: the association, 1915), pp. 255–58.

22 F. W. Reynolds, NUEA Conference, Chicago, 1919, *Proceedings* (Washington, D.C.: the association, 1919), p. 70.

23 William H. Lighty, NUEA Conference, St. Louis, 1923, *Proceedings* (Washington, D.C.: the association, 1923), pp. 54–64.

24 Louis Reber, NUEA Conference, Madison, Wisconsin, 1924, *Proceedings* (Washington, D.C.: the association, 1924), pp. 21–38.

25 Almere Scott, NUEA Conference, Salt Lake City, 1926, *Proceedings* (Washington, D.C.: the association, 1926), pp. 87ff.

26 Isaac Asimov, "Computerized Education in a Low Birth Rate Society," *Continuum* 44, no. 1, (September, 1979): 12.

27 George Canning, *The King's Message*, 1828.

28 Bernard Bailyn, *Education in the Forming of American Society* (New York: Vintage Books, 1960), p. 49.

29 Bailyn, *Education in the Forming of American Society*, pp. 91–95.

30 Frank Laubach and Sharif Al Mujahid, "Illiteracy of Adults," *International Encyclopedia of Higher Education*, vol. 5, ed. Asa S. Knowles (San Francisco: Jossey-Bass Publishers, 1977), p. 2108. See also: Paolo Freire, *The Pedagogy of the Oppressed* (New York: Herder and Herder, 1971).

31 Some of the material on pages 28–30 is adapted from the author's "Teaching-Learning Environments," in *Frontiers in Education*, eds. J. Biedenbach and L.

Grayson, (New York: The American Association of Electrical Engineering and the Institute of Electrical and Electronic Engineers, 1973), pp. 8–10. Used here with permission.

32 The word *surround* may have the ring of jargon. It is used because there is no other word that has the specific meaning needed in its context of use. "Surrounding" and "environment" are too broad and general in meaning. Surround derives its more limited meaning from two sources: a mainly British usage referring to something immediately surrounding an object (for example, "The paved surround of a swimming pool"), and a largely American usage referring to a band of illumination immediately surrounding an image on a screen. In this exposition, surround refers to the immediate area around the learner, in which he lives and works. Thus, the learner and his changing surround are, together, the environment for learning. Surround is commonly used by persons who work on the environment of learners and others. See *Webster's Third New International Dictionary*, s. v. "surround."

Chapter III: Teaching, Learning, Schooling, and Knowledge

1 Some of the material on pages 32–37, is adapted from the author's "The New Educational Technology," American Dietetic Association. *Journal* 53, no. 4 (1968): 325–28. Used here with permission.

2 Some of the material on pages 37–41, is adapted from the author's "Satellite, Cable and Education: Looking Beyond the Classroom," *Public Telecommunications Review*, July–August 1975, pp. 15–21, and from the author's "Satellite and Cable—No Highway in the Sky for Conventional Teaching and Learning," in *A Report on University Applications of Satellite-Cable Technologies* (Madison, Wis.: University of Wisconsin–Extension, 1976), pp. 1–7. Used with permission. Some material in this chapter is adopted from the author's *Learning Through Technology* (Hagen, W. Germany: Zentrales Institut für Fernstudienforschung, Papier 26). © by the author.

3 R. M. Gagne, "Learning Research and Its Implications for Independent Learning," in *The Theory and Nature of Independent Learning*, ed. G. T. Gleason (Scranton, Pa.: International Textbook Co., 1967), pp. 15–34.

4 Jacob Bronowski, *The Ascent of Man*. British Broadcasting Corporation, London, 1971. And book of same name (Boston: Little, Brown & Co., 1974). See especially the final television show and chapter, "The Long Childhood of Man."

5 *Passages* 5, no. 4, (April 1974): 19–20. The quotations attributed to Seattle were excerpted from a 1972 documentary film production of the Southern Baptist Convention's Radio and Television Commission (script by Ted Perry).

Chapter IV: Distance and Independent Learning

1 Critics and supporters of education may agree on the problems they perceive in schooling, but disagree on their causes and remedies. For another view, see

Fred M. Hechinger's "School-yard Blues, The Decline of Public Education." *Saturday Review*, 20 January 1979, pp. 20–22.

2 Henri Dieuzeide, *Educational Technology and the Development of Education* (Paris: UNESCO International Education Year (IEY) Special Unit, 1970), p. 9.

3 Otto Peters, *Der Fernunterricht* (Berlin: Pädagogisches Zentrum, 1973), n7ff.

4 Swedish Commission on Television and Radio in Education (TRU), *Distance Education* (Stockholm: TRU Commission, 1976), p. 11.

5 Heinz Schwalbe, "Distance Education, Home Study or Correspondence Education," *Epistolodidaktika*, 1 (London 1976): 39–42.

6 Schwalbe, "Distance Education," pp. 39–42.

7 Börje Holmberg, *Distance Education* (London: Kogan Page, 1977), p. 9.

8 I. Bruce Hamilton, *The Third Century; Postsecondary Planning for the Non-traditional Learner.* (New York: College Entrance Examination Board, 1976), p. 16.

9 For further comments on non-traditional learning, see the Preface.

10 John W. C. Johnstone, and Ramon J. Rivera, *Volunteers for Learning.* (Chicago: Aldine Publishing Co., 1965).

11 Charles A. Wedemeyer, "The Re-emergence of the Independent Learner," *Gyan Doot*, 4, no. 1. (1973): 3–8.

12 Charles A. Wedemeyer, "Independent Study," in *The Encyclopedia of Education*, vol. 4, ed. Lee C. Deighton (New York: Free Press, 1971), pp. 548–57.

13 Wedemeyer, "Independent Study," pp. 548–57.

14 Michael G. Moore, "Some Speculations on a Definition of Independent Study," in *Proceedings, Kellogg Seminar on Independent Learning in the Health Sciences* (Vancouver: Department of Adult Education, University of British Columbia, 1973), pp. 37–38.

15 J. B. MacDonald, "Independent Learning," in *The Theory and Nature of Independent Learning*, ed. G. T. Gleason (Scranton, Pa.: International Textbook Co., 1967), pp. 2, 11–12.

16 G. T. Gleason, ed., *The Theory and Nature of Independent Learning* (Scranton, Pa.: International Textbook Co., 1967), p. *v.*

17 Robert Dubin and Thomas C. Taveggia, *The Teaching-Learning Paradox* (Eugene: University of Oregon Press, 1968), pp. 29–30. See also Thomas C. Taveggia, "Goodbye Teacher, Goodbye Classroom, Hello Learning", *Journal of Personalized Instruction*, 2(1977) 2, 119–122. Fred S. Keller, "PSI (Personalized System of Instruction) and Reinforcement Theory", *The Keller Plan Handbook*, (Menlo Park, Calif: Benjamin, 1974).

18 P. L. Dressel and M. M. Thompson, *Independent Study* (San Francisco: Jossey-Bass Publishers, 1973), p. *vii.*

19 John Dewey, *Intelligence in the Modern World, John Dewey's Philosophy*, ed. Joseph Ratner (New York: Modern Library, 1939), pp. 619–27.

20 The summary statements are from: Gleason, *Theory and Nature of Independent Learning*, Gagne: pp. 15–30; MacDonald: p. 3, 9–12; Sears: pp. 35–48; Lee: pp. 51–63; Gleason: pp. 65–78; Jourard: pp. 79–101.

21 Holmberg, *Distance Education*, p. 9.

22 Michael G. Moore, *On a Theory of Independent Study*, Zentrales Institut für

Fernstudienforschung Papiere no. 16. (Hagen, W. Germany: Zentrales Institut für Fernstudienforschung, 1977), pp. 11–12. (English translation by Helmut Fritsch.)

23 Where, then, is the "environment for learning"? This question is discussed in Chapter II.

24 Moore, *On a Theory*, p. 11.

25 Moore, *On a Theory*, pp. 19–21.

26 H. A. Witkin, "Cognitive Styles in Learning and Teaching. In *Individuality in Learning: Implications of Cognitive Styles and Creativity for Human Development*, ed., S. Messick (San Francisco: Jossey-Bass Publishers, 1976). And: Leona E. Tyler, *Individuality* (San Francisco: Jossey-Bass Publishers, 1978), Chapter II, "Field Dependence and Independence," pp. 162–75.

27 Michael G. Moore, "The Cognitive Styles of Independent Learners." (Ph.D. diss., University of Wisconsin–Madison, 1976).

28 Malcolm S. Knowles, *Self-Directed Learning*. (New York: Association Press, 1975).

29 Carl Rogers, *Freedom to Learn*. (Columbus, Ohio: Merrill Publishing Co., 1959).

30 Moore, *On a Theory*, p. 17.

31 Howard R. Neville, (address to the National University Extension Association), *NUEA. Newsletter*, 14 April 1978, p. 3.

32 Christopher Lasch, *Haven in a Heartless World, The Family Besieged*. (New York: Basic Books, 1977), p. *xiv*.

Chapter V: Open Learning

1 C. O. Houle, *The External Degree*. (San Francisco: Jossey-Bass Publishers, 1973), p. 13.

2 Some of the material on pages 61–62 is adapted from the author's "The 'Open' School: Education's Runnymede?" *Educational Technology* 12, no. 1 (January 1972): 65–68. Used with permission.

3 Some of the material on pages 62–63 is adapted from the author's "Characteristics of Open Learning Systems," *Public Telecommunications Review* 1, no. 3 (December 1973): 53–55, and included with modifications in: National Association of Educational Broadcasters, *Open Learning Systems* (Washington, D.C.: NAEB, March 1974).

4 James Martin, "Open Learning Systems," (background paper for the National Association of Educational Broadcasters Advisory Committee on Open Learning, November 1973).

5 Norman Mackenzie, Richmond Postgate, and John Scupham, *Open Learning*. (Paris: UNESCO Press, 1975), p. 17.

6 Samuel Gould, *Diversity by Design*. (San Francisco: Jossey-Bass Publishers, 1973), p. *xv*.

7 Edgar Faure, *Learning To Be: The World of Education Today and Tomorrow*. (Paris: UNESCO Press, 1972).

8 For a fuller treatment of contextual change, see Chapter III, pp. 34–35.

9 Charles A. Wedemeyer and Michael Moore, "Wisconsin Open School Survey,"

in *The Open School,* ed. Clifford Wood (Madison, Wis.: Governor's Commission on Education, 1970).

10 Robert Dubin, and Thomas C. Taveggia, *The Teaching-Learning Paradox* (Eugene: University of Oregon Press, 1968). *See also* J. F. Gibbons, W. R. Kincheloe, K. S. Down, "Tutored Videotape Instruction: A New Use of Electronic Media in Education", *Science* 195 (1977) 1139–1146.

11 Some of the material on pages 64–65 is adapted from the author's "Independent Study," in *The Encyclopedia of Education,* vol. 4, ed. Lee C. Deighton. (New York: Free Press, 1971), pp. 548–57, and from "Independent Study," in *The International Encyclopedia of Higher Education,* vol. 5, ed. Asa S. Knowles (San Francisco: Jossey-Bass Publishers, 1977), pp. 2114–32. Used with permission.

12 Louis B. Wright, *Culture in the Moving Frontier.* (New York: Harper & Row Publishers, 1955), p. 230.

13 Wright, *Culture,* p. 224.

14 In 1891 the catalog of the University of Wisconsin reported the adoption of university correspondence study: "The scheme thus adopted is exceptionally comprehensive, embracing a combination of all leading lines of effort which have proved successful in *extending to the people* a portion of the benefits of university education" (emphasis added). Effective implementation, however, did not begin until 1906, when the University Extension Division was established and William H. Lighty was employed to organize correspondence study (Chester Allen and Charles A. Wedemeyer, *Extending to the People* [Madison, Wis.: University of Wisconsin–Extension, 1957], pp. 17, 20).

15 Mackenzie et al., *Open Learning,* p. 26.

16 Some of the material on pages 67–73, is adapted from the author's "Fourteen Preliminary Questions," *Adult Leadership* 24, no. 3 (November 1975): 85. Used with permission.

17 Charles A. Wedemeyer, "Permanent or Temporary Faculties in Open Institutions?", in *Zehn Yahre Deutsches Institut für Fern-studium,* ed. Günther Dohmen. (Weinheim and Basel: Beltz-Verlag, 1978), pp. 334–39.

18 NAEB, *Open Learning Systems.*

CHAPTER VI: The Implications of Non-Traditional Learning

1 Milton H. Miller Psychiatrist, University of Wisconsin–Madison, to the author, 30 July 1970.

2 Allen Tough, "Major Learning Efforts: Recent Research and Future Directions," mimeographed (Toronto: Ontario Institute for Studies in Education, 1977), p. 1. Also *Adult Education* 28 (Summer 1978): 250–63.

3 Allen Tough, *Why Adults Learn: A Study of the Major Reasons for Beginning and Continuing a Learning Project* (Toronto: Ontario Institute for Studies in Education, 1968), pp. 171–73. And: Allen Tough, *The Adult's Learning Projects: A Fresh Approach to Theory and Practice in Adult Learning* (Toronto: Ontario Institute for Studies in Education, 1971), pp. 6–15.

4 Tough, "Major Learning Efforts," p. 4.

5 Tough, "Major Learning Efforts," pp. 6–8.

6 Patrick R. Penland, "Individual Self Planned Learning in America," (final report of a project. Washington, D.C.: U.S. Office of Education, Office of Libraries and Learning Resources, 1977).

7 James Fair, "Teachers As Learners: The Learning Projects of Beginning Elementary-School Teachers" (Ph.D. diss., University of Toronto, 1973).

8 Cressy McCatty, "Patterns of Learning Projects Among Physical and Health Education Teachers," *Reporting Classroom Research*, 5, no. 2, (1976).

9 Nancy E. Kelley, "A Comparative Study of Professionally Related Learning Projects of Secondary School Teachers" (Master's thesis, Cornell University, 1976).

10 Nancy L. Miller, "Teachers and Non-Teaching Professionals As Self-Directed Learners." (Master's thesis, Cornell University, 1977).

11 Laurent O. J. Denys, "The Major Learning Efforts of Two Groups of Accra Adults" (Ph.D. diss., University of Toronto, 1973).

12 J. Woodall, "If I Were a Dean," *The Lancet* 1 (1978): 433.

13 "Feasibility Study for an Open University of America" mimeographed (Lincoln, Neb.: University of Mid-America, June 1980), p. 2.

14 Tough, "Major Learning Efforts," p. 1.

15 Mary-Claire van Leunen, "Pray for the Grace of Impatient Readers," *The Chronicle of Higher Education*, 16, no. 14 (30 May 1978): 19.

16 van Leunen, "Pray for the Grace of the Impatient Readers," p. 19.

17 Jack R. Frymier, "Motivation Is What It's All About," *Motivation Quarterly* 1, no. 1 (1970): 2.

18 Carl Rogers, *Freedom to Learn* (Columbus, Ohio: Merrill Publishing Co., 1959).

19 John F. A. Taylor, "Politics and the Neutrality of the University," *AAUP Bulletin*, December 1973. The issue of academic freedom was discussed by Lord Walter Perry, Vice Chancellor of the Open University, Walter James, Dean of the Open University Faculty of Education, and the author in a half hour video tape sponsored by The Open University, BBC, and the U.S. Endowment for the Humanities, London 1972. Copies of the video tape available at U.S. Information Agency libraries.

20 In 1977, instructors of a social studies course offered by the British Open University came under public criticism because of alleged one-sidedness.

21 Some institutional hazards are wryly presented by William C. Rogers in "Adult and Continuing Education: Snatching Defeat Out of the Jaws of Victory." *Continuum* 44, no. 1 (September 1979): 25–26.

Non-traditional institutions are vulnerable because they are different, and what is different doesn't easily fit into established educational processes and funding patterns developed by and for traditional institutions. Furthermore, new institutions are vulnerable simply because they are new, and lack strong constituencies to counter the established constituencies of traditional education. An interesting example of this double vulnerability (being new and different) is Athabasca University of Alberta, Canada. Athabasca is Alberta's only non-traditional university. Located in Edmonton, Athabasca was founded in 1970 and given degree-granting power in 1975. In March 1980 Athabasca officials presented to the Alberta government proposals for the improvement of its Edmonton facilities, only to learn that the government had already decided to move the university from Edmonton to Athabasca, a town about ninety miles to the north. Such a unilateral government decision undoubtedly reflects the influence of traditional university political constituencies into which the new institution was not wired. See Barbara Spronk, "A University is Moved," *Newsletter* of the International Council for Correspondence Education 9, no. 4 (April 1980): 14–16.

22 Quoted by Charles B. Stalford in *An Evaluative Look at Non-Traditional Post-secondary Education* (Washington, D.C.: National Institute of Education-U.S. Department of Health, Education and Welfare, September 1979) p. *iii*.

Administering a non-traditional institution may give an edge to persons with experience in applied (knowledge-as-means) universities with an emphasis on service. John Horlock, vice-chancellor of Britain's University of Salford, will become vice-chancellor of Britain's Open University in January 1981. Horlock sees his experience at Salford as an advantage in becoming the head of the Open University: "Universities exist to promote education, scholarship and research, in the service of society. The Open University serves the whole British community in precisely this way. . . . I am sure that my experience as head of a major 'applied' university [Salford] will help me in that objective [at the Open University]." (Quoted in "The British Open University appoints a new Vice-Chancellor," *Newsletter* of the International Council for Correspondence Education 9, no. 4 [April 1980]: 17.)

In the United States, the proposed American Open University would also have a broad service mission: "The mission of the American Open University is to assist adults in achieving educational, personal and career goals by offering, in a cost-effective manner, high quality educational opportunities that are accessible to adults and responsive to individual and emerging social needs." (University of Mid-America, "Mission, Goals and Objectives of American Open University" mimeographed [Lincoln, Neb.: the University, 6 October 1980], p. 1.) Clearly, the AOU envisioned will be a multidimensional non-traditional university with applied, knowledge-as-means administrative and operational characteristics.

23 Frank Bowen, Stewart Edelstein, and Leland Medsker, "The Identification of Decisionmakers Concerned with Non-traditional Degree Programs and an Analysis of their Informational Needs" in *An Evaluative Look at Non-traditional Post-secondary Education.* (Washington, D.C: NIE-HEW, September 1979), p. 119.

24 In 1975, the North Central Association of Schools and Colleges for the first time accredited a proprietary correspondence school after a full evaluation; the same school was reaccredited in 1978.

25 Gavriel Salomon, *Interaction of Media, Cognition and Learning.* (San Francisco: Jossey-Bass, Publishers, 1979), p. 216.

26 G. T. Gleason, ed. *The Theory and Nature of Independent Learning.* (Scranton, Pa.: International Textbook Co., 1967), pp. 10–11.

27 In the United States, only agricultural extension succeeded, through the de-

velopment of the "integrated" department, in overcoming the separation of extension faculty from regular faculty who hold all controls. The integrated department is frequently proposed as a model for new institutions.

28 Peter S. Cookson, "Adult Education Participation and Occupational Achievement: A Regression Analysis," *Adult Education* 29, no. 1 (Fall 1978): 37.

29 Norman Mackenzie, Richmond Postgate, and John Scupham, *Open Learning*. (Paris: UNESCO Press, 1975).

30 Lord Walter Perry, *Open University: A Personal Account of the First Vice Chancellor* (Milton Keynes, England: The Open University Press, 1976).

31 Tough, "Major Learning Efforts."

32 Malcolm Knowles, *Self-Directed Learning*. (New York: Association Press, 1975).

33 Ronald Gross, *The Lifelong Learner*. (New York: Simon and Schuster, 1977).

34 Information provided by Wisconsin State Department of Public Instruction, 1976.

Chapter VII: Technology and Non-Traditional Learning

1 James Ridgeway, "Computer-Tutor," *The New Republic* 154, no. 23 (4 June 1966): 19–22.

2 John Milton, *Paradise Lost*, bk. 1, line 330.

3 Paul F. Sharp, "Our Second Culture," *Phi Kappa Phi Journal*, Summer 1968, pp. 3–11, 17.

4 Joseph Wood Krutch, *More Lives Than One*. (Clifton, N. J.: William Sloane Associates, 1962), p. 353.

5 *Webster's Third New International Dictionary*, s.v. "subliminal": "2a: existing or functioning outside the area of conscious awareness: influencing thought, feeling or behavior in a manner unperceived by personal or subjective consciousness."

6 Eric Hoffer, "The Crowded Life," Public Broadcasting Service, 1 January 1978.

7 Gardner Quarton, "Controlling Human Behavior and Modifying Personality," in *Toward the Year Two Thousand: Work in Progress*, 2d edition, ed. Daniel Bell. (Boston: Houghton-Mifflin Co., 1968), p. 214.

8 Notable exceptions to short-term federal funding are to be found, however, in the continuing support for children's television ("Sesame Street," for example), in the National Institute of Education's long-range support of the University of Mid America, the regional open university model employing educational television, and in NIE continuing support of regional laboratories and research centers in education. For a case study of UMA, see: Norman Mackenzie et al. *Open Learning* (Paris: UNESCO Press, 1975), pp. 447–72.

9 A. G. Oettinger, and N. Zapol, "Will Information Technologies Help Learning?" *Teachers College Record*, Fall 1972.

10 L. P. Grayson, "Education Satellite: A Goal or a Gaol?" (Washington, D.C.: National Institute of Education, 1975).

11 Dave Berkman, "The Myth of Educational Technology," *Educational Forum*, May 1972, pp. 451–60. See also Berkman's "The Learning Industry and ITV," *Educational Broadcasting Review*, June 1971, pp. 19–24.

12 Michael G. Moore, "Investigation of the Interaction Between the Cognitive Style of Field Independence and Attitudes to Independent Study Among Adult Learners Who Use Correspondence and Self-Directed Independent Study." (thesis submitted in partial fulfillment of the Ph.D., University of Wisconsin–Madison, 1976), pp. 12–64. Some material in this chapter is adopted from the author's *Learning through Technology*. (Hagen, W. Germany: Zentrales Institute für Fernstudienerenforschung, Papier 26). © by the author.

13 Moore, "Investigation of the Interaction," pp. 49–50.

14 Malcolm S. Knowles, *Self-Directed Learning*. (New York: Association Press, 1975), p. 4.

15 Knowles, *Self-Directed Learning*, p. 4.

16 Knowles, *Self-Directed Learning*, p. 15.

17 Knowles, *Self-Directed Learning*, p. 14.

18 Lynn White, "Technology's Challenge," in *Technology in Western Civilization*, vol. 2, eds. Melvin Kranzberg and Carroll W. Pursell, Jr. (New York: Oxford University Press, 1967), p. 705.

19 Charles A. Wedemeyer, and Robert E. Najem, *AIM: From Concept to Reality. The Articulated Instructional Media Program at Wisconsin* (Syracuse, N.Y.: Syracuse University Publications in Continuing Education, 1969), pp. 8–11.

20 James Burke, *Connections*. (Boston: Little, Brown & Co., 1978), p. 295.

Chapter VIII: Instructional Design
in Non-Traditional Teaching and
Learning Systems

1 Donald P. Ely, "Educational Technology," *Media Adult Learning* 2, no. 3 (Spring 1980): 3.

2 Guthrie Moir, ed. *Teaching and Television* (Oxford: Pergamon Press, 1967).

3 Robert Theobald, "Higher Education and Cybernation," *NEA Journal* (March 1966): 26.

4 Robert E. Hoye, "Check Point to Teaching Splashdown," *Wisconsin Library Bulletin* 66, no. 2 (March–April 1970): 79.

5 Lee C. Deighton, ed. *The Encyclopedia of Education*. 10 vols. (New York: Free Press, 1971).

6 Steven Goodman, ed. *Handbook on Contemporary Education* (New York: R.R. Bowker Company, 1976).

7 Association for Educational Communications and Technology. "The Field of Educational Technology: A Statement of Definition," *Audiovisual Instruction*, 1972, pp. 17–38.

8 Some of the material in this chapter is adapted from the author's "Instructional Design," in *The Telephone in Education*, Compiled by Lorne A. Parker and Betsy Ricomini (Madison: The University of Wisconsin–Extension, 1976), pp.

161-169; and from the author's "Trouble at Castle Perilous: Applying Media and Technology to Instruction," *Educational Technology,* July 1971, pp. 19–24. Used with permission.

9 Donald P. Ely, "Educational Technology," p. 6.

10 Charles E. Silberman, *Crisis in the Schools.* (New York: Random House, 1970).

11 Marshall McLuhan, *Understanding Media: The Extensions of Man.* (New York: McGraw-Hill Book Co., 1964), pp. 7–21.

Chapter IX: Building and Evaluating Non-Traditional Institutions or Programs

1 *To Improve Learning.* (report to the President and the Congress of the United States. Washington, D.C.: U.S. Government Printing Office, 1970), p. 5.

2 Melvin Blase, *Institution Building: A Source Book.* (Beverly Hills, Calif.: Sage Publications, 1973), pp. 4–11.

3 Ripley S. Sims, "An Inquiry Into the Correspondence Educating Processes," mimeographed (report prepared with the support of UNESCO and the International Council of Correspondence Education, Madison, Wis., 1977), pp. 58–59.

4 Charles A. Wedemeyer, "Independent Study," in *The International Encyclopedia of Higher Education,* vol. 5, ed. Asa Knowles (San Francisco: Jossey-Bass Publishers, 1977), p. 2129.

5 Sims, "An Inquiry."

6 Renée Erdos, *Teaching by Correspondence.* (Paris: UNESCO Press, 1967).

7 Lord Walter Perry, *Open University: A Personal Account of the First Vice Chancellor* (Milton Keynes, England: Open University Press, 1976).

8 Dennis Gooler, "Criteria for Evaluating the Success of Nontraditional Postsecondary Education Programs," *Journal of Higher Education* 48, no. 1, (Jan.–Feb. 1977): 78–95.

9 Norman Mackenzie, Richard Postgate, and John Scupham, *Open Learning* (Paris: UNESCO Press, 1975).

10 Otto Peters, *Die didaktische Struktur des Fernunterrichts* (Weinheim, Federal Republic of Germany: Beltz-Verlag, 1973).

11 Börje Holmberg, *Distance Education.* (London: Kogan Page, 1977).

12 Donald Kaiser, "A Value-Standards Evaluation of an Independent Study Program," mimeographed (Madison: University of Wisconsin – Extension, 1976).

13 Sara M. Steele, "Contemporary Approaches to Program Evaluation" (report prepared for Educational Resources Information Center (ERIC) Clearing House on Adult Education, 1973), p. 89ff.

14 Steele, "Contemporary Approaches," p. 52ff.

15 Charles A. Wedemeyer, Michael Moore, and Clifford Wood (ed.), *The Open School.* (Madison, Wis.: Governor's Commission on Education, 1971), p. 12.

16 See Chapter III, page 38.

17 See Chapter III, page 40.

18 See Chapter IV, page 47; Chapter VI, p. 78.

19 John Dewey, *Theory of Valuation*. (Chicago: University of Chicago Press, 1939), pp. 49–51.

Chapter X: Lifespan Learning

1 Quoted in C. K. Ogden and I. A. Richards, *The Meaning of Meaning*, 4th ed. (New York: Harcourt, Brace & Co., 1936), p. 1, ante.

2 Ogden and Richards, *The Meaning of Meaning*, p. 1, ante.

3 Leonard Bloomfield, *Language*. (New York: Henry Holt and Co., 1933), p. 41.

4 Henri Dieuzeide, *Educational Technology and the Development of Education*. (Paris: UNESCO IEY Special Unit, 1970), p. 9. See also Michael G. Moore, *On a Theory of Independent Study*, (Hagen, W. Germany: Zentrales Institut für Fernstudienforschung, 1977), Papiere no. 16, p. 1.

5 U.S. Department of Health, Education and Welfare, *Lifelong Learning and Public Policy* (report prepared by the Lifelong Learning Project, Washington, D.C.: HEW, 1978), p. *iv*.

6 *Lifelong Learning and Public Policy*, p. 30.

7 Robert A. Luke, "Teacher Training for Adult Education," in *The International Encyclopedia of Higher Education*, vol. 2, ed. Asa S. Knowles (San Francisco: Jossey-Bass Publishers, 1977), pp. 163–64.

8 *Lifelong Learning and Public Policy*, p. 1.

9 Malcolm S. Knowles, "Andragogy Revisited II," *Adult Education* 30, no. 1 (1979): 52.

10 Huey B. Long, Kay McCrary, and Spencer Ackerman, "Adult Cognition: Piagetian Based Research Findings," *Adult Education* 30, no. 1 (1979): 14–15.

11 Robert A. Carlson, "The Time of Andragogy," *Adult Education* 30, no. 1 (1979): 53–54.

12 Robert A. Carlson, "The Time of Andragogy," p. 56.

13 See Chapter IX, section on "Learner Roles/Situations and Role Behaviors," pp. 144–48.

14 Howard Y. McClusky, "The Adult as Learner" in *Management of the Urban Crisis*, eds. Robert J. McNeill and Stanley F. Seashore. (New York: Free Press, 1971), p. 514. Quoted also by Keith Main in "The Power-Load-Margin Formula of Howard Y. McClusky as the Basis for a Model of Teachings" *Adult Education* 30, no. 1 (1979): 22.

15 Milton H. Miller, Quoted in Chapter VI, p. 75.

16 Frank Jessup, Unpublished lecture. University of Wisconsin–Madison, October 1967.

17 See Chapter VI, pp. 76–77.

18 See: J. S. Bruner, "Eye, Hand and Mind," in *Studies in Cognitive Development*, ed. D. Elkind and J. H. Flavell (New York: Oxford University Press, 1969). Also: J. S. Bruner, "Nature and Uses of Immaturity," *American Psychologist* 27, no. 8 (1977): 1–22. And: J. S. Bruner, "Organization of Early Skilled Action," *Child Development*, 44 (1977): 1–11.

19 Herbert J. Klausmeier, and Richard E. Ripple, *Learning and Human Abilities,* 3d ed., rev. (New York: Harper & Row Publishers, 1971), p. 7.

20 Klausmeier and Ripple, *Learning and Human Abilities,* p. 9.

21 Klausmeier and Ripple, *Learning and Human Abilities,* p. 10.

22 Earl S. Schaefer, "Need for Early and Continuing Education," in *Education of the Infant and Young Child,* ed. Victor H. Denenberg (New York: Academic Press, 1970), pp. 61–62.

23 Lewis J. Lipsitt, "Learning in Infancy," in *The Encyclopedia of Education,* vol. 5, ed. Lee C. Deighton. (New York: Free Press, 1971), p. 447.

24 Lipsitt, *Encyclopedia of Education,* pp. 447–48.

25 Schaefer, "Need for Early and Continuing Education," pp. 62–63, 79.

26 Schaefer, "Need for Early and Continuing Education," p. 70.

27 Sir John C. Eccles, *The Understanding of the Brain.* (New York: McGraw-Hill Book Co., 1973), p. 222.

28 Eccles, *The Understanding of the Brain,* p. 221.

29 Eccles, *The Understanding of the Brain,* p. 191.

30 Richard Peterson et al., *Lifelong Learning in America: An Overview of Current Practices, Available Resources, and Future Prospects* (San Francisco: Jossey-Bass Publishers, 1979), p. 15.

31 Educational Policy Research Center, *The Learning Force.* (Syracuse, N.Y.: Educational Policy Research Center, 1970).

32 *Lifelong Learning and Public Policy,* p. iv.

33 *Webster's Third New International Dictionary,* s.v. "span."

34 Leona E. Tyler, *Individuality.* (San Francisco: Jossey-Bass Publishers, 1978), p. 3.

35 John Dewey so stressed the responsibility of the teacher as shaper of the learning experiences, that one consequence has been the reinforcement of the concept that learning must follow teaching.

36 *Webster's Third New International Dictionary,* s.v. "idiosyncratic": "peculiar to the individual."

37 Malcolm Knowles, *Self-Directed Learning.* (New York: Association Press, 1975), pp. 14–17.

38 Klausmeier and Ripple, *Learning and Human Abilities,* pp. 7–8.

39 *Webster's Third New International Dictionary,* s.v. "maturation."

40 Tyler, *Individuality,* p. 57.

41 Tyler, *Individuality,* p. 54.

42 Tyler, *Individuality,* p. 54.

43 Prof. Robert Clasen, University of Wisconsin–Extension–Madison, to the author, 11 February 1974.

44 Figure 13 was suggested by Dr. Robert Clasen, professor of education, University of Wisconsin–Extension–Madison, in a memo to the author, 11 February 1974. In addition to the suggestions made by Clasen, the author received useful comments from Dr. Michael Moore, then a professor at St. Francis Xavier University, Nova Scotia, and Dr. James Martin, associate director, Independent Study Programs for Health Care Trustees, University of Minnesota.

Chapter XI: Education for What?

1 George O. Klemp, Jr., "Three Factors of Success," in *Relating Work and Education*, ed. D. W. Vermilye (San Francisco: Jossey-Bass Publishers, 1977), p. 107.

2 See Chapter VI, "Implications of Non-Traditional Learning," the section on "Dual Mission."

3 Charles A. Wedemeyer, and Robert E. Najem, *AIM: From Concept to Reality, The Articulated Instructional Media Program at Wisconsin* (Syracuse, N.Y.: Syracuse University Press Publications in Continuing Education, 1969), p. 57.

4 See Chapter IX, "Building and Evaluating Non-Traditional Institutions and Programs," the section on "Learner Roles and Role Behaviors."

5 Mortimer J. Adler, "Work, Education and Leisure," in *Relating Work and Education*, ed. D. W. Vermilye (San Francisco: Jossey-Bass Publishers, 1977), p. 35.

6 Allen Tough, "Major Learning Efforts: Recent Research and Future Directions," *Adult Education*, 28 (Summer 1978): 250–63.

7 Rosella Linskie, "Cultural Values as they Relate to Learning," in *Speaking About Adults* eds. R. Phillip Carter and Verl M. Short (DeKalb, Ill.: Northern Illinois University Press, 1966), p. 15ff.

8 Howard R. Bowen, "Values, The Dilemma of Our Time, and Education," in *Relating Work and Education*, ed. D. W. Vermilye (San Francisco: Jossey-Bass Publishers, 1977), p. 34.

9 Adler, "Work, Education and Leisure," p. 53.

10 Russell Edgerton, "Education, Work and FIPSIE," in *Relating Work and Education*, ed. D. W. Vermilye (San Francisco: Jossey-Bass Publishers, 1977), p. 119.

11 Thomas F. Brady, "Learner-Instruction Interaction in Independent Study Programs." (Ph.D. diss., University of Wisconsin–Madison, 1976), pp. 16–19.

12 Arthur G. Wirth, "The Philosophical Split," in *Relating Work and Education*, ed. D. W. Vermilye (San Francisco: Jossey-Bass Publishers, 1977), p. 16.

13 James O'Toole, "The Purposes of Higher Learning," in *Relating Work and Education*, ed. D. W. Vermilye (San Francisco: Jossey-Bass Publishers, 1977), p. 10.

14 Erik Erikson, *Childhood and Society.* (New York: W. W. Norton & Co., 1950), p. 272. See also his *Insight and Responsibility* (New York: W. W. Norton & Co., 1964).

15 Richard I. Evans, *Dialogue with Erik Erikson.* (New York: Harper & Row Publishers, 1967), p. 51.

16 George E. Vaillant, *Adaptation to Life* (Boston: Little, Brown & Co., 1977), p. 350.

17 Robert J. Havighurst, *Developmental Tasks and Education* (New York: David McKay, 1952).

18 Robert J. Havighurst, "Changing Status and Roles During the Adult Life Cycle: Significance for Adult Education," in *Sociological Backgrounds of Adult Education*, ed. Hobert W. Burns (Syracuse: Center for the Study of Liberal Education for Adults, 1964).

19 Norma M. K. Roberts, "The Human Developmental Needs of Adults Across

the Lifespan with Implications for Higher Education" (Ph.D. diss., University of Wisconsin–Madison, 1978), Chapter III.

20 Learning stages are discussed in Chapter III.

21 *Webster's Third New International Dictionary.* s. v. "concern." Examples supplied by the author.

22 See discussion of "Learner Role Behaviors," Chapter IX, pp. 141–48.

23 Florence B. Stratemeyer et al. *Developing a Curriculum for Modern Living* (New York: Teachers College Press, 1957).

24 Sir Peter Venables (Chairman), *Report of the Committee on Continuing Education* (Milton Keynes, England, Open University Press, 1976), p. 104.

25 Jean R. Renshaw, "The Company and the Family," in *Relating Work and Education,* ed. D. W. Vermilye (San Francisco: Jossey-Bass Publishers, 1977), p. 217.

26 Willard Wirtz, "Education for What?" in *Relating Work and Education,* ed. D. W. Vermilye (San Francisco: Jossey-Bass Publishers 1977), p. 270.

27 *Webster's Third New International Dictionary,* s.v. "liberal arts."

28 Paul Hirst, "Liberal Education," in *The Encyclopedia of Education,* vol. 5, ed. Lee C. Deighton (New York: Free Press, 1971), pp. 505–6.

29 Robert Hutchins, *The Learning Society* (New York: Praeger Publishers, 1968). Quoted by Willis H. Harman, "Future Work, Future Learning," in *Relating Work and Education,* ed. D. W. Vermilye (San Francisco: Jossey-Bass Publishers 1977), p. 249.

30 Howard R. Bowen, "Values, the Dilemmas of our Time, and Education," in *Relating Work and Education,* ed. D. W. Vermilye (San Francisco: Jossey-Bass Publishers, 1977), pp. 32–33.

31 Harold C. Martin, "Colleges of Arts and Sciences," in *The Encyclopedia of Education,* vol. 1, ed. Lee C. Deighton (New York: Free Press, 1971), p. 349–55.

32 Harold Howe II, "Basic Issues in American Education," in *The Encyclopedia of Education,* vol. 1, ed. Lee C. Deighton (New York: Free Press, 1971), p. 201.

33 Irving Allen Dodes, "General Mathematics," in *The Encyclopedia of Education,* vol. 6, ed. Lee C. Deighton (New York: Free Press, 1971), p. 137.

34 Howe, "Basic Issues in American Education," p. 201.

35 Kurt F. Wendt et al., "Business Education: Extension Courses," in *The Encyclopedia of Education,* vol. 1, ed. Lee C. Deighton (New York: Free Press, 1971), p. 545.

36 C. P. Snow, *The Two Cultures and the Scientific Revolution* (Cambridge: Cambridge University Press, 1959). See also Snow's *The Two Cultures — A Second Look* (Cambridge: Cambridge University Press, 1963).

37 Charles A. Wedemeyer, "The Next Frontier: Potentials and Problems of International-Intercultural Education via Satellites," (paper delivered at the University of Wisconsin Space Science Colloquium, 1969), p. 4.

38 Robert M. Pirsig, *Zen and the Art of Motorcycle Maintenance* (New York: Bantam Books, 1976), pp. 15–18.

39 Robert Greene, *Friar Bacon and Friar Bungay,* 1594.

40 Pirsig, *Zen and the Art of Motorcycle Maintenance,* p. 306.

41 Arthur W. Chickering, "Vocations and the Liberal Arts," in *Relating Work and*

Education, ed. D. W. Vermilye (San Francisco: Jossey-Bass Publishers, 1977), p. 139.

42 John Dewey, *Experience and Education* (New York: Macmillan Co., 1938), p. 1.

43 C. Richard Soderberg, "A Note on Engineering Education," in *Applied Science and Technical Programs* (Washington, D.C.: National Academy of Science, Government Printing Office, 1967), pp. 399–413.

44 Edgar Weinberg, "Technological Change and Education," in *The Encyclopedia of Education*, vol. 9, ed. Lee C. Deighton (New York: Free Press, 1971), p. 121.

45 Frederick A. Olafson, "The Humanities and Education," in *The Encyclopedia of Education*, vol. 4, ed. Lee C. Deighton (New York: Free Press, 1971), p. 523.

46 Arthur R. King, Jr. and John A. Brownell, *The Curriculum and the Discipline of Knowledge* (New York: John Wiley & Sons, 1966), pp. 33–34.

47 Hirst, "Liberal Education" pp. 505–9.

48 James O'Toole, *Work, Learning and the American Future* (San Francisco: Jossey-Bass Publishers, 1977), p. 154.

49 Samuel Gould, "The Intellectual Role of Universities," in *The Encyclopedia of Education*, vol. 9, ed. Lee C. Deighton (New York: Free Press, 1971), pp. 354–358.

50 Wendt et al. "Business Education: Extension Courses," p. 545.

51 Howard R. Bowen, "Values, the Dilemmas of our Time, and Education," in *Relating Work and Education*, ed. D. W. Vermilye (San Francisco: Jossey-Bass Publishers, 1977), p. 34.

52 Gould, "The Intellectual Role of Universities," p. 358.

53 A. J. Cropley, ed., "Lifelong Education: Issues and Questions." *Lifelong Education: A Stock Taking* (Hamburg: UNESCO Institute for Education, 1979), p. 22.

Chapter XII: Back Door Learning in the Learning Society

1 Carl Sandburg, *The People, Yes* (New York: Harcourt Brace and Co., 1936), pp. 18–19. Used with permission of the publisher.

2 Tom Wayman, "Longshoremen are Also Authors and Artists," *In These Times*, 14–20 November 1979, p. 13.

3 "Musings," a column in *Second Thoughts* 2, no. 2 (October 1979): 11.

4 Ronald Gross, "The Converse of MCE (Mandatory Continuing Education)." *Second Thoughts* 2, no. 2 (October 1979): 11.

5 Alvin C. Eurich, "Reflections on University Research Administration." *Sponsored Research in American Universities and Colleges*, ed. S. R. Strickland (Washington, D.C.: American Council on Education, 1968), pp. 1–6.

6 Huey B. Long, *Continuing Education of Adults in Colonial America* (Syracuse, N.Y.: Syracuse University Press Publications in Continuing Education, 1976), p. 1.

7 Long, *Continuing Education of Adults in Colonial America*, p. 3.

8 Long, *Continuing Education of Adults in Colonial America*, p. 75.

9 Alexis de Tocqueville, *Democracy in America* (New York: Alfred A. Knopf, 1944), p. 317.

10 Charles Dickens, *American Notes and Pictures from Italy* (New York: Oxford University Press, n.d.), pp. 80–81.

11 Frederick Jackson Turner, *The Frontier in American History* (New York: Henry Holt, 1921), pp. 145, 305.

12 Joseph E. Gould, *The Chautauqua Movement* (Albany: State University of New York Press, 1961), pp. 98–99. Used with permission of the publisher.

13 Gould, *Chautauqua*, pp. *vii–viii*.

14 Gould, *Chautauqua*, p. 13.

15 Gould, *Chautauqua*, p. 99.

16 Charles A. Wedemeyer and Robert E. Najem, *AIM: From Concept to Reality, The Articulated Instructional Media Program at Wisconsin* (Syracuse: Syracuse University Press Publications in Continuing Education, 1969).

17 Samuel B. Gould and K. Patricia Cross, *Explorations in Non-Traditional Study* (San Francisco: Jossey-Bass Publishers 1972).

18 National Association of Educational Broadcasters, *Open Learning Systems.* (Washington, D.C.: NAEB, March 1974).

19 For example: Charles A. Wedemeyer, Michael Moore, and Clifford Wood (ed.), *The Open School* (Supplement to final report of the commission. Madison, Wis.: Governor's Commission on Education, 1971).

20 Norman Mackenzie, Richard Postgate, and John Scupham, *Open Learning* (Paris: UNESCO Press, 1975).

21 Gould, *Chautauqua*, p. 100.

22 K. Richmond, "The Concept of Continuous Education," in *Lifelong Education: A Stock Taking*, ed. A. J. Cropley (Hamburg: UNESCO Institute for Education, 1979), p. 64.

23 P. V. Delker, "Government Roles in Lifelong Learning," *Journal of Research and Development in Education* 7 (1974): 24–33.

24 A. J. Cropley, ed., "Lifelong Education: Issues and Questions" in *Lifelong Education: A Stock Taking* (Hamburg: UNESCO Institute for Education, 1979), p. 10.

25 Carl Rogers, "Learning to be Free." *NEA Journal* 52, no. 3, (March 1963): 28.

26 Luis R. Holtzclaw, "The Adult Learner's Need for Inner Freedom," *Lifelong Learning* 3, no. 1, (September 1979): 24.

27 R. Wrocznski, "Learning Styles and Lifelong Education," *International Review of Education* 20 (1974): 464–73.

28 Cropley, "Lifelong Education: Issues and Questions," p. 17.

29 B. Suchodolski, "Lifelong Education at the Crossroads," in *Lifelong Education: A Stock Taking*, ed. A. J. Cropley (Hamburg: UNESCO Institute for Education, 1979), p. 38.

30 James Lynch, *Lifelong Education and the Preparation of Educational Personnel* (Hamburg: UNESCO Institute for Education, 1977), p. 7.

31 Douglas M. Windham, Norman D. Kurland, and Florence H. Levinsohn, eds., *Financing the Learning Society* (Chicago: University of Chicago Press, 1978), pp. 304–5.

32 A. J. Cropley, ed., "Lifelong Education: Some Theoretical and Practical Con-

siderations," in *Lifelong Education: A Stock Taking* (Hamburg: UNESCO Institute of Education, 1979), p. 103.

33 Cropley, "Lifelong Education: Some Theoretical and Practical Considerations" p. 104.

34 Jeffrey L. Fox, "Creative Approach to Genesis" (commentary on the work of William Day), *Science News* 16, no. 19 (10 November 1979): 334.

35 Richmond, "The Concept of Continuous Education," p. 72.

36 Richmond, "The Concept of Continuous Education," p. 72.

37 Hazel Henderson, "A New Economics," in *Relating Work and Education*, ed. D. W. Vermilye (San Francisco: Jossey-Bass Publishers, 1977), p. 235.

38 Lynch, *Lifelong Education*, pp. 3, 20, 23.

39 Habeeb and Elizabeth S. Ghatala, "How can we best Motivate Students as a Group and Individually?" *The Proceedings* of the International Council for Correspondence Education vol. 2 (London: Tuition House, 1979), pp. 250–57.

40 Paul Lengrand, "Prospects of Lifelong Education," in *Lifelong Education: A Stock Taking*, ed. A. J. Cropley (Hamburg: UNESCO Institute of Education, 1979), p. 23.

41 Lengrand, "Prospects of Lifelong Education," pp. 28–29.

42 Lengrand, "Prospects of Lifelong Education," p. 29.

43 Quoted by Lengrand, "Prospects of Lifelong Education," p. 74, from a paper now in press by W. K. Richmond entitled "After Piaget: a Dialogue with Michael Huberman."

44 Earl S. Schaefer, "Need for Early and Continuing Education," in *Education of the Infant and Young Child*, ed. V. H. Denenburg (New York: Academic Press, 1970), p. 78.

45 Paul Dickson, "Any Fool Can Make a Rule," *Reader's Digest*, March 1979, p. 99.

46 A. Pflüger, "Lifelong Education and Adult Education: Reflections on Four Current Problem Areas," in *Lifelong Education: A Stock Taking*, ed. A. J. Cropley (Hamburg: UNESCO Institute of Education, 1979), p. 98.

47 Roger Reynolds, "The Man Who Fell to Earth" *Reader's Digest*, January 1980, p. 52.

48 Isaac Asimov, "Computerized Education in a Low Birth Rate Society" *Continuum*, 44, no. 1 (September 1979): 13.

Selected Bibliography

Alford, Harold J. *Continuing Education in Action.* New York: John Wiley & Sons, 1968.

Allen, W. H. "Intellectual Abilities and Instructional Media Design." *AV Communications Review* 23 (1975): 139–70.

Asimov, Isaac. "Computerized Education in a Low Birth Rate Society." *Continuum* 44, no. 1 (September 1979): 5–13.

Bååth, J. A. *Correspondence Education in the Light of Contemporary Teaching Models.* Malmo: Liber Hermods, 1979.

Bailyn, Bernard. *Education in the Forming of American Society.* New York: Vintage Books, 1960.

Beeby, C. E. *Qualitative Aspects of Educational Planning.* Paris: UNESCO Press, 1969.

Bengsten, Urban. "Interest in Education Among Adults with Short Previous Formal Schooling." *Adult Education* 30, no. 3, (1980): 131–51.

Bereday, George G. *Universities for All.* San Francisco: Jossey-Bass Publishers, 1973.

Blanchard, Everard B. *A New System of Education.* Homewood, Ill.: ETC Publications, 1975.

Blase, Melvin. *Institution Building: A Source Book.* Beverly Hills: Sage Publications, 1973.

Bloom, Benjamin S.; Hastings, J. T.; and Madaus, G. F. *Handbook on Formative and Summative Evaluation of Student Learning.* New York: McGraw-Hill Book Co., 1971.

Brady, Thomas F. "Learner-Instruction Interaction in Independent Study Programs." Ph.D. dissertation, University of Wisconsin–Madison, 1976.

Bronowski, Jacob. *The Ascent of Man*. Boston: Little, Brown & Co., 1974.

Brubacher, John S. *A History of the Problems of Education*. New York: McGraw-Hill Book Co., 1947.

Bruce, Hamilton I. *The Third Century: Postsecondary Planning for the Non-traditional Learner*. New York: College Entrance Examination Board, 1976.

Bruner, Jerome S. *The Process of Education*. New York: Vintage Books, 1960.

Burke, James. *Connections*. Boston: Little, Brown & Co., 1978.

Burns, Norbert W., ed. *Sociological Backgrounds of Adult Education*. Syracuse: Center for the Study of Liberal Education for Adults, 1970.

Carnegie Commission on Higher Education. *Less Time, More Options*. New York: McGraw-Hill Book Co., 1971.

Carnegie Commission on Higher Education. *Toward a Learning Society*. New York: McGraw-Hill Book Co., 1973.

Carnegie Council on Policy Studies in Higher Education. *Three Thousand Futures: The Next Twenty Years for Higher Education*. San Francisco: Jossey-Bass Publishers, 1980.

Chickering, Arthur. "Adult Development — Implications for Higher Education." *Designing Diversity, 1975*. proceedings of the Second Conference on Open Learning and Non-Traditional Study. Washington, D.C. (1975): 203–19.

Chickering, Arthur. "Dimensions of Independence." *Journal of Higher Education* 25 (1964): 38–41.

Cohen, Sol. "The History of American Education, 1900–1976: The Uses of the Past." *Harvard Educational Review* 46, no. 3, (1976): 298–330.

Conant, James Bryant. *The Education of American Teachers*. New York: McGraw-Hill Book Co., 1963.

Coombs, P. H. *The World Educational Crisis: A Systems Analysis*. New York: Oxford University Press, 1968.

Cropley, A. J., ed. *Lifelong Education: A Stock Taking*. Hamburg: UNESCO Institute for Education, 1979.

Cross, Wilbur, and Florio, Carol. *You Are Never Too Old to Learn*. New York: McGraw-Hill Book Co., 1978.

Crossland, Fred E. *Minority Access to College*. New York: Schocken Books, 1971.

Darrow, Helen F., and Van Allen, R. *Independent Activities for Creative Learning*. New York: Teachers College Press, 1961.

Denenberg, Victor H., ed. *Education of the Infant and Young Child*. New York: Academic Press, 1970.

Dewey, John. *Experience and Education*. New York: Macmillan Co., 1938.

Dewey, John. *Theory of Valuation*. Chicago: University of Chicago Press, 1939.

Dieuzeide, Henri. *Educational Technology and the Development of Education*. Paris: UNESCO IEY Special Unit, 1970.

Dill, William R.; Wallace, B. S.; and Elton, E. J. "Strategies for Self Education." *Harvard Business Review* 43 no. 6 (1965): 119–30.

Dohmen, Günther; Wedemeyer, Charles A.; and Rebel, Karlheinz. *Offenes Lernen und Fernstudium*. Deutsches Institut für Fernstudien an der Universität Tübingen. Weinheim und Basel: Beltz Verlag, 1976.

Dressel, P. L., and Thompson, M. M. *Independent Study.* San Francisco: Jossey-Bass Publishers, 1973.

Dubin, Robert, and Taveggia, Thomas C. *The Teaching-Learning Paradox.* Eugene: University of Oregon Press, 1968.

Dubos, René. *So Human an Animal.* New York: Charles Scribner's Sons, 1968.

Eccles, Sir John C. *The Understanding of the Brain.* New York: McGraw-Hill Book Co., 1973.

Edstrom, L. O.; Erdos, R.; and Prosser, R. *Mass Education.* Uppsala, Sweden: Dag Hammerskjold Foundation, Almkuist and Wiksell, 1970.

Educational Policy Research Center. *The Learning Force.* Syracuse, N.Y.: Educational Policy Research Center, 1970.

Elam, Stanley, and McLure, W. P. *Educational Requirements for the 1970's.* New York: Praeger Publishers, 1967.

Ellsworth, R. E., and Wagener, H. D. *The School Library: Facilities for Independent Study in the Secondary School.* New York: Educational Facilities Laboratory, 1963.

Ellul, Jacques. *The Technological Society.* New York: Vintage Books, 1964.

Erdos, Renée. *Teaching by Correspondence.* Paris: UNESCO Press, 1967.

Erikson, Erik. *Childhood and Society.* New York: W. W. Norton & Co., 1950.

Erikson, Erik. *Insight and Responsibility.* New York: W. W. Norton & Co., 1964.

Eurich, Alvin C. *Campus 1980.* New York: Delacorte Press, 1968.

Evans, Richard I. *Dialogue with Erik Erikson.* New York: Harper & Row Publishers, 1967.

Evans, R. I., and Leppman, P. K. *Resistance to Innovation in Higher Education.* San Francisco: Jossey-Bass Publishers, 1968.

Faure, Edgar. *Learning To Be: The World of Education Today and Tomorrow.* Paris: UNESCO Press, 1972.

Flinck, R. *Correspondence Education Combined with Systematic Telephone Tutoring.* Kristianstad: Hermods, 1978.

Freire, Paolo. *The Pedagogy of the Oppressed.* New York: Herder and Herder, 1971.

Gagne, Robert M. *The Conditions of Learning.* New York: Holt, Rinehart & Winston, 1965.

Gagne, Robert M., ed. *Learning and Individual Differences.* Columbus, Ohio: Charles E. Merrill Books, 1967.

Gardner, John W. *Self-Renewal: The Individual and the Innovative Society.* New York: Harper & Row Publishers, 1964.

Glatter, R.; Wedell, E. G.; Harris, W. J. A.; and Subramian, S. *Study by Correspondence.* London: Longmans, Green and Co., 1971.

Gleason, G. T., ed. *The Theory and Nature of Independent Learning.* Scranton, Pa.: International Textbook Co., 1967.

Goodlad, John I. *School, Curriculum and the Individual.* Waltham, Mass.: Blaisdell Publishing Co., 1966.

Gooler, Dennis. "Criteria for Evaluating the Success of Nontraditional Postsecondary Education Programs." *Journal of Higher Education* 48, no. 1 (1977): 78–95.

Gould, Joseph E. *The Chautauqua Movement*. Albany: State University of New York Press, 1961.

Gould, Samuel. *Diversity by Design*. San Francisco: Jossey-Bass Publishers, 1973.

Gould, Samuel B., and Cross, K. Patricia. *Explorations in Non-Traditional Study*. San Francisco: Jossey-Bass Publishers, 1972.

Grattan, C. Hartley. *In Quest of Knowledge*. New York: Association Press, 1955.

Gross, Ronald. *Future Directions for Open Learning*. Washington, D.C.: U.S. Department of Health, Education and Welfare, National Institute of Education, and University of Mid America, 1979.

Gross, Ronald. *The Lifelong Learner*. New York: Simon and Schuster, 1977.

Hack, Walter G. et al. *Educational Futurism 1985*. Berkeley, Calif.: McCutcheon Publishing Co., 1971.

Harrington, Fred Harvey. *The Future of Adult Education*. San Francisco: Jossey-Bass Publishers, 1977.

Harris, W. J. A. *The Distance Tutor*. Manchester, England: University of Manchester Monographs, 1972.

Havighurst, Robert J. *Developmental Tasks and Education*. New York: David McKay Co., 1952.

Heidt, E. U. *Instruction Media and the Individual Learner*. London: Kogan Page, 1978.

Hesburgh, T. M.; Miller, P. A.; and Wharton, C. R. *Patterns for Lifelong Learning*. San Francisco: Jossey-Bass Publishers, 1973.

Holmberg, Börge. *Distance Education*. London: Kogan Page, 1977.

Houle, C. O. *The External Degree*. San Francisco: Jossey-Bass Publishers, 1973.

Houle, Cyril O. *The Inquiring Mind*. Madison, Wis.: University of Wisconsin Press, 1963.

Hutchins, Robert. *The Learning Society*. New York: Praeger Publishers, 1968.

Jessup, Frank W., ed. *Lifelong Learning*. Oxford: Pergamon Press, 1969.

Johnstone, John W. C., and Rivera, R. J. *Volunteers for Learning*. Chicago: Aldine Publishing Co., 1965.

Kabwasa, Antoine, and Kaunda, Martin M. *Correspondence Education in Africa*. London: Routledge and Kegan Paul, 1973.

Kidd, J. Roby. *How Adults Learn*. New York: Association Press, 1959.

Kindervatter, Suzanne. *Non-Formal Education as an Empowering Process*. Amherst, Mass.: University Center for International Education, 1979.

Klausmeier, Herbert J., and Ripple, Richard E. *Learning and Human Abilities*. 3d ed., rev. New York: Harper & Row Publishers, 1971.

Knowles, Malcolm S. *The Modern Practice of Adult Education*. New York: Association Press, 1970.

Knowles, Malcolm S. *Self-Directed Learning*. New York: Association Press, 1975.

Knox, Allan B.; Grotelueschen, A.; and Sjogren, D. D. "Adult Intelligence and Learning Ability." *Adult Education* 18, no. 3 (1968): 188–96.

Knox, Allen. *Adult Development and Learning*. San Francisco: Jossey-Bass Publishers, 1977.

Koenig, Kathryn, and McKeachie, W. J. "Personality and Independent Study." *Journal of Educational Psychology* 50 (June 1959): 132–34.

Koestler, Arthur. *The Act of Creation.* New York: Macmillan Co., 1969.

Kranzberg, Melvin, and Pursell, Carroll W., eds. *Technology in Western Civilization.* 2 vols. New York: Oxford University Press, 1967.

Kulich, Jindra. "An Historical Overview of the Adult Self-Learner." *Journal of the International Congress of University Adult Education* 9, no. 3 (September, 1970): 22–31.

Lasch, Christopher. *Haven in a Heartless World, The Family Besieged.* New York: Basic Books, 1977.

Lawson, K. H. *Philosophical Concepts and Values in Adult Education.* 2d ed. Milton Keynes, England: Open University Press, 1979.

Livingstone, D. W. "Some General Tactics for Creating Alternative Educational Futures." *Interchange* 4, no. 1 (1973): 1–9.

Long, Huey, B. *Continuing Education of Adults in Colonial America.* Syracuse, N.Y.: Syracuse University Press Publications in Continuing Education, 1976.

Loughary, John W. *Man-Machine Systems in Education.* New York: Harper & Row Publishers, 1966.

Lynch, James. *Lifelong Education and the Preparation of Educational Personnel.* Hamburg: UNESCO Institute for Education, 1977.

Mackenzie, Norman; Postgate, Richard; and Scupham, John. *Open Learning.* Paris; UNESCO Press, 1975.

Mackenzie, Ossian, and Christensen, E. L. *The Changing World of Correspondence Study.* University Park, Pa.: Pennsylvania State University Press, 1971.

Malcolm, Andrew. *The Tyranny of the Group.* Totowa, N. J.: Littlefield, Adams and Co., 1975.

Medsker, Leland et al. *Extending Opportunities for a College Degree.* Berkeley, Calif.: Center for Research and Development in Higher Education, 1975.

Meierhenry, Wesley C., ed. *Learning Theory and AV Utilization.* Washington, D.C.: Special Issue of *AV Communication Review* 9, no. 5 (1961).

Meyer, Peter. *Awarding College Credit for Non-College Learning.* San Francisco: Jossey-Bass Publishers, 1975.

Moir, Guthrie, ed. *Teaching and Television.* Oxford: Pergamon Press, 1967.

Moore, Michael G. "The Cognitive Styles of Independent Learners." Ph.D. dissertation, University of Wisconsin Madison, 1976.

Moore, Michael G. *On a Theory of Independent Study.* Zentrales Institut für Fernstudienforschung Papiere no. 16. Hagen, W. Germany: Zentrales Institut für Fernstudienforschung, 1977.

McLuhan, Marshall. *Understanding Media: The Extensions of Man.* New York: McGraw-Hill Book Co., 1964.

National Association of Educational Broadcasters. *Open Learning Systems.* Washington, D.C.: NAEB, March 1974.

National Institute of Education. *An Evaluative Look at Non-Traditional Post-Secondary Education.* Washington, D.C.: National Institute of Education–U.S. Department of Health, Education and Welfare, 1979.

National Research Council. *Telecommunications for Metropolitan Areas: Opportunities for the 1980's.* Washington, D.C.: National Academy of Sciences, 1978.

Newman, Frank (Chairman). *Report on Higher Education*. Washington, D.C.: U.S. Department of Health, Education and Welfare, 1971.

Newman, Michael. *The Poor Cousin: A Study of Adult Education*. London: George Allen and Unwin, 1979.

Ohmer, Milton. *Alternatives to the Traditional*. San Francisco: Jossey-Bass Publishers, 1973.

O'Toole, James. *Work, Learning and the American Future*. San Francisco: Jossey-Bass Publishers, 1977.

Perry, Lord Walter. *Open University: A Personal Account by the First Vice Chancellor*. Milton Keynes, England: Open University Press, 1976.

Peters, Otto. *Die didaktische Struktur des Fernunterrichts*. Weinheim, Federal Republic of Germany: Beltz Verlag, 1973.

Peters, Otto. *Der Fernunterricht*. Berlin: Pädagogishes Zentrum, 1973.

Pirsig, Robert M. *Zen and the Art of Motorcycle Maintenance*. New York: Bantam Books, 1976.

Ritterbush, Philip C. *Let the Entire Community Become Our University*. Washington, D.C.: Acropolis Books, 1972.

Rogers, Carl. *Freedom to Learn*. Columbus, Ohio: Merrill Publishing Co., 1959.

Rosen, David; Brunner, Seth; and Fowler, Steve. *Open Admissions: The Promise and the Lie of Open Access to American Higher Education*. Lincoln, Neb.; Nebraska Curriculum Development Center, 1973.

Rossi, Peter H., and Biddle, B. J. *The New Media and Education*. New York: Doubleday & Co., 1967.

Salomon, Gavriel. *Interaction of Media, Cognition and Learning*. San Francisco: Jossey-Bass Publishers, 1979.

Schramm, Wilbur; Coombs, P. H.; Kuhnert, F.; and Lyle, J. *New Educational Media: Case Studies for Planners*. 3 vols. Paris: UNESCO Press, 1967.

Schueler, Herbert, and Lesser, G. S. *Teacher Education and the New Media*. Washington, D.C.: American Association of Colleges for Teacher Education, and the National Education Association, 1967.

Scott, Peter. *Strategies for Postsecondary Education*. New York: John Wiley & Sons, 1975.

Shannon, Theodore J., and Schoenfeld, Clarence A. *University Extension*. New York: Center for Research in Education, 1965.

Silberman, Charles E. *Crisis in the Schools*. New York: Random House, 1970.

Sims, Ripley S. *An Inquiry into the Correspondence Educating Processes*. A report prepared with the support of UNESCO and the International Council for Correspondence Education. Madison, Wis.: Ripley Sims, and UNESCO, 1977.

Skinner, B. F. *The Technology of Teaching*. New York: Appleton-Century-Crofts, 1968.

Spicer, Edward H. ed. *Human Problems in Technological Change*. 1952. Reprint. New York: John Wiley & Sons, 1967.

Swedish Commission on Television and Radio in Education (TRU). *Distance Education*. Stockholm: TRU Commission, 1976.

Tax, Sol et al. *Anthropological Backgrounds of Adult Education*. Syracuse, N.Y.: Center for the Study of Liberal Education for Adults, 1968.

Taylor, Harold. *Students Without Teachers — The Crisis in the University.* New York: Avon Books, 1969.

Titmus, Colin et al., *Terminology of Adult Education.* In English, Spanish, French. Paris: UNESCO Press, 1979.

Tough, Allen. *The Adult's Learning Projects: A Fresh Approach to Theory and Practice in Adult Learning.* Toronto: Ontario Institute for Studies in Education, 1971.

Tough, Allen. "Major Learning Efforts: Recent Research and Future Directions." *Adult Education* 28 (Summer, 1978): 250–63.

Tough, Allen. *Why Adults Learn: A Study of the Major Reasons for Beginning and Continuing A Learning Project.* Toronto: Ontario Institute for Studies in Education, 1968.

Turner, Frederick Jackson. *The Frontier in American History.* New York: Henry Holt, 1921.

Tyler, Leona E. *Individuality.* San Francisco: Jossey-Bass Publishers, 1978.

U.S. Commission on Instructional Technology. *To Improve Learning.* Washington, D.C.: U.S. Government Printing Office, 1970.

U.S. Department of Health, Education and Welfare. *Lifelong Learning and Public Policy.* A report prepared by the Lifelong Learning Project. Washington, D.C.: HEW, 1978.

Vaillant, George E. *Adaptation to Life.* Boston: Little, Brown & Co., 1977.

Venables, Sir Peter (Chairman). *Report of the Committee on Continuing Education.* Milton Keynes, England: Open University Press, 1976.

Vermilye, Dyckman W., ed. *Learner-Centered Reform.* San Francisco: Jossey-Bass Publishers, 1975.

Vermilye, D. W., ed. *Relating Work and Education.* San Francisco: Jossey-Bass Publishers, 1977.

Verner, Coolie, and Millard, F. W. *Adult Education and the Adoption of Innovations.* Vancouver: University of British Columbia, 1966.

Wedemeyer, Charles A. "Independent Study." In *The Encyclopedia of Education,* edited by Lee C. Deighton, vol. 4, pp. 548–57. New York: Free Press, 1971.

Wedemeyer, Charles A. "Independent Study." In *The International Encyclopedia of Higher Education,* edited by Asa S. Knowles, vol. 5, pp. 2114–32. San Francisco Jossey-Bass Publication, 1977.

Wedemeyer, Charles A. "The New Educational Technology." *American Dietetic Association. Journal* 53, no. 14 (1968): 325–28.

Wedemeyer, Charles A. "The 'Open' School: Education's Runnymede?" *Educational Technology* 12, no. 1 (January 1972): 65–68.

Wedemeyer, Charles A. "Satellite, Cable and Education: Looking Beyond the Classroom." *Public Telecommunications Review,* July-August 1975, pp. 15–21.

Wedemeyer, Charles A.; Moore, Michael; and Wood, Clifford (ed.). *The Open School.* Madison, Wis.: Governor's Commission on Education, 1971.

Wedemeyer, Charles A., and Najem, Robert E. *AIM: From Concept to Reality, The Articulated Instructional Media Program at Wisconsin.* Syracuse, N.Y.: Syracuse University Press Publications in Continuing Education, 1969.

Wedemeyer, Charles A., and Starkweather, John A. "I Am Joe's School." *Education* 92, no. 4 (1972): 119–29.

Whitehead, Alfred North. *The Aims of Education and Other Essays.* New York: Macmillan Co., 1959.

Windham, Douglas M.; Kurland, N. D.; and Levinsohn, F. H., eds. *Financing the Learning Society.* Chicago: University of Chicago Press, 1978.

Witkin, H. A. "Cognitive Styles in Learning and Teaching." In *Individuality in Learning: Implications of Cognitive Styles and Creativity for Human Development,* edited by S. Messick. San Francisco: Jossey-Bass Publishers, 1976.

Wright, Louis B. *Culture in the Moving Frontier.* New York: Harper & Row Publishers, 1955.

Index

Academic: attitude to change, 16; respectability, continuing theme in extension, 24; tenure and freedom, 81; traditional, locked into classroom model, 213

Access: need through lifespan, 60; improved by media, 61. *See also* Opportunity

Ackerman, Spencer, 165

Adler, Mortimer J., 181–82

Adult: attitude to education, 65; reasons for learning, 77; as learner via media, 107; non-traditional learner, 165–66; blends opposing cultures, 197. *See also* Education, Adult; Learning, adult

Advising and Counseling: need for, 152

Allen, Chester, 229n14

American Dream, 219

American Open University, 218, 231n22

Androgogy, 165. *See also* Education, adult; Learning, adult

Appalachian Education Satellite Program, 218

Aristotle (384–322 B.C.), 37, 189–98 *passim*

Arthurian legends, 117

Articulated Instructional Media (AIM): first experimental model for open university, 204–5

Asimov, Isaac, 27, 219

Association for Educational Communication and Technology, 121

Athabasca University, 34, 231n21

Audio-visual services, 110, 116

Back door learners: demand equitable treatment, 78. *See also* Non-traditional learners

Back door learning: syndrome, 216. *See also* Non-traditional learning

Bacon, Francis (1561–1626), 193

Bacon, Roger (1214–1292), 192, 198

Bailyn, Bernard, 28

Behavior: modification, by maps or models, 106; problems, coping with through learning, 206

Berkman, David, 109

Binkeley, Robert, 200

Birge, E. A., 24

Blake, William, 191

Blase, Melvin, 133

Bloomfield, Leonard, 162

Bouchard, Thomas, 11

Bowen, Frank, 85

Bowen, Howard R., 182, 197

Brady, Thomas F., 237n11

British Broadcasting Corporation (BBC), 230n19

Bronowski, Jacob, 19, 43, 58

Brownell, John A., 196

Bruner, J. S., 235n18

Buber, Martin, 21

Burke, James, 115

Campbell, Donald, 10

Campbell, Joseph, 20

Canning, George (1770–1827), 27

Carlson, Robert A., 165

Carnegie Corporation, 204

Change: in societal contexts, 64, 88, 201

Changed concepts: products of communication, 162

Chaplin, Charlie, 191

Chautauqua, 16, 23, 66, 201, 203; paved way for extension, community colleges, adult education, 203; became a university in 1883, 203

Chicago TV College, 53

Chickering, Arthur W., 194

Chief Seattle, 43–4

Chronicle of Higher Education, 16

Churches: democratization of education, 201. *See also* Religious schools

Churchill, Winston, 29

Clasen, Robert, 177

Classroom: resistance to new models, 37; met needs of earlier societies, 37; major cultural artifact; 37–8; real space-time

Classroom (*continued*)
  model, 38; incompatible with distance, 39; time constraints of, 43; false analogue for non-traditional learning, 71
College Entrance Examination Board, 49, 204
Commission on Non-Traditional Study, 204
Communications: richer outside of school, 31-2; improvements resisted by educators, 32; ended space-time relationship of teaching-learning, 34; links separated teachers and learners, 100; technologies of are extensions of culture, 103; regulatory agencies not responsible of education, cultural development, 107; variable in teaching-learning models, 112; multiple paths needed, 114; penetrate learner networks, 151; essential element in teaching-learning models, 103; affects change, 162. *See also* Federal Communications Commission
Community College of Vermont, 54
Comparative studies: as evaluation, 136; of traditional and non-traditional learning, 215-16
Conceptual matrix: modeling non-traditional institutions, 140-43
Concerns: as motivators for learning, 186; used in planning curricula, 186; universal, 187; inter-related, 187; place learner in center of curriculum, 188; may lead to common learnings, 198. *See also* Curriculum
Consumers: cast into technological serfdom, 193
Content: debate over values of, 189
Continuing education: similar to educación permanente, xxvii; survival priority of, 4. *See also* Adult education; Lifelong education; Lifespan education
Cookson, Peter S., 92
Cooperative Extension Service, 22
Copernican revolution in education: the learner at center of the educational process, 78, 148, 161-2
Copernicus, Nicolaus (1473-1543), 161-2
Correspondence Schools: incredulity of educators, 213
Correspondence study: programs for independent learners, xxv; first formally structured program for independent learners, 50-51; seed bed for open learning, 61; enabled learners to overcome space, time, social and economic barriers, 65-6; ingredient in open learning systems, 67; alternate to schooling, 67. *See also* Independent study; Home study; Distance learning; Non-traditional learning
Cropley, A. J., 207
Cross, K. Patricia, 17, 85
Culture: inherited by victims and beneficiaries, 161; learned, elements in self-identity, 195; the basic learning culture, 198
Curriculum: states ends of education, 183; determined from top down, 183; needs integration of liberal and technical-vocational contents, 184; age basis for determining, 184; unsuited to non-traditional learner, 189; polarity of "two cultures", 192; towards blend of liberal arts, technical-vocational, 208
Cybernation, 117

Dawkins, Richard, 11
Day, William, 241n34
Delker, P. V., 207
Denys, Laurent O. J., 77
Dependence: alters behavior, affects self-identity, 176
de Tocqueville, Alexis (1805-1859): American pioneers not culturally deprived, 202
Deutsches Institut für Fernstudien, 134
Dewey, John (1859-1952), 23, 52, 67, 95, 156, 165, 194, 195
Dieuzeide, Henri, 47
Dickens, Charles (1812-1870): astonished at self learning in America, 202
Distance learning: characteristics of, xxvi; kinds of distance in learning, 39; distance education defined, 48-50. *See also* Non-traditional learning; Open learning; Independent learning
Dodes, Irving A., 191
Down, K. S., 229n10
Dressel, P. L., 52
Drucker, Peter, 201
Dubin, R., 52
Dubos, René, 10, 12, 19, 21

Eccles, Sir John: on nature-nurture, 11–12; on learning, 108, 174
Edelstein, Stewart, 85
Edgerton, Russell, 182
Edison, Thomas A., 204
Edman, Irwin, 181–2
Educación Permanente, xxvii
Education: adult, xxvi, 107; reflects view of humanity, 10; innovation in 1960s–70s, 26; accountability of, 26; as personal right, 27; changed societal contexts of, 34–35; present task of, 35; synonymous with schooling, 37, 167; Copernican revolution in, 47, 56; venerated, 66; unresponsive to technology, 101; common roots of, via technology, 106; a person-centered process, 118; lifelong, statistics regarding, 169; non-traditional provides new dimension, 180; instrumental for most learners, 181; means or end, 182; age-fragmented, 183; dichotomized, 194; lifespan, not confined to children, youth, 197; means of productivity, 201; democratization of, 215. See also Learning
Educational Communications, 25. See also Communications
Educational institutions: as cultural artifacts condition acceptance of change, 69. See also Institutions, educational
Educational media: non-school format less restrictive, 105–6
Educational Policy Center, Syracuse, N.Y., 170
Educational quality: treatment different for traditional or non-traditional learners, 216
Educational Radio, 25. See also Radio and television education
Educational Resources Information Center (ERIC), 111
Educational System: essentially undesigned, patchwork of programs poorly linked and overlapping, 163. See also Systems design; Educational technology
Educational technology: educational purpose, xviii; compared to Progressivism, 95–96; result of changed societal contexts, 96; advocated by business, 96–97; advocated by government, 97; to reach Great Society objectives, 98; advocated by administration, 98; spurred by help to developing nations, 98; needed for non-traditional learning, 99; as tools of education, 100; human element important in, 101; primarily communications technologies, 102; greater impact outside of schooling, 105; could restore, strengthen popular culture, 106; non-school use of, 107; need of in adult education, 107; problems impede success, 108–9; teacher reasons for not accepting, 109; cautious optimism, 110; non-traditional learning gives fresh assessment of, 110; frustrations for teachers, learners, 112; articulated structure needed, 114; humanist use of, 115; includes instructional design, 116; misunderstood concept, 116; confused ends and means, 117; systems approach of, 118; defined as system, 132. See also Technology; Technology of use; Systems design
Educational Testing Service, 49, 204
Educational theory: children and youth prominent in, 164. See also Learning theory
Educators: importance as humanists, 15; need training in non-traditional learning, 209. See also Faculty; Teachers; Academic
Einstein, Albert, 182
Elementary and Secondary Act of 1965, 97
Elkind, D., 235n18
Ely, Donald P., 116, 123
Empire State College, 14, 54
Erdos, Renée, 135
Erikson, Erik, 185
Ethical Culture Society, 14, 23
Eurich, Alvin, 201
Evaluation: summative, 135–36; as function of institution building, 136; formative or developmental, 137
External studies, xxvi, 54

Faculty: temporary vs. permanent, 89; development, key to instructional design, 122. See also Academics; Educators; Teachers
Fair, James, 77
Farmer's Institutes, 65
Faure, Edgar, 64

Federal Communications Commission, 104–5
Fernuniversität, 54, 134
Flavell, J. H., 235n18
Ford, Henry, 204
Formative evaluation: in institution building, 137–38; in Stage 1 model building, 151; for learner profiles, 153; as means towards institutional ends, 156–58. See also Evaluation
Free University of Iran, 54
Freire, Paolo, 29
Freud, Sigmund, 67
Franklin's subscription library, 23. See also Libraries; Public libraries
Frymier, Jack R., 80

Gagne, R. M., 39, 52–53
Ghatala, Habeeb and Elizabeth, 210
Gibbons, J. F., 229n10
Gleason, G. T., 52, 53
Gooler, Dennis, 135
Gould, Joseph E., 203, 204, 205
Gould, Samuel, 63–64, 197–98
Grayson, Lawrence P., 109
Great Society, 97–98
Gross, Ronald, 200

Hamilton, William, 11
Harper, William Rainey, 24, 66
Harrington, Fred Harvey, 12, 13, 17
Havighurst, Robert J., 185
Hechinger, Fred M., 227n
Henderson, Hazel, 209
Higher education: a new configuration of learners, 77–78. See also University; Post secondary education
Higher Education Act of 1965, 97
Hirst, Paul, 196
Hoffer, Eric, 20, 106, 182
Holistic view of learning, 170, 179. See also Learning
Holmberg, Börje, 49, 55–56, 135
Holtzclaw, Luis R., 207
Home: as place for learning, 208. See also Learning environment
Home Study: program for independent, distance learners, xxv, 54; See also Independent study; Correspondence study; Distance learning; Non-traditional learning

Homo Sapiens: learning for survival, 19. See also Man
Horlock, John, 231n22
Houle, Cyril, 60
Howe, Harold II, 191
Hoye, Robert, 118
Huberman, Michael, 211
Humanism: future of, 196
Huxley, Aldous, 191
Huxley, Thomas Henry, 10

Independence: reciprocal, 115; human growth towards, 177
Independent learning: hierarchy of freedoms, 52; link with learning and personality theory, 57; one kind of lifespan learning, 175; potentially most advanced learning, 177; traditional in Colonial society, 202. See also Distance learning; Non-traditional learning
Independent study: programs for independent learners, xxv; part of lifelong education, 9; internal and external, 51; product of autonomy and distance, 51–52; defined, 51–53; relationship to open learning, 67. See also Correspondence study; Home study; Distance learning; Non-traditional learning
Infant: as learner, 167; potentially for learning after birth, 168; uses survival, surrogate, and independent kinds of learning, 176–77. See also Lifespan learning; Survival learning; Surrogate learning, Independent learning
Innovation: lack of conceptual framework, theory, 6; search for better theoretical base, 17
Institution building: uncertainty of means, ends, 156; using systems design and formative evaluation, 214. See also Systems design; Formative evaluation
Institutional concept: in institution development, 137; summative and formative evaluation in development, 154
Institutional model and modeling: for development of non-traditional program, institution, 138–40; non-traditional model based on learner role behaviors, 141; traditional model based on institutional roles, 144; matrix for development

of non-traditional model, 156–57. *See also* Instructional design

Institutional policy: reflects instrumental view of learning, 182

Institutions, educational: symbiotic elements in social system, 90; confused within, misunderstood without, 197. *See also* Educational institutions

Instruction: new guidelines for, 36. *See also* Teaching

Instructional Design: special process of educational technology, 116; defined, 119; reasons for, 119–20; principles of, 120–21; as systems approach, 121; hypothetical application of, 121–30; faculty development phase, 123–26; software development phase, 126–28; hardware procurement phase, 128–30; evaluation and feedback, 130; system for achieving human purposes, 130

Integrated department, 231*n*27

Intelligence: randomly distributed, 99, 100

International Commission on Terminology: proposed for non-traditional education, 55. *See also* Terminology

International Council for Correspondence Education (ICCE), 135

James, Walter, 230*n*19

James, William (1842–1910), 24, 67

Jessup, Frank, 166, 167

Johnstone, J. W. C., and R. J. Rivera Report, 51

Jourard, Sidney, 53

Kaiser, Donald, 135

Kelley, Nancy E., 77

Kincheloe, W. R., 229*n*10

King, Arthur R., Jr., 196

Klausmeier, Herbert J., 167, 173

Klemp, George O., Jr., 180

Knowledge: diffusion of lags behind need, 18; perceptions of undergoing change, 43–44; as end, a powerful mystique, 88; for the good and moral life, 194; structure of changing, 210; as end and means, 211; knowledge intensive society, 219; as means, 231*n*22. *See also* Content; Curriculum

Knowles, Malcolm S., 57, 112–13, 165

Krutch, Joseph Wood, 20–21, 102

Kulich, Jindra. 9

Kurland, Norman D., 208

Lasch, Christopher, 58

Laubach, Frank, 28

Learner: in non-traditional programs characterized by autonomy, distance, xxvi; non-traditional and lifespan, 20; prodded by preachers, printers and teachers, 28; with surround as environment for learning, 30–31; changing needs of, 35; has less fear of changed learning models, 42; field dependent or independent, 56–57; self-direction and autonomy of, 61; different cognitive styles of, 61; part-time exceeds full-time, 77; self concept of, 80; dependency altered by distance from teacher, 111; growth towards independence, 112; central in design of educational technology, 113; central in teaching-learning, 115; as variable in off-campus courses, 134; role behaviors of in modeling institutions, 144; traditional and non-traditional roles, situations compared, 145–47; cyclical role behaviors of, 148; unique differences of, 163; experiences wholeness of education through life, 163; in range between dependent and independent, 172; may be dependent in school, independent outside, 175; central to learning society, 178–79; responsive to concerns, 186; when dependent is extrinsically motivated, 186; as self-educated is persistent folk model, 201; reactive mode in school, 207; central to learning, 212

Learning: non-traditional, definition of, xxv; urgency regarding, 3, 8; as renewable resource, 3; non-traditional, questions to be faced, 4–5; theories about are culture bound, based on values, beliefs, 7–8; significant for survival, 12; at back door, 18–20; importance of self-motivated, 21; back door, has left mark on American society, 27–28; new era redresses old wrongs, 27; environment for, 29–30; not dependent upon social interaction, 39; stages of, 42; is idiosyncratic, 43; with maturity, independence, 57–58;

Learning (*continued*)
  as natural, effective, 61; self-initiated, 75; most adult learning planned by adults, 76; clearer picture of adult learning emerging, 76; major source outside school via technology, 111; effect of technology on, 111; autonomy regarding, 112; via technology requires learner initiative and autonomy, 113; as developed humanness, 113; power of, 113; changing era of, 115; is lifespan in scope, 155; holistic view of needed, 166–67, 170, 179; definition of, 168; cultural bias for schooling as learning, 168; continues birth to death, 169; broader than schooling, 172; as lifespan, 172, 206; related to reality of self and pseudo-reality of schooling, 173; related to maturation, 174; in lifespan, survival, surrogate and independent learning in jumbled sequence, 174–78; urgency of reflected in non-traditional approaches, 205, 206; all of should be recognized, 206; as normal, natural process, 207; towards humanistic ends, 208; a natural survival behavior, 208; most assumptions about are inappropriate, 208–9; as natural, is intrinsic, applied, evaluated, 219; persistent, erroneous belief that must follow teaching, 236*n*35. *See also* Non-traditional learning
Learning and teaching: conceptually and operationally separate, 172
Learning environment: learner and surround, 212
Learning, independent: characteristics of, xxv. *See also* Independent study; Home study; Correspondence study; Distance learning
Learning Society: now essential, 3; on threshold of, 170; earlier, 201; non-traditional learning most genuine ingredient, 219
Learning theory: Piagetion theory re: adult learning, 165; present theory incomplete, 171, 208, 209
Lee, Dorothy, 53
Lengrand, Paul, 210, 211
Levinsohn, Florence H., 208
Lewin, Kurt, 10
Library, 110, 201, 203. *See also* Public libraries

Liberal arts: debate over, blend with technical-vocational education, 184, 189, 190; efforts to combine, 195, 196; affected by non-traditional education, 197
Lifelong learning, xxvii; new vantage points, 163; reflects add-on view of continuing education, 163–64. *See also* Lifespan learning; Continuing education; Educación permanente
Lifelong Learning Project, 163, 164, 169, 170
Lifespan learning: and continuing education, xxvii; blend of traditional and non-traditional, 59; sphere of, 105; as concept, 170, 171; jumbled sequence of, 176; kinds of learning at different intensity levels, 176–77; elements of, not hierarchical or sequential, 177; from a relationship-with-others viewpoint, 177–78; blend of schooling and non-school learning, 183; three kinds of, survival, surrogate, and independent, 212. *See also* Survival learning; Surrogate learning; Independent learning
Lighty, William H., 24, 25, 66
Lincoln, Abraham, 204
Linskie, Rosella, 181
Lippsitt, Lewis J., 168, 174
Long, Huey B., 165, 201
Luke, Robert A., 164
Lyceum, 65, 66, 201
Lynch, James, 210

McCathy, Cressy, 77
McClusky, Howard Y., 166, 235*n*14
McCrory, Kay, 165
MacDonald, J. B., 52, 53
Mackenzie, Norman, 63, 67, 135
Mackintosh, Sir James, 19
McLuhan, Marshall, 48, 105, 131
McNeil, Donald, 14
Main, Keith, 235*n*14
Man: learning animal, 206. *See also* Homo Sapiens
Mandated Continuing Education (MCE), 205
Martin, James, 236*n*44
Massachusetts Institute of Technology, 115
Masterpiece Theatre, 105
Maturation: related to learning, 174
Means: agents of instruction, 34
Medsker, Leland, 85

Meiklejohn, Alexander, 24
Memorial University of Newfoundland, 54
Miller, Milton H., 75, 166
Miller, Nancy L., 77
Minnesota Metro, 14, 54
Moir, Guthrie, 117
Moore, Michael G., 51, 56, 57, 111, 112, 235n4, 236n44, 240n19
Morrill Act, 1862, 21
Motivation: intrinsic, plumbs self, 180; as need-state, prerequisite to behavior, 180
Moulton, Richard, 24
Mujahid, Sharif al, 28
Mumford, Louis, 191

Najem, Robert E., 237n3, 240n16
National Alliance for Voluntary Learning, 205
National Association of Educational Broadcasters, 62
National Defense Education Act 1958, 97
National Institute of Education, 62, 110, 232n8
National Public Radio, 111
National Research Council: Report, educational services in 1980s, 3-4
National University Extension Association, 24, 25, 55
Need-state: fundamental to lifespan learning, 198
Needs: randomly distributed, 99, 100
Neville, H. R., 5
New England, American Tract Society, 23
New institutions: arise because old institutions unresponsive, 70. See also Institutions; Non-traditional institutions
New York Regents Degree Program, 14
Nietzsche, Friedrich Wilhelm (1844–1900), 161
Non-traditional faculty: tenure with exclusions, 89. See also Educators; Faculty; Teachers
Non-traditional institutions: knowledge-as-means mission, 83; research at, 84–85; creativity as important as quality, 90; governance, 91; pay price for dependence, 133; employ systems design, 134; conceptual matrix for modeling, 140–43; systems development, 141; unconventional modeling required, 144, 147;

model based on learner role behaviors, 151, 153, 154, 155; systems model, 155; need for, 206; vulnerability of, 231n21. See also Institutions; New institutions
Non-traditional learner: traditional requirements inappropriate, 134; role behaviors, 147, 148; centrality of, 148, 149, 150; reach through appropriate networks, 151; advising and counseling, 152; non-start phenomenon misunderstood, 153; profile by formative evaluation, 153; failures of, 154; examination hazard, 154; successful, coping with, 155; most pursue learning as means, 181; a yeasty element in society, 182; select range of curricula, 184; loneliness of, 199; accomplishments disparaged or ignored, 200; a great national resource, 200. See also Learner
Non-traditional learning: accomplishments of, 28; reasons for increase in, 47; three major types of, 47–48; ambiguity of terminology, 51–54; growth towards independence, 59; new development in education, 60; principles of, 60, 61; changing systems of education, 74; implications for learners, 75–78; allied with schooling, 77; implications for teachers, 78–81; implications for academic department, 81; implications for institutions, 82–92; implications regarding mission, 82–85; knowledge-as-means vs. knowledge-as-end, 83; dual missions, 83–84; implications for operations, administration, 85; skepticism regarding evaluative data, 85–86; implications for curriculum, instruction, rewards, 86; reduces dependency of learners, 86; options and choices, 87; diffusion, access, communication, 87; faculty governance, renewal, creativity, 87–90; permanent or temporary faculty for, 87–91; opposition to, 88; funding and support, 91; needs equal basis of subsidy, 92; affects all education, 92; access and opportunity for distance learners, 101, 206; non-starts and non-completions, 134; pressures to emulate traditional, 134; new dimensions and purposes, 180, 183; broad range of learning, 200; significant factor in American innovation, self-reliance, productivity,

Non-traditional learning (*continued*) 201; means of removing class distinctions, 203; progress and innovation in 1960s–1970s, 204, 205; relationship to general learning theory, 206; opposite of schooling, 207; model for revitalizing all learning, 207, 219; through the lifespan, 211; special processes of, 215; recognition sometimes refused, 216; needs acceptance, 217; best hope, new institutions, 217; credentialism, 218. *See also* Learning; Open learning; Distance learning; Independent learning

Non-traditional programs: compared with traditional, 134

North Central Association of Schools and Colleges, 231*n*

Oettinger, A. G., 109

Ogden, C. K., 235*n*

Olafson, Frederick A., 196

Open learning: characteristics of, xxvi; recognition of, 61, 68; defined, 61–62; expands freedoms of learners, 62; systems characteristics, 62–63; congruence with changed societal contexts, 64; grafted to university extension and correspondence study, 65; relationship to independent learning, 65–67; questions to consider before creating, 67–72; curriculum for, 68; target populations, 68; mission, objectives, 68; academic resources, availability, 68–69; learner effect on policy, 69; strategies for support, 69; teaching, learning, examining functions, 69; rewards, acceptance, accreditation, 70; communications, diffusion, access, 70; aggregation level and cost-benefits, 71; fees and subsidy, 71–72; relationships, other institutions, 72; independent or public utility status, 72; staff, student training, 72; opposite of traditional education, 73. *See also* Non-traditional learning; Independent learning; Distance learning

Open University (British), 6, 14, 54, 65, 81, 134, 187, 204, 230*n*20, 231*n*22

Opportunity to learn: uneven and unequal, 99; effect of restricted access to teachers, 101. *See also* Access

Orwell, George, 191

O'Toole, James, 184, 196

Oxford University, 33, 166

Paradise Lost, 98

Peabody awards, 105

Penland, Patrick R., 77

Perry, Lord Walter, 6, 7, 135, 230*n*19

Peters, Otto, 49, 135

Peterson, Richard, 236*n*30

Pflüger, A., 217

Piaget, J., 165

Pirsig, Robert M., 192, 194

Plato (427–348 B.C.), 32, 34, 37, 38, 39, 99, 100, 189, 190

Poincaré, Raymond (1860–1934), 161

Post-secondary education: value-laden questions asked, 82. *See also* Adult education; Continuing education; Non-traditional learning

Progressive education, 95–96

Providers: of educational programs in U.S., 14–15

Public Broadcasting Service, 111

Public libraries: role in continuing education, xxvii, 23. *See also* Library; Redwood library

Quarton, Gardner, 106

Queen Elizabeth II, 65

Radio and television education, 61

Reber, Louis, 24, 25

Redwood Library of Newport, Rhode Island, 23

Regents Degree Programs, 54

Religious schools, 22. *See also* Churches

Renshaw, Jean R., 188

Reynolds, Roger, 218

Richards, J. A., 235*n*

Richmond, K., 209

Ridgeway, James, 97

Ripple, Richard E., 167, 173

Roberts, Norma M. K., 185

Rogers, Carl, 57, 80, 207

Rogers, William C., 230*n*21

Ruskin, John, 191

Salomon, Gavriel, 87

Sandburg, Carl, 199

Schillace, R., 6

Schaeffer, Earl S., 167, 168, 212

Schoenfeld, Clarence, 24

Schooling: part of lifespan learning, 3; thought to be synonymous with learning, 37; cannot educate alone, 105; tends to produce dependent learners, 173; not the same as learning, 207; cultural artifact, 207. See also Learning; Non-traditional learning; Open learning; Independent learning; Distance learning

Schools: ancient reasons for, 30; lead to dependencies, hamper maturation, 58, 59; distributed unevenly, 99; modeled on job archetype, 183

Schwalbe, Heinz, 49

Schweitzer, Albert, 21

Sears, Pauline, 53

Self-concept: learned, 80

Sesame Street, 105, 232n8

Shannon, T. J., 24

Sharp, Paul, 100

Silberman, Charles E., 123

Sims, Ripley S., 133

Smith-Hughes Act of 1917, 21

Smith-Lever Act of 1914, 22

Smith, Mike, 20

Snow, C. P., 191, 192, 195

Society: co-beneficiary of any learning, 92; changes in education by year 2000, 197

Socrates (469–399 B.C.), 34, 37

Soderberg, C. Richard, 195

Spronk, Barbara, 231n21

Stalford, Charles B., 231n

Sunday School Society, 23. See also Chautauqua; Churches; Religious education

Surrogate learning: a category of lifespan learning, 175; occurs in schools where learner yields to authority, becomes dependent, 175; low impact of, despite cost, 177. See also Lifespan learning; Schooling; Independent learning

"Surround": part of environment for learning, 226n

Survival learning: a category of lifespan learning, 173; natural learning, driven intrinsically, affected by extrinsic factors, 175; important throughout life, may inhibit other kinds of learning, 177. See also Lifespan learning; Schooling; Independent learning

Swedish Commission on Television and Radio in Education (TRU), 49, 134

Swedish Institute of Public Opinion Research (SIFO), 64

Swift, Jonathan (1667–1745), 18, 19, 79, 198

Systems design and development, xxviii, 141. See also Formative evaluation; Educational systems; Non-traditional learning; Open learning

Taveggia, T. C., 52

Teachers: self-concept, 40, 41, 79, 80, 172; new roles for, 78, 210. See also Academics; Educators; Faculty

Teaching: Platonic model, 32; Greek values in form and mystique, 34; model for non-traditional programs, 148. See also Instruction

Teaching-Learning: environments not the same, 30, 31; traditionally connected real-time activities, 32; in space-time chained relationship, 33, 99; communication revolution shattered space-time relationship, 34; separate acts not dependent upon physical presence, 37, 54, 100, 101; essential elements of, 38; model to accommodate physical distance, 40; activities require dual systems, 86. See also Teaching; Learning; Instruction; Non-traditional learning

Technical-vocational education: need for, 191

Technology: hero and villain, 27, 192, 213; relationship to learning, 30; alters learner surround, 31; not alien to learning, 31; challenge to, 87, resisted by educators, 96, 97, 105; can become end in itself, 102; as means to humane ends, 102; not value-neutral, 103; cultural contexts affect use, 104; perceived as aid for conventional education, 104; intricate technology of human being excels man-made technology, 114; places constraints on teachers and learners, 114; need not dehumanize learning, 115; disparaged as applied science, 193; equalizes opportunity, access in non-traditional learning. See also Educational technology; Technology of use

Technology of use: part of educational technology, xxviii; needs input from human-

Technology of use (*continued*)
ists, 114. *See also* Technology; Educational technology
Terminology: of non-traditional learning is ambiguous, 54; has little logical integrity, 55; use of affected by user self-concept, 55
Theobold, Robert, 117
Thompson, M. M., 52
Thorndike, Edward L., 164
Tough, Allen, 76, 79, 167, 170, 181
Trivers, Robert, 11
Turner, Frederick Jackson, 203
"Two cultures": small bridgeheads between, 196; may merge into new ethic, 198
Tyler, Leona E., 171, 174, 176, 228*n*26

United Nations Scientific, Educational and Cultural Organization (UNESCO), 135, 205
United States Endowment for the Humanities, 230*n*19
United States Information Agency, 230*n*19
United States Office of Education, 97
Universities: new models depart from traditional, 14; vestiges of medievalism remain, 33; missions of, need separation by concept space, 83–85; need appropriate educational purpose, 197–98
University extension: provides opportunity and access, xxvii, 14; rise of, 22–26; concept from Britain, 23; called academic sideline, 24; an essential function of university, 24; shift of emphasis, 25; function of, 27; mentioned, 61, 65, 84, 87, 110, 121, 217; returning credit courses to residence, 84; incomplete control over programs, 89; not to harm universities, 132, 133, 134; lack of control over credit programs and rewards, 134. *See also* Non-traditional education; Distance learning; Open learning; Correspondence study; Independent learning, study
University of Chicago, 24

University of London, 69
University of Lund, 134
University of Mid-America, 14, 54, 218, 231*n*22, 233*n*8
University of South Africa, 54
University of the South Pacific, 54, 217
University of Wisconsin, 24, 166, 204
University of Wisconsin Extension Division, 24
University Without Walls, 14

Vaillant, George E., 185
Values: hunger for, 106; value rigidity, 194; are learned, part of self-concept, 195
van Hise, Charles R., 24
van Leunen, Mary Claire, 79
Veblen, Thorstein, 21
Venables, Sir Peter, 187

Ward, Lester Frank (1814–1913), 24
Weinberg, Edgar, 195
Weiner, Norbert, 117
Weisner, Jerome B., 115
Wendlandt, Billie, 181
Wendt, Kurt F., 197
Western Reserve University, 200
Westril, Clas, 64
Wheeler, Nicholas A., 12
White, Lynn, 114
Whitehead, Alfred North (1861–1947), 23
Windham, Douglas M., 208
Wirth, Arthur G., 184
Wirtz, Willard, 189
Witkin, H. A., 56
Wood, Clifford, 240*n*19
Woodall, J., 77
Wright, Louis B., 66
Wrocznski, R., 240*n*27

Yankelovich, David, 64
Youth: attitudes toward education, 64

Zapol, N., 109